THE ORIGINAL RADIO DRAMA

Other Star Wars books available:

THE ART OF STAR WARS - A NEW HOPE EPISODE IV
THE ART OF STAR WARS - THE EMPIRE STRIKES BACK EPISODE V
THE ART OF STAR WARS - THE RETURN OF THE JEDI EPISODE VI
THE ART OF STAR WARS GALAXY
THE ART OF STAR WARS GALAXY 2
STAR WARS - THE ORIGINAL RADIO DRAMA

STAR WARS: THE EMPIRE STRIKES BACK

THE ORIGINAL RADIO DRAMA

**Based on Characters and Situations
Created by George Lucas**

Brian Daley

TITAN BOOKS

STAR WARS: THE EMPIRE STRIKES BACK
THE ORIGINAL RADIO DRAMA

ISBN 1 85286 644 6

Published by
Titan Books Ltd
42-44 Dolben Street
London SE1 0UP

First Titan edition September 1995
2 4 6 8 10 9 7 5 3 1

Published originally in the United States by Ballantine Books Inc.

British Library Cataloguing-in-Publication Data.
A catalogue record for this book is available from the British Library.

Printed and bound in Great Britain by Cox and Wyman Ltd, Reading, Berkshire.

To Mary Lylah "Mel" Sahr,
the Heroine who,
in cliff-hangers galore,
rescued NPR's *Star Wars* and *Empire*
from the Forces of Chaos

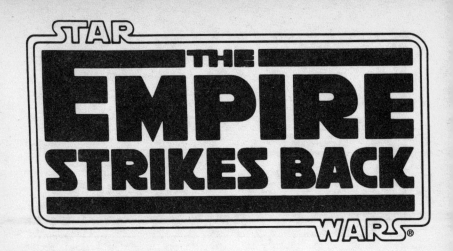

THE ORIGINAL RADIO DRAMA

INTRODUCTION

It wasn't until The Empire Struck Back in midtown Manhattan that we found out about droids being fueled by bananas. That was also where Yoda suddenly got four feet taller and Luke Skywalker considered dressing like Sky Masterson of *Guys and Dolls*. That was where the cast and other players from the National Public Radio *Star Wars* serial had reunited and taken on some new crewmates to record a ten-episode version of the second leg of George Lucas's sf magnum opus. We were at A & R Studios, a place with a very different feel to it from Los Angeles and Westlake Audio, where we'd recorded *Star Wars* in the summer of 1980.

I was looking forward to it even more than I had the first one. Scripting and being in on the recording of *Star Wars* had been tremendous fun; having written two novels in the interim, I was looking forward to the collaboration of working on another NPR drama.

As with the first serial, radio adaptation offered time to expand upon the movie. *Empire* the motion picture shows Han finding a delirious, wounded Luke on the subzero ice fields of Hoth as a storm closes in. Han sticks his friend in a gutted tauntaun to keep him warm while he erects an emergency shelter. The next time we see them is when the snowspeeder search teams find them the following day.

For the radio dramatization, having the two thrown together in close quarters and life-threatening danger was too good to pass up. It offered a chance to show their bantering, but more importantly their underlying friendship. After all, these are two guys who happened to run into each other one Mos Eisley day and ended up serving together in a war.

Then there was the face-off between Darth Vader and Han and Chewbacca inside Cloud City. Vader stopped Han's blaster bolts with a gloved palm as if they were spitballs. The blaster was snatched from Han's hand to the Sith Lord's. Troops rushed in, and the scene ended. I'd written a trilogy about Han and Chewie in addition to adapting the first NPR drama, and thought there'd probably be more to the scene than that. As Han tells Vader herein, "Don't flatter yourself! *You* ain't the biggest thing me 'n' the *Wookiee* ever tackled, pal!"

Our adaptation of *Star Wars* had been the most successful NPR drama ever. Arbitron ratings said 750,000 listeners heard the shows, 11% of them between ages 12 and 17—nearly four times average for the network. Another 50% were between 25 and 39, as compared to the usual 35% for the network. The shows generated fifty thousand phone calls and letters. NPR named the series as one of the primary causes of its 40% audience increase over that year. Overall growth of drama listenership was 135%. I'd been traveling the country when the first serial aired and heard *Star Wars* in so many different places that it seemed the sky was a big *Star Wars* radar net.

Calculating roughly, it had cost about 47 cents per listener, or 3.6 cents per audience member per episode—not counting subsequent airings. In terms of public broadcasting funds and donations from NPR sponsors and backers, that seemed a good buy.

The critics liked it, too. *The Los Angeles Times* called the series a "fun, spine-tingling, mind-bending piece of escapist entertainment that doesn't miss the visuals a bit."

And George Lucas approved, which made me feel even better because the laurels ultimately are due to him and his creation.

So we all had our fingers crossed for an *Empire* sequel. The project was finally put into motion when John Bos joined NPR as director of performance programming. John saw *Star Wars* and the proposed *Empire* as a way to anchor a six-days-a-week fare of radio drama offerings. To fill the other slots, he began cultivating programming like Karl Schmidt's *Earplay* shows from Madison, Wisconsin. John also brought in the twelve-part BBC radio version of *The Hitchhiker's Guide to the Galaxy* in all its demented brilliance. He was sure that if he got quality programming on the air an audience would find it. Events proved him right.

Bos got *Empire* rolling in association with KUSC, the affiliate station at George Lucas's alma mater in Los Angeles. George once again "sold" the enormously valuable radio rights to public broadcasting for the sum of one dollar, as he had done with *Star Wars*. I began to outline scripts that would be vetted by Anita Gross at Lucasfilm as well as director John Madden and sound producer Tom Voegeli. We decided on ten episodes rather than thirteen, due to both time and budget constraints. After story conferences in November 1981, I spent the majority of that winter in the Catskills, turning a movie continuity script into discrete radio chapters. The Catskills winter made writing the frozen Hoth scenes easier. But I don't think the generous folks at the Hensonville courthouse ever really understood what I was using their photocopy machine for.

Recording took place in New York City the following June. Principal players from the first serial were back, with the addition of Billy Dee Williams reprising his role as Lando Calrissian. The consensus was that the New York taping sessions were more fun than the Los Angeles ones. Mel Sahr—who cast both series, handled production coordination and made the project happen by working tirelessly—told me she felt the New York go-around was more intimate, more collegial for the actors. In Los Angeles, she said, some actors had passed on supporting roles in *Star Wars* because they were unwilling to commit to a daytime job. "They wanted to sit by the phone, hoping they'd get called for a pilot." New York was much the opposite: Actors appearing in various plays and shows had free time during the day. They were usually delighted to come into the studio, take a role or two or three, work with peers, and practice their craft.

In Los Angeles, despite the renowned laid-back attitude, Ann Sachs, who played the NPR drama's Princess Leia, had gotten a sense that some supporting players were eager to complete their part and get on to the next thing—do a day's work and head home. "In New York people worked harder," she recalls of supporting players who had numerous motion picture and TV credits. "And at the same time they had more of a sense of fun. They were relaxed, they wanted to try new things, redo scenes another way." Ann was proving her own range at the time: She was Leia by day and by night was a star in the Jules Feiffer play *A Thinkpiece* at the Circle Rep.

Recently I had to ask her about her/Leia's first encounter with Billy Dee/Lando. When the *Millennium Falcon* arrives at Cloud City, Lando shows up and gives the Princess a suave hello. In the studio, Billy Dee looked at Ann and turned on that famous killer charm, full bore. In a moment that passed into legend, she decided to just enjoy it, the heck with her next line. Of course, the scene had to be redone.

"It was really seductive," she said, laughing. "He's a charmer, that one. It's that laser vision he has. He'll look at you as if you're the only woman on the planet."

Or the floating Tibanna-gas mine.

In an interview for *The New York Times*'s "Metropolitan Diary" column, Tony Daniels talked about how odd it was to be out in the *Star Wars* galaxy all morning and then find himself in a busy midtown deli at lunchtime. Mark Hamill added that, "If you're doing radio, and you're in New York City, you feel you should be playing the part. I'd like to be wearing a 40's suit and a fedora, so I could stroll on over to Lindy's with Fred Allen."

Sky Masterson, meet Luke Skywalker.

When the column appeared on June 16, 1982, it included a cartoon by Bob Gale. Seated at a counter were Threepio with a bemused look on his face as he contemplated a burger and fries with ketchup, Yoda in a fedora and trenchcoat that made him resemble Walter Winchell, and Darth Vader perusing a menu whose cover read "JOE'S DINER." A definite keeper.

Actor Jay Sanders kidded Ann about her earphones, calling them her Leia hairdo. I'd go home to the Upper East Side at night and tell friends about this hysterically funny guy, David Alan Grier, whose improvs almost made me rupture a spleen. John Pielmeier, the award-winning playwright of *Agnes of God*, dropped by to play a couple of Rebel parts. Jerry Zaks, now one of New York's most successful directors, tackled roles ranging from Coordinator Droid to Guard. And I got to do a bit part as a stormtrooper, helping heave Han Solo into the Cloud City slammer. When I pitched John Madden a rewrite wherein my character rescues the galaxy and marries Leia, though, he thought it would be taking a mite too much dramatic license.

I suppose I should explain about bananas and droids.

For *Empire,* Anthony Daniels was once again See-Threepio, the role he had created in the movies and the first series. It became a ritual for Mel Sahr to make sure fresh bananas were available at the studio every morning for energy and because they kept Tony's stomach from rumbling in a way that, he said, might've resembled robotic grinding noises but would have given sound producer Tom Voegeli an ulcer. So that's how bananas came to be known as "droid fuel."

They worked. Tony did a splendid job in carrying not only his own part but a good share of Artoo-Detoo's. A major portion of the little astro-droid's existence lies in Threepio's interchanges with him and Tony's gift for making everyone believe his counterpart was standing right there next to him.

Mark Hamill, the little robot's second most frequent companion, showed the same knack in the X-wing and Dagobah scenes. Ann, Billy Dee, and Perry King were also marvelous at keeping Artoo (and Chewie) "in the scene," but it was Threepio's manner and Tony's conjuring that most anchored Artoo's existence.

It was very pleasant to hear Tony approve of how Threepio was treated in the expanded *Empire.* In the radio drama, the golden interpreter is thrown together with Leia, Han, and Chewie for adventures aboard the *Falcon,* during which Threepio is often and loudly vexed with reckless Han. The way I saw it, that wasn't because the droid was *trying* to be a pain and a kvetch. Luke ordered him to look after Leia, and he's simply doing his level best to keep Solo from needlessly endangering her life. Threepio was never as gratuitously grouchy as some observers imply. He was built with a basic mission that was often difficult or impossible to carry out, through no fault of his own. Communication, facilitation, aiding the courteous and cordial flow of human social and diplomatic contact—those can be pretty tough in the midst of a galactic war, and he was frequently under demands that voided the manufacturer's warranty. "Goldenrod" 's highest values call for mutual respect and uncommon courtesy. In the *Star Wars* galaxy, that can be a pretty brave stand.

Tony Daniels again acted his part inside a windowed isolation booth so that his voice could be processed later. This time around we made sure his lines and speeches were shorter, since Threepio doesn't breathe and Tony therefore couldn't be heard to inhale or exhale. As before, he did stiff, robotic arm and torso movements to keep himself completely in character.

The booths were busy places. *Empire*'s climax is a lightsaber duel between Luke and Vader, which meant putting Brock Peters, radio's Darth, in isolation so his voice could be processed and his breathing could be added later, and positioning Mark just out-side. That way they could see each other, deliver lines, and make sounds to indicate physical exertion at just the right moments—with the sputter and crash of energy blades to be mixed in after-ward. Their battle royal sounded magnificent when broadcast.

Things got cold on Hoth but sweltering on Dagobah, and casting the mysterious swamp planet's most famous citizen be-came a crisis. Fortunately for Mel Sahr, she didn't have to find a look-alike to portray Yoda, the nine-hundred-year-old, dwarfish Jedi Master. But then, sound-alikes weren't all that common either.

Frank Oz of Muppet fame, who'd done voice and animation for the Yoda construct in the movie, was the ideal choice, but he was in England. One odd but tempting solution came up when Mark demonstrated that he did a *great* Yoda. John Madden almost went for it despite the technical headaches of having Mark play both roles in many and protracted scenes with himself. Mark was ready to tackle it, a unique radio tour de force.

When Yoda finally appeared, however, he came in the form of John Lithgow—Academy Award nominee for *The World According to Garp*, star of *Harry and the Hendersons* and *Cliffhanger*, and a Tony Award winner on the New York stage.

Madden was at that time directing Lithgow in a play called *Be-*

yond Therapy, rehearsing for Broadway. They were joking around when it emerged that Lithgow, too, did a dead-on Yoda. John Lithgow laid down all his lines, opposite Mark, in a single *long* day. He'd just delivered his last one when his voice *went.* Zap! Nothing left but a croak like a Dagobah bullfrog. That's what they call a trooper.

To do the scenes in the Hoth emergency shelter, with Luke wounded by the wampa ice creature and a storm howling outside, Perry King and Mark got down onto the floor into some "radio scenery" Tom Voegeli had rigged up. It consisted of blankets draped over chairs, like a kid's imaginary fort. The arrangement not only gave Voegeli the sound qualities he needed, but gave Perry and Mark a claustrophobic setting in which Luke and Han could quarrel and joke.

Like *Star Wars, Empire* required wild lines for background actors in various scenes. Wild lines are those indistinct remarks, exclamations, and conversations that create crowd atmosphere and let the listener hear a hubbub. Wild lines had to be written rather than ad-libbed because it would have jarred the audience to hear someone improvise, "Let's do lunch. I'll have my Ugnaughts call your Ugnaughts." Or, "Let's face it, is the techno-cyberpunk comb-over thing not working for Lobot's bald spot, or what?"

Wild lines were often bureaucratic, procedural stuff, but sometimes they were fun, as in this background dialogue on Hoth Base:

REBEL #10: Hold it! Where's the transfer-circuit adjuster I left lyin' right here? Who took it?

REBEL #11: It's being used to repair the *Millennium Falcon.*

REBEL #10: Oh it is, huh? Who does Solo think he is? I got a good mind to go over there and take it right back outta his hand. What does he think, he owns this base? In fact, I think I *will* go over there and—

REBEL #11: It was the Wookiee who took it.

REBEL #10: Uh, Chewbacca?

REBEL #11: You know any others? Well? Gonna go over and yank it out of his paw?

REBEL #10: Well, now, there must be another one around here someplace . . .

With taping completed, Tom Voegeli again retreated to his postproduction studios in Minnesota. As before, he was using sound resources generously shared by Lucasfilm's three-time Academy Award winner, Ben Burtt. Months of work went into editing, addition of music and sound effects, and so on. A single scene could take Tom days.

Included here is a page from the first episode, as marked by Tom, to show how complex and time-consuming his labors were. He explained, "If a scene required all kinds of comlink sounds or motor sounds for Artoo-Detoo or whatever, that all got premixed to a stereo finished-dialogue track. And to that I orchestrated music, and to *that* I did effects. When the effects got extremely complicated, those were premixed to a stereo composite, so I was just dealing with one stereo track.

"So the sample page is one scene showing what all the composites were. My notations say 'Track 3 and 4 vox throughout cockpit.' [LOWER LEFTHAND CORNER.] Those are the master dialogue tracks. In almost all cases there are two numbers side by side, meaning the tracks were stereo pairs, left and right, of these various composites that might have taken ten or twelve individual tracks each to assemble. Otherwise I would have run out of track capacity and the mix would have become too complicated.

"The dialogue tracks are probably the most easy-to-understand component, because you have the live action characters recorded in stereo. But to that you have Darth Vader added, for example. He's on another track and has to be put on, has to have his breathing added. Say Artoo happened

1-1

1	ANNCR:	OPENING CREDITS.
2	MUSIC:	OPENING THEME.
3	NARRATOR:	A long time ago in a galaxy far, far
4		away, there came a time of revolution,
5		when rebels united to challenge a
6		tyrannical Empire. Now, it is a dark
7		time for the Rebellion. Evading the
8		dreaded Imperial Starfleet, a group of
9		freedom fighters, led by Luke Skywalker,
10		has established a secret base on the
11		remote ice world of Hoth. But the evil
12		Lord Darth Vader, obsessed with finding
13		young Skywalker, has dispatched
14		thousands of "probe droids" - automated
15		hunting machines - into the far reaches
16		of space.
17	SOUND:	X-WINGS, TRANSPORTS ZOOMING BY, UNDER.
18	NARRATOR:	Now, a small space convoy of rebel
19		transport ships and snubfighter escorts
20		seeks to bring desperately-needed
21		supplies and reinforcements to Hoth.
22		SCENE 1-1 NARRA'S COCKPIT
23		
24	SOUND:	NARRA'S COCKPIT SOUNDS COME UP. ALL
25		OTHER LINES ARE OVER COMLINK.
26		

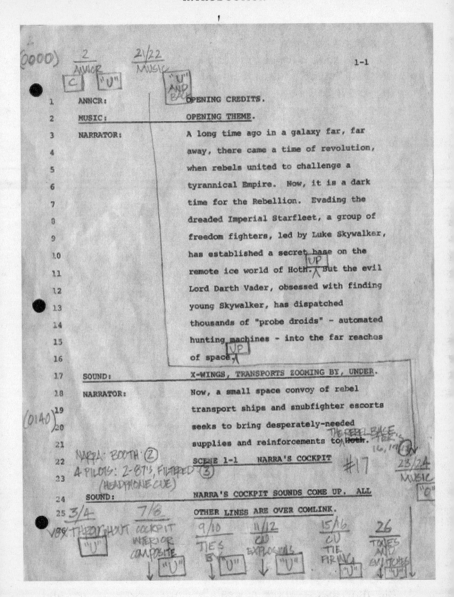

(0000)   2   21/22
         ANNCR   MUSIC
         C   "U"   "U" AND END

UP

UP

(0140)

NARRA: BOOTH (2)
4 PILOTS: 2-BT's, FLARED (3)
(HEADPHONE CUE)

THE REBEL BASE
16, 17   #17   23/24 MUSIC "O"

3/4   7/6   9/10   11/12   15/16   26
VBX THRU'OUT   COCKPIT INTERIOR COMPOSITE   TIES BY   EXPLOSIONS   CU TIE FIRING   TIES AND EXPLOSIONS
"U"   "U"   "U"   "U"   "U"   "U"

to be in the same scene; he gets added with all of his various 'dialogue' and motors.

"Say you now have eight tracks to build up the dialogue. I would then premix all that dialogue, panning and, as Ben Burtt would say, 'worldizing.' Meaning taking the dry, mechanical Artoo sounds, for example, and putting them in the same *space* as the rest of the dialogue, so it sounds like he's in the scene—and also 'moving' him electronically in stereo.

"I would finish that for a scene and then mix it to a brand new stereo pair. There are also notes as to how the original dialogue was recorded, and some 'keeper take' numbers. So this sample page shows the track layout of the final mix of all the composites of music and dialogue."

As Tom Voegeli was working on the show, NPR's public-information machine cranked up. Jan Hausrath, who'd done production chores during the recording sessions, got a blizzard of articles and features into print and broadcast media. One of the most innovative things NPR did was to get celebrated chef Craig Clairborne to create his own version of "Yoda's Incredible Herb Stew" (aka "Rootleaf"), which the little Jedi Master served up to Luke at the hut on Dagobah. The recipe ran in magazines and newspapers across the country; I wonder how many people tried it?

The Empire Strikes Back debuted on NPR on Valentine's Day, 1983. Like its predecessor it was well received, despite suffering the same disadvantage: Local NPR affiliates slipped it into their schedules any which way they pleased, so the series was denied the huge advantage of national PR that could mention a specific timeslot.

Still, the series did extremely well. Soon after, talks began for the *Return of the Jedi* series. But it was about then that NPR funding took severe hits from Reaganomics cutbacks, and the project had to be abandoned.

But now that a whole new audience has come of age and enjoyed the first two series, both as rebroadcasts on NPR and complete sets of the episodes on tape, talk has resurfaced of finally finishing the trilogy. Along with audiences new and old, I look forward to that possibility. While taping *Empire,* Mark Hamill said, "It's nice to head for the stars again." He spoke for a lot of us.

Brian Daley
Pines on Severn, Maryland
December 1994

EPISODE ONE:

"FREEDOM'S WINTER"

CHARACTERS:

Luke	Rieekan	Renegade Four
Han	First Rebel	Narra
Leia	Coordinator Droid	Renegade Seven
Threepio	Second Rebel	Renegade Three
Artoo	Deck Officer	Renegade Two
Ben	Command Center	Needa
Chewbacca	Sentry	Imperial Officer

ANNOUNCER: OPENING CREDITS.

Music: Opening theme.

NARRATOR: A long time ago in a galaxy far, far away there came a time of revolution, when Rebels united to challenge a tyrannical Empire. Now, it is a dark time for the Rebellion. Evading the dreaded Imperial starfleet, a group of freedom fighters, led by Luke Skywalker, has established a secret base on the remote ice world of Hoth. But the evil Lord Darth Vader, obsessed with finding young Skywalker, has dispatched thousands of "probe droids"—automated hunting machines—into the far reaches of space.

Sound: X-wings, transports zooming by, under.

NARRATOR: Now, a small space convoy of Rebel transport ships and snubfighter escorts seeks to bring desperately needed supplies and reinforcements to Hoth.

SCENE 1-1   NARRA'S COCKPIT

Sound: Narra's cockpit sounds come up. All other lines are over comlink.

COMMANDER NARRA: Renegade Flight, this is Renegade Leader. I'm getting interference on my sensors. It just might be Imperial jamming, so maintain close visual scanning. Renegade Four, stay closer to your transport ship.

RENEGADE FOUR: I copy, boss. It's probably just the atmospherics, cluttering the sensors.

17

NARRA: Transport ships, keep close together. We go to hyper-space as soon as we're out of Derra IV's gravity field. Fighters, stick close to the convoy and keep your eyes open, all of you.

RENEGADE SEVEN: Renegade Leader, this is Renegade Seven. Boss, I have a visual sighting—a number of small spacecraft coming at high velocity, from sector four.

NARRA: Can you identify them?

RENEGADE SEVEN: They're moving awfully—Imperial TIE fight-ers! Must be twenty of 'em!

NARRA: Renegade Flight, this is Renegade Leader. Prepare to engage the TIE fighters. Transport ships, go to hyperdrive as soon as you're clear of—

RENEGADE THREE: This is Renegade Three! Boss, there's an-other bunch of 'em dead ahead on our course. They're breaking for attack!

RENEGADE TWO: This is Renegade Two! More TIEs approach-ing from sector eight!

RENEGADE THREE: They're all over the place! Here they come!

Sound: TIE fighters swoop in firing.

NARRA: Renegade Three, Four, Five, and Six: Get up and clear the way for the transports. The rest of you protect the convoy.

Sound: Another TIE, firing, passes.

NARRA: Keep close to your wingmen! Transports, run for it! Max-imum acceleration! All right, Renegade Flight, hit 'em!

Sound: Narra's ship zooms, fires. TIEs and snubs maneuver and dogfight.

RENEGADE THREE: Watch it, Renegade Two!

RENEGADE TWO: I see him!

Sound: Zooming, firing, all under next.

RENEGADE FOUR: One on your tail, Renegade Seven! Scissor right! Scissor right!

RENEGADE SEVEN: Here I come! Get 'im off me!

Sound: Snub firing.

RENEGADE FOUR: Got 'im!

RENEGADE SEVEN: Boss, we can't stop 'em! There're too many!

Sound: Distant explosion.

RENEGADE THREE: Boss, they just got Ketku!

NARRA: Protect the transports! The transports *have* to get through! Repeat, the transports have to—

Sound: Explosion.

RENEGADE SEVEN: Boss, they're all over us! They just got transport number two!

RENEGADE THREE: I'm hit! Lost both portside engines!

NARRA: Keep going!

Sound: Dogfighting, etc.

RENEGADE THREE: This is Renegade Three; there're four TIE fighters on me! Help me, somebody! Can't shake 'em!

Sound: Renegade Three explodes.

RENEGADE THREE: SCREAMS, SUDDENLY CUT OFF.

NARRA: Renegade Three!

RENEGADE TWO: He's gone, boss . . .

RENEGADE FOUR: There's no way out! They're all around us!

Sound: Explosion.

RENEGADE TWO: The lead transport just blew!

RENEGADE SEVEN: Boss, there's a bunch of 'em headed for you!

NARRA: Try to make a run for it!

Sound: TIEs firing, shrieking.

NARRA: All ships: This is Commander Narra. Break contact and escape if you can! Break contact and run for it—

Sound: TIEs, firing. Explosions in Narra's cockpit.

NARRA: SCREAMS.

Sound: Fades to silence.

SCENE 1-2   IMPERIAL DESTROYER BRIDGE

Sound: Sounds of Imperial Destroyer bridge come up. Instrumentation, crew's wild lines, etc.

IMPERIAL OFFICER: *(APPROACHING)* Captain Needa!

NEEDA: Yes, Lieutenant?

IMPERIAL OFFICER: Sir, Starfleet Headquarters reports that a Rebel convoy has been completely destroyed near Derra IV.

NEEDA: At least *someone* is seeing a little action. Let's hope that *we* do, before the Rebellion is completely obliterated. What is the status of our probe-droid operation?

IMPERIAL OFFICER: The probe droids we've launched so far report no Rebel activity—no human activity, for that matter—on any of the planets they've reconnoitered.

NEEDA: And the next launch-group?

IMPERIAL OFFICER: All the probes are targeted and ready to go. The ship is now in position. Shall I give the order to launch?

NEEDA: No, Lieutenant. I just received a priority signal from Lord Vader's flagship. We have new information to program into the probes' data banks and sensors.

IMPERIAL OFFICER: That could delay the launch for some time, Captain Needa. May I ask what the new information is?

NEEDA: It seems that Lord Vader is more eager than ever to locate this "Skywalker." He has also placed great emphasis on discovering the whereabouts of a starship called the *Millennium Falcon*.

IMPERIAL OFFICER: I'll have the new material programmed into the probes immediately, sir.

NEEDA: Lord Vader has also revised the targeting list. Have the operations people retarget probe droids for the planets Allyuen, Tokmia, and Hoth.

IMPERIAL OFFICER: *Hoth*, sir? But Captain Needa, that's an ice planet!

NEEDA: I am aware of that, Lieutenant.

IMPERIAL OFFICER: Sir, the Rebels' last base was on a tropical planet. Their equipment and supplies are mostly suited for jungle conditions.

NEEDA: Are you questioning a directive from Lord Vader, Lieutenant?

IMPERIAL OFFICER: No, sir, of course not!

NEEDA: That is very, very prudent of you. Perhaps Lord Vader has information he doesn't deign to share. Or, it may be that he is following his intuition. In any event, it is always dangerous to differ with him.

IMPERIAL OFFICER: I'll attend to it right away, sir. These changes won't take very long.

NEEDA: Carry on.

IMPERIAL OFFICER: Tech crews, stand by! *(MOVING OFF)* Prepare to retarget probe droids for planets Allyuen, Tokmia . . . *and Hoth*!

Sound: Bridge fades.

SCENE 1-3   REBEL BRIEFING ROOM

Sound: Rebel briefing room comes up.

FIRST REBEL: *(AS SOUND COMES UP)*—but the techs have assured me that they can have the speeders adapted, ready to operate here on Hoth, within another day at the most, Princess Leia.

LEIA: And the base defenses?

FIRST REBEL: Nearly complete, at least as complete a defensive and offensive system as we can manage right now. Lieutenant Commander Skywalker and the others have practically all the sensors in place for a regional warning network. As time allows, we can expand it.

GENERAL RIEEKAN: How do we stand on cold-weather clothing and other gear?

FIRST REBEL: We've managed to procure or improvise enough for everyone in the base, General Rieekan. And so, Your Highness; gentlemen; that's our current status.

RIEEKAN: We're short of just about everything, including sleep, but we've almost completed drilling of the ice caverns, and the base is close to completion. And when the convoy arrives, we'll be in far better shape. Is there anything else, gentlemen?

STAFF: GENERAL MURMURS, NEGATIVE.

RIEEKAN: Your Highness? Have you anything to add?

LEIA: Just one thing, General Rieekan: I think that everyone in

Hoth Base is bearing up as bravely now as they ever did in battle. I hope that all of you here will pass that along for me.

STAFF: GENERAL THANKS AND REASSURANCES THAT THEY WILL.

RIEEKAN: Our next staff meeting will be at the same time tomorrow. We all have a great deal to accomplish by then. Dismissed.

Sound: Chairs moving back from the table.

STAFF: CONVERSING IN LOW TONES AS THEY EXIT.

LEIA: They're all worried, even though they're trying not to let it show.

RIEEKAN: They know that there's a lot to be done yet, and that this base is the Rebellion's best chance to regroup and reorganize. Maybe its last.

FIRST REBEL: *(OFF)* General Rieekan! Urgent message for you, sir! They're decoding it now.

RIEEKAN: *(MOVING OFF)* Pardon me, Your Highness. I'll be right back.

LEIA: I'll speak to you later, General Rieekan. I have to make certain that—

LUKE: *(APPROACHING)* Leia! Hey, Princess, wait up!

LEIA: Hello, Luke.

LUKE: Glad I caught you. I was wondering—how you were getting along. I haven't seen much of you lately.

LEIA: I—we're trying to pull things back together. Everyone's been so busy . . .

LUKE: Yeah; me, too. That's why I told See-Threepio and Artoo-Detoo to stay close to you, help out when they could.

LEIA: *You* told them—to help *me*?

LUKE: They're glad to do it. I mean they used to belong to my uncle, but they sort of belong with both of us, now.

LEIA: I guess so.

LUKE: Leia, I'm not due to go back outside for a while yet.

HAN: *(FROM OFF)* Hey, is this the staff conference?

LUKE: Uh, I was thinking, if you had a little time . . .

LEIA: Luke, I really have to see about some things that just can't—

HAN: *(APPROACHING)* Where is everybody? Luke! Hey, kid!

LUKE: Oh. H'lo, Han. Hi, Chewbacca.

CHEWBACCA: GRUNTS A GREETING.

HAN: Where'd the general go?

LUKE: He was headed over to—

HAN: Aw, never mind; Her Overwhelmingly Highnessness here'll do.

LEIA: Now what, Han?

HAN: Have me 'n' Chewie been pulling our weight around here or not?

LUKE: CLEARS HIS THROAT.

LEIA: Han, what's wrong with you? Nobody ever said that you and Chewbacca weren't—

HAN: When the *Millennium Falcon* got shot up, that last time around, I knew I'd have to wait in line for repairs. But they've got the base's defensive generators in place now, and the ion cannon.

CHEWBACCA: GROWLS, REMINDING HIM.

HAN: Huh? Oh yeah, and like Chewie says: the trenches and gun emplacements are all set up, too.

LUKE: "AHEMS," RATHER MORE LOUDLY.

LEIA: They still have to make sure the energy field is working, and adapt the snowspeeders to conditions on Hoth. Those just take priority right now, even over the *Falcon*.

HAN: Look, I need a starship that *works*. I got her messed up helpin' you Rebels; the least you could do is—

LEIA: Aren't you a Rebel, Han? Or do you and Chewbacca still consider yourselves independent operators?

CHEWBACCA: GROANS.

HAN: Look, we get a little jittery when the *Falcon* doesn't work right. And you need her, too. All you've got here in Hoth Base are some X-wing fighters and a few transport ships.

LEIA: Yes. We need ships. We need provisions. We need clothing, equipment . . .

LUKE: Han, most of the techs and engineers are dead on their feet, and they still can't keep up with all the work that has to be finished before the base can be—

HAN: Luke, me and the Wookiee would've had the *Falcon* fixed already, by ourselves. Except that I've been riding all over this snowball with *you*, pal, on those stupid, smelly, ornery tauntauns!

LEIA: Those warning sensors have to be set in place, and you and Luke are the best riders we have.

HAN: I've heard all this before, if you'll remember . . .

LUKE: Han, nobody twisted your arm to sign on with the Rebellion. Aren't you the one who's always saying that a deal's a deal?

CHEWBACCA: SNORTS GRUFFLY.

HAN: Well—are you saying it was part of the deal for the *Falcon* to be sitting there, outta commission, when—

RIEEKAN: *(APPROACHING)* Glad to see you're so full of energy,

25

Captain Solo. It can't be much fun, being out in that freezing wind day after day.

HAN: Oh, uh, hello, General. Sir.

CHEWBACCA: MUTTERS A GREETING.

RIEEKAN: Hello, Chewbacca. Your Highness, it's just as well you're still here. They just decoded the message. In fact, you all might as well hear this.

LUKE: What is it, General? What's wrong?

RIEEKAN: A huge force of TIE fighters jumped Commander Narra and the convoy off Derra IV. Cut them to pieces. There were no survivors.

LEIA: Oh, no . . . We need them so badly. We need every one of them so badly.

CHEWBACCA: HOOTS MOURNFULLY.

HAN: Quiet, Chewie . . .

RIEEKAN: Luke, this bumps you to commander.

LUKE: I—the boss was a great man . . . great pilot.

HAN: It's a rotten way to step into somebody's shoes, Luke—*I know*. But you can handle the job. That's why you've got it.

LEIA: Luke, I know how much you respected Commander Narra. But he respected you, too; that's why he put you in command of Rogue Flight.

RIEEKAN: This means no resupply, at least for a while, and no snubfighter reinforcements either. Rogue Flight's just about all we've got.

LUKE: Then we're gonna need whatever else we have. General, can you spare some techs to help Chewbacca work on the *Falcon*? Or even some repair droids? Whatever you can manage.

RIEEKAN: I'll do what I can, Luke. *(MOVING OFF)* I'll be in the command center, Your Highness.

LEIA: I'll join you shortly.

HAN: Let's go, Luke. We're a little early, but we've got a lotta sensors to place today. I'll get the tauntauns saddled and we can go work on our suntans. C'mon, Chewie. *(MOVING OFF)* Don't forget your heavy-duty underwear, kid!

CHEWBACCA: GROWLING AS HE MOVES OFF.

LEIA: Luke, I'm glad you're here. We'll need you more than ever, now.

LUKE: The boss was one of the best—he was one of the best we had.

LEIA: I know.

LUKE: *(MOVING OFF)* I'd better catch up with Han. There's so much to do . . .

LEIA: I'll see you later, Luke.

Sound: Base fades.

SCENE 1-4 HOTH EXTERIOR

Sound: Exterior Hoth, winds, etc., come up. Luke's tauntaun approaches, making its sounds, galloping.

LUKE: *(APPROACHING)* Okay, girl. Hold up, hold up now! That's it, girl . . .

Sound: The tauntaun slows and stops, but shifts and stamps nervously, complaining and balking.

LUKE: Easy, girl! Easy! What's wrong with you?

Sound: The tauntaun balks.

27

LUKE: Just calm down, old girl! Time for a communications check, then we'll get going again.

Sound: Luke activates his wrist comlink.

LUKE: Echo Three to Echo Seven, commo check. Echo Three to Echo Seven. Han, old buddy, do you read me?

HAN: *(OVER COMLINK)* Loud and clear, Luke. What's up?

LUKE: I haven't picked up any life readings out here so far. How about you?

HAN: Are you kidding? There isn't enough life on this ice cube to fill a space cruiser. All I'm picking up is chilblains and saddle-sores.

Sound: Luke's tauntaun acts up again, shuffling and stamping, rearing, etc.

LUKE: My tauntaun's been acting up. She's really skittish—nervous.

HAN: Hey, I came across a carcass. It looked like one of those wampa ice beasts made a kill a day or two ago.

LUKE: A wampa?

HAN: Yeah. Watch yourself, Luke. Those wampas'll go after anything they can find.

LUKE: I read you, Han. What's your location?

HAN: I'm at the end of the canyon, where the glacier narrows down. You?

LUKE: I'm at the top of the ridge line.

HAN: I placed all my sensors—I'm going back to the base.

LUKE: Right. I'll be with you shortly. There's a meteorite that hit the ground near here—I want to check it out. It won't take long.

HAN: Hurry up; it's gettin' colder. Looks like a bad storm's kickin' up. I'm gonna go thaw out my saddlesores. See you at the base.

LUKE: This is Echo Three, out.

Sound: Luke's comlink deactivates. Tauntaun complains.

LUKE: All right, baby. We're going home soon. Calm down!

Sound: The tauntaun stamps and gobbles.

LUKE: Hey, steady, girl!

Sound: Tauntaun frightened.

LUKE: What's gotten into you? You smell something? What's the matter—

Sound: The wampa ice beast as it pounces on Luke and his mount.

LUKE: Wampa! *No!*

Sound: Frightened bleating of the tauntaun as it stamps. Wampa roars, striking Luke. Impact of the swipe.

LUKE: CRIES OUT AS HE'S STRUCK—ENDS ABRUPTLY.

Sound: Luke lands in the crusty snow. The wampa roars again. Impact as it strikes the tauntaun. Tauntaun's death gurgle and fall. Wampa growls. Exterior fades.

SCENE 1-5   REBEL HANGAR

Sound: Interior of Rebel caverns comes up. Machinery, wild lines, utility vehicles, etc.

FIRST REBEL: *(APPROACHING)* Princess Leia! Your Highness!

LEIA: Yes? What is it?

FIRST REBEL: Princess Leia, General Rieekan presents his compliments and would like to see you in the command center as soon as possible.

LEIA: I'll be right there. *(CALLING TO DISTANCE)* Threepio! Artoo-Detoo!

THREEPIO: *(APPROACHING)* Yes, Your Highness?

Sound: Artoo's sounds and Threepio's servomotors as the droids come to POV.

LEIA: Do either of you know if Luke and Han have gotten back yet?

THREEPIO: They haven't returned as yet, Your Highness, but they are due at any moment.

LEIA: Would you tell them I'd like to speak to them?

THREEPIO: Most certainly, Your Highness. Oh, and Artoo-Detoo and I moved your new communication unit into your quarters.

ARTOO: BEEPS.

THREEPIO: Artoo says that it is functioning perfectly.

LEIA: Thank you both. You've been a great help.

ARTOO: WHISTLES A "YOU'RE WELCOME."

THREEPIO: A pleasure to be of service, Your Highness. Is there anything else we can do?

LEIA: Not just now. *(MOVING OFF)* But please see that Luke and Han get my message.

THREEPIO: *(CALLING AFTER)* You may rely upon us!

ARTOO: TWEEDLES A WARNING.

THREEPIO: How's that again, Artoo? *Who's* coming?

ARTOO: ANSWERS.

THREEPIO: Oh, yes, it's that bothersome coordinating droid again. Honestly, Artoo, it's *degrading* that a droid with speech capability should be such an officious dullard!

Sound: Coordinator droid approaching.

COORDINATOR DROID: *(APPROACHING WOODEN, LUSTER-LESS VOICE)* Unit Artoo-Detoo. Unit See-Threepio. Confirm.

ARTOO: BRIDLES.

THREEPIO: Quite right, Artoo! *(TO COORDINATOR DROID)* You know perfectly well who we are!

COORDINATOR DROID: Unit Artoo-Detoo, unit—

THREEPIO: Very well, very well! Confirmed! And stop referring to us as "units"!

COORDINATOR DROID: Unit Artoo-Detoo reassigned to cavern-drilling operations. Unit See-Threepio reassigned to communications center.

ARTOO: SHOCKED AND ANGERED. BEEPING.

THREEPIO: I'll handle this, Artoo! *(TO COORDINATOR DROID)* Now, just you see here! Artoo and I are personal aides-de-camp to Commander Skywalker and the Princess Leia Organa!

COORDINATOR DROID: Irrelevant. Reassignment is ordered.

THREEPIO: Do you have any idea to whom you are speaking,

31

you lout? Why, my counterpart and I were the ones who saved the Death Star plans! And we helped rescue the princess.

ARTOO: BURBLES A REMINDER.

THREEPIO: What, Artoo? Oh yes. *(TO COORDINATOR DROID)* And I'll have you know that Artoo here was in that X-wing fighter when our master blew up the Death Star! Confirm *that*, you rusting bureaucrat!

COORDINATOR DROID: Data not relevant.

THREEPIO: *Not relevant, is it?* Then allow me to tell you what *is* relevant. We have been given an errand by the Princess Leia Organa herself. If you want to countermand her order, go argue with her!

COORDINATOR DROID: The Princess Leia Organa?

THREEPIO: *Confirmed!* So, go bother her. She'll probably have you deactivated.

ARTOO: GIVES THE COORDINATOR DROID A RASPBERRY.

COORDINATOR DROID: Reassignment rescinded.

THREEPIO: Hah! That's more like it! Bad enough that we have to live in these ice caverns, without having to contend with the likes of you. Why, just now we found the princess's room freezingly cold. If we hadn't turned up the heating system, she might have caught—

COORDINATOR DROID: Confirm: heat increased?

THREEPIO: —her death of—eh? That's what I said, isn't it? If she and our master didn't have us to look after them, there's no telling—

COORDINATOR DROID: Error. Error. Increased heat causes melting of cavern walls. Malfunction possible. Damage possible.

THREEPIO: What? Oh! Oh, dear! Come along, Artoo! I hope it's not too late! What have you *done*?

ARTOO: *(MOVING OFF WITH THREEPIO)* MAKES PROTESTING NOISES.

THREEPIO: *(MOVING OFF)* What do you mean, *my* fault? *You're* the one who adjusted the heating system. Oh, this is dreadful!

Sound: Base fades.

SCENE 1-6 HOTH CAVE

Sound: Hoth winds come up in background, in wampa's cave.

LUKE: *(PANTING, MOANING. VOICE ECHOES)* What—where . . . *(GROANS)*

Sound: Comlink activates.

LUKE: Echo . . . Echo Three, Echo *Three*, to Echo Seven. Come in, Han—Han . . . I was—Han, I was attacked by a wampa. I'm in—in its cave. Dunno where . . . I'm wounded.

Sound: The comlink as Luke turns the gain higher.

LUKE: Han . . . do you—d'you copy? Stuck . . . I'm stuck in here. The wampa—it left me frozen to the cave ceiling, by my feet . . .

Sound: Growl of the wampa, distance.

LUKE: *(RAGGED WHISPER)* Wampa! Han, the wampa's coming back! *(GROANS)* My lightsaber—it's on the cave floor. I can see it, but . . . *(MOANS WITH THE EFFORT)* Can't reach it. Can't reach it . . .

Sound: The wampa is closer.

LUKE: *(CHANTS SHAKILY)* The Jedi and his lightsaber. The lightsaber and the Jedi. *(MORE EVENLY)* The two are one. The Force binds us.

Sound: Nearby, the lightsaber trembles, vibrating like a tuning fork.

LUKE: The Force binds us. The Force calls my lightsaber to me.

Sound: Lightsaber's vibration rises in pitch and intensity.

LUKE: The Force—

Sound: Wampa, closer now.

LUKE: —calls my lightsaber—

Sound: Tuning-fork vibration peaks.

LUKE: —to me!

Sound: The lightsaber, breaking free, rings as it zips through the air and slams into Luke's palm.

LUKE: Got it!

Sound: He activates it. Lightsaber hums as he swings it. Ice shatters and the blade hisses and spits. Ice falls to the cave floor.

Sound: Luke's impact as he hits the floor. The saber deactivates.

LUKE: GROANS, PANTS.

Sound: Comlink activating.

LUKE: *(PANTING, HUSHED)* Han, come in. I got myself down, but—

Sound: The wampa charges, roaring. Lightsaber activates.

LUKE: *(REACTING TO CHARGE, INDICATING EFFORT OF THE SLASH.)*

Sound: Lightsaber moans as Luke slashes with it, then flares as it cuts. Wampa's roar changes to a howl of pain. The saber cuts again. Wampa's howl changes to death rattle, then silence, as it falls heavily to the cave floor. The lightsaber deactivates.

LUKE: PANTS.

Sound: Comlink.

LUKE: Hello, Han—base camp—anybody! Wampa's dead. I killed . . . killed it. *(GROANS)* No good staying here in the cave. Tauntaun's nowhere around . . . I've got no—no survival gear. *(INDICATES EFFORT OF RISING)* Just in case somebody's receiving, I'll leave my comlink keyed open. *(MOVING OFF UN-STEADILY)* Nothing I can—nothing I can do but try to make it back on foot . . .

Sound: Hoth winds rise, fade.

SCENE 1-7   REBEL HANGAR

Sound: Rebel base—hangar section comes up: repairs, servicing, construction, background conversations, etc. There is the hailing sound of a comlink.

SECOND REBEL: *(OVER COMLINK)* Outpost four to Deck Officer. Outpost four to Deck Officer.

DECK OFFICER: Deck Officer here.

SECOND REBEL: We have a positive ID on that tauntaun rider. It's Captain Solo. We passed him through the defensive zone. He'll be at your location any time now.

DECK OFFICER: Right. I'll pass the word. *(CALLING OFF)* Sentry!

SENTRY: *(OFF)* Yes, sir!

DECK OFFICER: You can let that tauntaun rider in right away.

SENTRY: *(OFF)* Right, sir!

Sound: Deck officer activates his comlink.

DECK OFFICER: Command center, this is the Deck Officer.

COMMAND CENTER: *(OVER COMLINK)* Command center here.

DECK OFFICER: Captain Solo's back, sir. No sign of Commander Skywalker yet.

COMMAND CENTER: Right. Have Solo report here at once.

DECK OFFICER: Will do. Deck Officer out.

Sound: As Deck Officer switches off his comlink, Han approaches on his tauntaun, which is galloping, snorting, etc.

DECK OFFICER: One of you men take his reins!

SENTRY: *(OFF)* Here, I'll take 'em.

Sound: As Han dismounts, tauntaun gobbles.

HAN: *(OFF)* Thanks.

DECK OFFICER: Captain Solo!

HAN: *(APPROACHING)* Yeah? What can I do for you?

DECK OFFICER: They want you and Commander Skywalker in the command center, Captain.

HAN: Tell 'em I'll be along in a bit. Luke'll be back any minute. Is my ship fixed yet?

DECK OFFICER: I don't think so, sir. They had to pull the techs off her for some problems they're having with the snowspeeders.

HAN: Oh, swell. That really takes the prize.

DECK OFFICER: Your first mate is working on the *Falcon*, though.

HAN: Thanks. Tell command I'll be there right after I check on my ship.

DECK OFFICER: General Rieekan and the princess wanted to see you as soon as you got—

HAN: Look, you just go and officer your deck, will you? *(MOVING OFF)* I've got a starship to think about.

Sound: Music up, then fades.

SCENE 1-7A   REBEL HANGAR

Sound: Different, closer sound of tools (plasma welding torch). Chewbacca growls softly to himself as he works.

HAN: *(APPROACHING)* Chewie! Where are you?

CHEWBACCA: BARKS AN IRRITATED ANSWER.

HAN: How's it goin'?

CHEWBACCA: YAMMERS A COMPLAINT.

HAN: Well, don't jump all over me about it. We'll just have to finish the job by ourselves.

CHEWBACCA: SNARLS.

HAN: Awright, don't lose your temper. I'll be right back to give you a hand.

CHEWBACCA: A MIFFED QUESTION.

HAN: I dunno; somethin' at the command center. I might as well tell 'em we're gonna be leaving.

CHEWBACCA: ROAR.

HAN: Forget it! I've made up my mind. *(MOVING OFF)* Maybe when Luke gets back he can help us with the *Falcon*.

Sound: Base fades.

SCENE 1-8 HOTH EXTERIOR

Sound: Exterior, Hoth: blizzard. Sounds of Luke stumbling through the snow.

LUKE: PANTS, NEARLY DONE IN.

Sound: Luke's comlink.

LUKE: Base, base—this is Skywalker . . . Ah . . .

Sound: Comlink off.

LUKE: PANTING AS HE TRIES TO GO ON. GROANS AS HE GOES DOWN.

Sound: Luke sprawls in the snow.

BEN: *(FAINTLY AT FIRST. OTHERWORLDLY)* Luke . . .

LUKE: Hmm? Sound—sounded like—

BEN: Luke . . . Hear me, Luke.

LUKE: Huh? Ben? *Ben!*

BEN: Yes. Listen to me, Luke.

LUKE: Ben, I see you, but—how—it can't be!

BEN: It *is*, Luke.

LUKE: But . . . you died! I saw you die!

BEN: Listen carefully, Luke. There is not much time. You must go to the Dagobah system.

LUKE: Dagobah—Dagobah system. Ben . . . I don't understand . . .

BEN: There you will learn from Yoda, the Jedi Master who instructed me.

LUKE: Yoda. Dagobah.

BEN: This is vital, Luke. You must not fail. *(FADING)* You must not fail!

LUKE: Ben! Wait! Don't leave me!

Sound: Luke thrashing in the snow on hands and knees.

LUKE: Ben! Where did you go? Ben, help me! Help me! *Ben!*

Sound: Hoth winds rise, then fade.

NARRATOR: An Imperial probe droid now hunts the Rebels on the frozen wastes of Hoth. Injured, suffering from shock and exposure, Luke Skywalker can go no further. Help of a sort, and a new quest for the young Jedi, have come from the Force. But these may not be enough to help him survive the deadly Hoth night.

Music: Up and under closing credits.

ANNOUNCER: CLOSING CREDITS.

EPISODE TWO:
"THE COMING STORM"

C H A R A C T E R S :

Luke   Chewbacca
Leia   Rieekan
Han   Deck Officer
Threepio   Sentry
Artoo

ANNOUNCER: OPENING CREDITS.

Music: Opening theme.

NARRATOR: A long time ago in a galaxy far, far away there came a time of revolution, when Rebels united to challenge a tyrannical Empire. Now, it is a dark time for the Rebellion.

Sound: Hoth winds.

NARRATOR: The freedom fighters have established a base inside the ice caverns on the frozen planet Hoth. Luke Skywalker, patrolling the Hoth wasteland for Imperial probe droids, has been injured by a savage wampa ice beast. Wandering in a delirium, nearly at the end of his endurance, he has seen the image of his Jedi instructor, and been told that he must seek further training. But Obi-Wan Kenobi's ghostly figure has faded from sight, leaving Luke alone to face the terrible Hoth blizzard.

SCENE 2-1 HOTH EXTERIOR

Sound: Luke trudging, with Hoth winds under.

LUKE: *(BREATHING HARD)* Ben! Ben, come back.

Sound: Luke falls.

LUKE: *(GRUNTS WITH PAIN OF IMPACT)* Where are you? . . . Did I . . . did I just imagine you? Getting so hard to see . . . So cold. Dagobah. Dagobah. Was that what you said, Ben? Yoda—have to try to find Yoda . . . Yes. Yes . . . So tired . . . so cold.

Sound: Hoth winds fade.

SCENE 2-2 REBEL COMMAND CENTER

Sound: Rebel command center up.

LEIA: What was it you wanted, General Rieekan?

RIEEKAN: We had a signal on the sensors a few minutes ago, Princess Leia. But it's gone now; reception's getting worse in this storm.

LEIA: A life-form?

RIEEKAN: An energy source. The monitors said it seemed to be transmitting, and moving as well.

LEIA: Could it have been distortion? Or equipment malfunction?

RIEEKAN: The monitors only had it on their scopes for a moment—then they lost it. They could have been wrong.

LEIA: Well, we should make sure. Perhaps we should send out a patrol?

RIEEKAN: Our snowspeeders still aren't ready, and sending people out in this storm on tauntauns would cost us lives.

LEIA: What do you recommend?

RIEEKAN: Solo and Skywalker are due back soon. They're the last men we have out there. When they return, we seal the shield doors and keep a close watch on the sensors, to see if whatever it was shows up again.

LEIA: If it does?

RIEEKAN: Well, it will depend on when and where it does. There's not a great deal that we can do with night coming on.

LEIA: I suppose that's true.

HAN: *(APPROACHING)* General Rieekan?

RIEEKAN: Over here, Solo.

HAN: All your sensors are in place, General. I couldn't see any sign of life out there except some old wampa kills.

RIEEKAN: Good work, Solo. You look done in.

HAN: Yeah, it's gettin' pretty frosty out there. But at least you'll know if somebody comes sniffin' around lookin' for this base.

LEIA: We hope.

RIEEKAN: Has Commander Skywalker reported in yet?

HAN: No. He's checking out a meteorite that hit near him, up at the top of the ridge line. He'll be back any time now.

LEIA: Another meteorite?

RIEEKAN: Yes, with all the meteor activity in this star system, it's going to be difficult to spot approaching ships.

HAN: Yeah, there's plenty of junk floating around in this part of space. That's kind of why you picked it, isn't it?

LEIA: Perhaps when we have more ships and people we can place surveillance satellites in orbit.

RIEEKAN: Perhaps, Your Highness. But I don't expect reinforcements for some time.

HAN: Uh, General, look, I know it isn't a great time to bring this up, but me and Chewie are making arrangements to leave. We can't stay with the Rebellion any longer.

LEIA: Han!

RIEEKAN: I'm very sorry to hear that, Captain. We've come to rely a great deal on you both, and on the *Millennium Falcon*.

HAN: As you know, there's a price on my head. If I don't pay Jabba the Hutt what I owe him, I'm a dead man.

RIEEKAN: Yes, I know. A death mark is not an easy thing to live with.

HAN: Yeah, or *through*.

RIEEKAN: Well, you're a good fighter, Solo. I hate to lose you. But good luck to you, and to Chewbacca as well.

HAN: Thanks, General. We both think you're a pretty good commanding officer, too.

RIEEKAN: Thank you, Han. *(TO LEIA)* Your Highness, I'll keep you informed if anything develops.

LEIA: Thank you, General.

HAN: Well, Your Highness, I guess this is it.

LEIA: That's right. This is it.

HAN: Phew! Well, don't get all mushy on me! So long, Princess. *(MOVING SLIGHTLY OFF)* I'll see you around, one of these days.

LEIA: Han, wait.

HAN: *(APPROACHING AGAIN)* Yes, Your Highnessness?

LEIA: I thought you said you had decided to stay with the Rebellion? I thought you were going to help us here on Hoth.

HAN: That bounty hunter we ran into on Ord Mantell? Well, he changed my mind. Strangers blazing away at me from all directions have always made me a little nervous.

LEIA: Everybody in the Rebellion is under a death sentence, if the Empire wins.

HAN: Ah, but not like this! Jabba's put a price on my head that's three times what I owe him, and it's kind of hard for me and the Wookiee to hide. We tend to be known everywhere, by the wrong kind of people. Every worm with a blaster's daydreaming about burning me down.

LEIA: You're safe here.

HAN: *(LAUGHS)* Listen, I set foot on any populated planet in the

Empire, I'm a target. It's like bein' in prison. And, one day they're bound to find me anyhow.

LEIA: Then, say good-bye! You're an expert at saying good-bye, aren't you, Han? You've had so much practice!

HAN: Look, I've got to settle this thing with Jabba the Hutt. I'm not gonna be any good to the Rebellion or anyone else until I do.

LEIA: We need you here, Han.

HAN: *We* need?

LEIA: The Rebel Alliance.

HAN: Why don't you stop talking for the Alliance and talk for yourself for once? What do *you* need, Leia?

LEIA: I don't have the slightest idea what you're talking about.

HAN: *(TSKS)* No, I guess you probably don't, at that. Looks like you never will, huh?

LEIA: And what, precisely, is it that I'm supposed to know, O Source of Wisdom? What are you trying to imply?

HAN: Come on! When're you gonna quit playin' games? You want me to stay because of the way you feel about me!

LEIA: Yes! I feel that you're a great help to the Alliance. I feel that you're a natural leader. If it wasn't for you we'd never have—

HAN: Uh, uh. We both know what I'm talking about. How come it's so hard for you to admit it?

LEIA: Han . . .

HAN: Huh? Huh?

LEIA: Has anybody ever mentioned anything to you about your ego problem?

HAN: Hah? C'mon! You look so pretty when you're blushing!

47

LEIA: You're imagining things.

HAN: Am I, Leia? Then why'd you call me back? 'Fraid I was gonna leave without giving you a good-bye kiss?

LEIA: You?

HAN: Me!

LEIA: I'd sooner kiss a Wookiee!

HAN: Well, I can arrange that, but you better move fast. Good-bye!

LEIA: Good-bye!

HAN: You could use a good kiss! *(MOVING OFF)* Let us all in on it, Princess; doesn't it ever get boring up there on that pedestal?

LEIA: Ohhh!

Sound: Command center fades.

SCENE 2-3   HOTH EXTERIOR

Sound: Hoth winds come up, Luke still plodding.

LUKE: *(BREATHLESS)* Ben? . . . Ben? So hard to . . . must keep . . . must keep trying . . .

Sound: Luke falls.

LUKE: *(GRUNTS)* Can't do it, Ben. Can't make it. I'm sorry. Tried; I tried, Ben . . .

Sound: Hoth winds fade.

SCENE 2-4   REBEL HANGAR

Sound: Base hangar noises come up.

HAN: *(APPROACHING)* Chewie! Hey, Chewie! You got the *Falcon* fixed yet?

CHEWBACCA: RESPONDS.

HAN: I want out of this place. We're gettin' off this snowball right now, before they close the shield door for the night.

CHEWBACCA: WOOFS AN INTERROGATIVE.

HAN: Because I'm sick of this planet, that's why! Because Jabba's hunting for our heads! Because I'm an expert at saying good-bye! Now, warm her up and let's raise ship!

CHEWBACCA: BARKS.

HAN: What?

CHEWBACCA: BARKS AGAIN.

HAN: You took *what* apart? What're you doing fine-tuning the hyperdrive now? Look at that mess! Are you crazy?

CHEWBACCA: SNARLS A LITTLE MENACINGLY.

HAN: Okay, calm down! We've still got a while before they shut the shield door. You close up the vector guides and I'll put the transition rig back together.

CHEWBACCA: OBJECTS.

HAN: All I wanna do is get us outta here, Chewie. Put 'em back together the best way you can, just so they'll get us to our next stop.

Sound: Tool noises as they work.

CHEWBACCA: HOOTS A QUESTION.

HAN: Who, Her Royalness? Never mind what she said. Remind me to tell you about hobnobbing with the upper classes some time! It's such fun!

THREEPIO: *(APPROACHING)* Don't you try to blame me, Artoo! I didn't actually ask you to turn on the heating system. I merely commented that it was freezing in the princess's chamber.

ARTOO: *(APPROACHING)* TWEEDLES.

HAN: Oh, great. Just what we needed. Here come the Loose Wiring Brothers.

THREEPIO: But it's supposed to be freezing in there!

ARTOO: QUERIES.

THREEPIO: I really don't know how we're going to dry out all her clothes.

ARTOO: BLAAATS AT HIM.

THREEPIO: Oh, switch off, you little runt!

CHEWBACCA: YIPS.

HAN: What are you doing, Chewie? Are you a saboteur? You think I want to spend the rest of my life here, fur-face?

CHEWBACCA: UTTERS AN ANGRY DENIAL TO HAN.

THREEPIO: Oh, Captain Solo, Artoo and I have been looking for you, sir.

HAN: Listen, Chewie, those vector guides'll do for now. Just get 'em back in place and let's button up the hull!

THREEPIO: Captain Solo . . .

CHEWBACCA: GROWLS.

HAN: I don't want 'em perfect. I don't want 'em pretty—

THREEPIO: Princess Leia has been trying to get you on the comlink, Captain.

HAN: I want 'em *now*! *(TO THREEPIO)* Whoa there. What'd you say, Threepio?

THREEPIO: I have been attempting to draw your attention to the fact that the Princess Leia has been trying to reach you by comlink now for—

HAN: I turned my comlink off. I don't want to talk to her anymore. It's bad for my disposition.

THREEPIO: Indeed! Well, Artoo and I are to inform you that the Princess Leia is worried about Master Luke. She doesn't know where he is.

HAN: I don't know where he is, either. D'you see him around here anyplace?

THREEPIO: That's just the point, Captain. Nobody knows where Master Luke is.

ARTOO: WHISTLES AN ANXIOUS CONFIRMATION.

HAN: What d'you mean "nobody knows," Threepio? He was only a couple minutes behind me when I rode in.

THREEPIO: Well, that is, you see, sir—

HAN: *(TO OFFICER)* Deck Officer! Deck Officer! C'mere, will you?

THREEPIO: Excuse me, sir, but might I inquire as to whether you—

HAN: Will you shut up for a second—

Sound: Han clamps his hand over the metal robot faceplate.

THREEPIO: MAKES MUFFLED, HIGHLY MIFFED SOUNDS, PROTESTING.

DECK OFFICER: *(APPROACHING)* Yes, sir, Captain Solo? What can I do for you?

HAN: You can tell me where Commander Skywalker is.

THREEPIO: MUFFLED SOUNDS.

DECK OFFICER: I haven't seen him. Is that droid malfunctioning, sir?

HAN: Not any more than usual.

DECK OFFICER: Then why are you holding your hand over his vocal slot?

HAN: He's got a cough!

THREEPIO: OBJECTS STRENUOUSLY, GAGGED.

HAN: Now, what about Luke?

DECK OFFICER: Commander Skywalker hasn't come through the main shield door. It's possible that he came in through the south entrance.

HAN: It's *possible*? *It's possible?* Well, why don't you just go and find out if it really happened, huh?

THREEPIO: MUFFLED, AGREEING VIGOROUSLY.

DECK OFFICER: Very well, Captain, as soon as I get the rest of—

HAN: It's gettin' dark out there, friend, and cold, in case you didn't notice.

DECK OFFICER: I'm aware of that. I joined up with the Rebels because I notice things, sir. *(MOVING OFF)* I'll go and check on the commander at once.

HAN: *(CALLING AFTER HIM)* Okay. Look, and thanks, pal!

THREEPIO: MUFFLED PLEA TO BE UNHANDED.

HAN: Hmm?

ARTOO: SAYS "LET HIM GO."

HAN: Oh, sure, Artoo. Sorry, Threepio.

THREEPIO: Thank you, Captain Solo, although there was really no need for that, I'm sure. What's happened to Master Luke, I should like to inquire?

HAN: You go ahead and inquire all you like, Threepio. *(MOVING OFF)* It never does any good around this deep freeze. Seal her up, Chewie! I'll be right back.

THREEPIO: Really, Artoo, have you ever seen such an impossible man?

ARTOO: SAYS "NO."

THREEPIO: Come along. Let's find the Princess Leia and tell her what's happened.

ARTOO: AGREES.

THREEPIO: We shall keep you posted on any new developments, Chewbacca!

CHEWBACCA: GROWLS THANKS.

THREEPIO: Between ourselves, Artoo, I think that Master Luke is in considerable trouble. This planet is even more hostile than that awful Tatooine.

ARTOO: GOES ALONG WITH THAT, MOVING OFF.

THREEPIO: *(MOVING OFF)* I'm so worried about him! This is what we get for allowing Master Luke to go off on his own without us to look after him . . .

Sound: Sounds of hangar bay fade.

SCENE 2-5   REBEL ENTRANCE

Sound: Sounds of entranceway rise, with winds in background.

HAN: *(APPROACHING)* What'd you find out? Where is he?

DECK OFFICER: Sir, Commander Skywalker hasn't come in the south entrance either. No one has heard from him since his last communication check with you.

HAN: He was clear up on the ridge line then.

DECK OFFICER: He might have forgotten to check in.

HAN: Luke? Unlikely. Where he grew up, people learn to be careful. I'm going looking for him.

DECK OFFICER: But Captain Solo—

HAN: Have the techs got those snowspeeders working? I'd use the *Falcon*, but she's on downtime right now.

DECK OFFICER: The snowspeeders aren't ready yet. We've been having all kinds of trouble adapting them to the cold. The techs are running up a bunch of replacement parts; they should be ready by morning.

HAN: Well, morning ain't likely to do Commander Skywalker very much good, is it? Isn't there anything in this whole base that'll fly?

DECK OFFICER: Nothing that can handle a Hoth blizzard, sir. Those winds would smash you down before you got halfway out to the end of—

HAN: All right, forget it. I'll have to ride out and look for him on a tauntaun. *(MOVING OFF)* C'mon, move it! We haven't got much time!

DECK OFFICER: *(MOVING OFF AFTER HIM)* Captain Solo! General Rieekan gave orders that no one is to leave the base!

Sound: Sounds fade.

SCENE 2-6 REBEL HANGAR

Sound: Up in another part of the hangar, with tauntauns nearby.

HAN: *(APPROACHING)* This one here'll have to do; it's still saddled. Tell the command center that I'll keep in touch with them over comlink band alpha.

DECK OFFICER: Wait! General Rieekan doesn't want anybody leaving the base!

HAN: Lieutenant . . .

DECK OFFICER: Sir?

HAN: Lieutenant, what'd you just call me?

DECK OFFICER: Uh, "sir"?

HAN: Right. Now get outta my way.

DECK OFFICER: But the temperature's dropping too rapidly. Even a tauntaun couldn't survive for long.

HAN: Yeah, and my friend's out there someplace. I'm giving you a direct order, to make it easy for you. I'm taking full responsibility, so *don't waste my time*!

DECK OFFICER: I'm afraid I can't let you do this. I have my standing orders, Captain Solo.

HAN: Lieutenant, have you ever seen my first mate? About three times your size? Covered with fur? Got a bad temper?

DECK OFFICER: Why, everybody in the base knows Chewbacca, sir.

HAN: Then get this: If you or anybody else tries to stop me from riding that tauntaun out of here, there's gonna be a fight. And even if you *do* stop me, Chewie's gonna take it real bad.

DECK OFFICER: But General Rieekan has clearly instructed me that no one—

HAN: And do you think General Rieekan wants a quarter of a ton of roarin'-mad Wookiee running around his base?

DECK OFFICER: I'm reasonably certain that he doesn't, sir.

HAN: Smart boy. Stand aside!

Sound: Tauntaun gobbles as Han mounts it, its feet shifting.

DECK OFFICER: I'm trying to save your life! Your tauntaun will freeze before you reach the first marker, even if you don't! Even with an insulated suit, if you're on foot out there, you're dead!

HAN: Then I'll see you in hell!

Sound: Han reins the tauntaun around.

HAN: Here we go, girl! Give me your best! Hya!

Sound: The tauntaun reacts to Han's proddings, gobbling as it races off.

HAN: *(MOVING OFF RAPIDLY)* Hya!

Sound: Comlink activating.

DECK OFFICER: Sentry post one, this is the Deck Officer.

SENTRY: *(OVER COMLINK)* Sentry post one, here.

DECK OFFICER: Tauntaun rider approaching your post.

SENTRY: I see him, sir!

DECK OFFICER: Permit him to pass.

SENTRY: Understood, sir.

Sound: Base sounds fade.

SCENE 2-7   HOTH EXTERIOR

Sound: Hoth winds come up.

LUKE: *(MOANING)* Dagobah . . . Dago . . . bah . . .

HAN: *(FROM OFF)* Luke! Luke!

Sound: Distant tauntaun.

LUKE: What? . . . Ben? . . .

Sound: Tauntaun approaches.

HAN: Luke! *(TO HIS TAUNTAUN)* Whoa, girl; hold up.

Sound: Tauntaun stops, wheezing and whining, stamping. She's plainly in a bad way.

HAN: *(DISMOUNTING)* Luke! Speak to me, kid! C'mon! Sit up!

LUKE: Ben . . . no; Han. Han? . . .

HAN: Yeah, yeah, it's me.

LUKE: So cold, Han; so cold . . . so cold . . . before . . . Warmer now . . .

HAN: *Warmer?* No, Luke! That means you're freezing! Fight it! Don't go to sleep on me!

LUKE: MOANS.

HAN: Don't do this to me, Luke! Come on, give me a sign, here!

Sound: The tauntaun gives a gurgle nearby.

HAN: Huh? *(TO THE TAUNTAUN)* No, girl! Don't you give me problems, too!

Sound: The tauntaun's death rattle and the sound of its fall.

HAN: Luke, stay with me. *Stay with me, kid!*

LUKE: Trying, Han. Ben . . .

HAN: The tauntaun's dead, Luke. I've got to get the emergency shelter up. Gotta keep you warm in the meantime. Are you listening? Wake up!

LUKE: Dagobah . . .

HAN: Where's your lightsaber? I need it.

Sound: Metal snap-ring at Luke's belt as Han grabs the lightsaber.

LUKE: Ben said . . . Yoda . . .

HAN: Not much time. There's only one way to keep you warm till the shelter's up.

Sound: The lightsaber activates, swings.

HAN: Sorry about this, old girl.

Sound: Gooey sounds as the tauntaun is sliced open and its innards pour forth. Lightsaber deactivates.

HAN: Luke, I'm gonna have to shove you inside the tauntaun's carcass, until the shelter's up. *Do you hear me?*

LUKE: Dagobah system . . .

HAN: Luke, I want you to keep still in there, understand? Just keep still and don't go to sleep!

LUKE: Yes . . . I understand, Han . . .

HAN: Here we go—*(GRUNTS WITH THE EFFORT OF DRAGGING LUKE)*

Sound: Luke being dragged.

HAN: This may smell bad, kid—

Sound: Luke being deposited in the tauntaun, pressed in, to slurping sounds.

LUKE: Yoda . . . ah . . . find him . . .

HAN: *(WITH EFFORT)*—but it'll keep you alive until I can get the shelter built.

Sound: Slurping sounds stop. Luke now mostly inside the carcass.

HAN: *(PANTING)* Ah. Ah. And I thought . . . these tauntauns smelled bad . . . on the outside!

Sound: Equipment being detached from the tauntaun's saddle, assembled.

HAN: All right, Solo . . . let's see . . . just how good you really are.

Sound: Hoth winds rise, then fade.

SCENE 2-8 HOTH SHELTER

Sound: Muted wind howling. Point of view from inside shelter.

HAN: Hold still, Luke; I gotta give you a stim-shot.

Sound: Small pneumatic noise as Han gives him the injection.

HAN: Just hang on, Luke. That shot oughta take hold and bring you around in a second or two.

Sound: Comlink activating.

HAN: This is Solo to base, Solo to base.

Sound: Static, interference, etc.

HAN: Command center, I don't know if you can read me, but I've got Luke. He's alive, but my tauntaun's down for good. We're in an emergency shelter. Do you copy?

Sound: Static.

HAN: The storm's kicking up pretty bad. I don't know if this hut can take it. Just come for us as soon as you can.

Sound: Luke stirs.

LUKE: GROANS.

HAN: I've got the homing beacon on. Just do your best for us, you guys.

Sound: Comlink shutting off.

LUKE: Han?

HAN: Lay quiet, Luke; there's not much room in here.

LUKE: *(CHATTERING WITH COLD)* Han, I can't see!

HAN: You're snowblind, Luke. But it'll pass. We'll get you taken care of soon, I promise. And keep that thermal wrap around you; we've gotta warm you up a little at a time.

LUKE: Han—*(LAUGHS)* It would be you. How'd you find me?

HAN: Snoozing in the snow, that's how I found you.

LUKE: Nice going. You have some sense of timing, Solo. Where are we?

HAN: Emergency shelter, north side of the glacier field.

Sound: The winds howl outside, making the shelter creak.

LUKE: You think this thing will hold up?

HAN: I'm sort of hoping for the best, buddy.

LUKE: We picked a great time to field-test it, huh?

HAN: Perfect. How you feeling?

LUKE: Oh, terrific. Why don't we go outside and get in some calisthenics before it gets too dark?

HAN: Nah. I hate fresh air.

LUKE: I've had my share for today, too. How'd you get here?

HAN: Tauntaun; wasn't any other way. She didn't make it, though.

LUKE: So we're here until the weather breaks?

HAN: That's about it.

LUKE: Wouldn't you know it, I forgot my knitting.

HAN: We could always play tag.

LUKE: *(GROANS)* No, I think I'll pass on the athletics. Can't feel much.

HAN: Aw, you're gonna be okay. There's not a lot more I can do for you with the medi-kit, but they'll put you through nerve therapy, float you in a regenerative tank, and you'll be as good as—

LUKE: Too bad the nearest one's a couple of kilometers from here through a blizzard.

HAN: No more talking like that! You're gonna make it, y'hear? What happened to your face? You look like you walked into a turboprop.

LUKE: A wampa ice beast. It jumped me on the ridge and killed my tauntaun.

HAN: How very rude, as Threepio would say. I hope you killed it right back.

LUKE: It seemed like the right thing to do at the time . . . *(SNIFFS)* What smells so bad in here?

HAN: You. You spent a little time inside my tauntaun while I was having a house-raising party.

LUKE: I guess you can cancel all my social engagements for the evening.

Sound: The winds rise as the shelter complains from the stress.

LUKE: Here's where we find out about survival equipment performance under stress.

HAN: You were mumbling about Ben when I found you.

LUKE: I went through strange dreams, or a hallucination or— something. I'm not sure exactly what happened to me, Han.

HAN: Don't let it throw you. Just keep still; that stim-shot's gonna take a lot out of you.

Sound: The shelter creaks again to the winds.

LUKE: What's your excuse this time, Han?

HAN: Huh? For what?

LUKE: Coming out after me. This time you can't even claim it was for the money.

HAN: I'll figure something out, Luke.

LUKE: I bet you will.

Sound: Shelter creaking, high wind.

HAN: This hut is gonna hold, Luke, and you're gonna make it.

LUKE: Y'know, when General Rieekan told me the boss was killed off Derra IV, and told me that I'm squadron commander now—

HAN: Yeah?

LUKE: It hit me kind of hard.

HAN: Yeah, I noticed.

LUKE: Yeah, and I walked away, to come on this patrol, without remembering to say good-bye to Leia. I wish I'd gotten to say good-bye to her, Han.

HAN: I've got an idea, pal: Why don't you just settle down and relax? And tomorrow—you can say hello to her instead.

Sound: Wind, creaking. Fades.

SCENE 2-9   REBEL HANGAR

Sound: Base sounds up, with winds outside the open shield door.

LEIA: *(APPROACHING)* Has there been any sign of Luke or Han, Threepio?

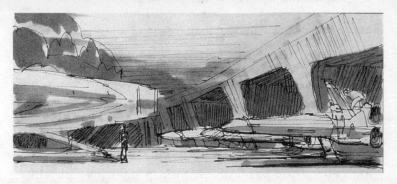

THREEPIO: None, Your Highness. Artoo maintained sensor scan outside the shield door for as long as he could, but our joints began freezing up.

ARTOO: BURBLES.

THREEPIO: Artoo has informed me that the communications center has been unable to get in contact with them. The storm is interfering with reception.

ARTOO: TWEEDLES.

THREEPIO: Oh, be quiet, you stupid little short circuit! Master Luke will be all right. He'll be quite all right, and so will Captain Solo. You'll see!

CHEWBACCA: YOWLS, OFF.

LEIA: What's Chewbacca doing?

THREEPIO: He has been keeping a vigil at the shield door since Captain Solo failed to report back, Your Highness. It was all we could do to dissuade him from going after them.

LEIA: I'm surprised you managed to, Threepio.

THREEPIO: It was already dark by that time, Your Highness. Moreover, Chewbacca could hardly ride a tauntaun, and has no idea which way the captain was going. Still, he very nearly went out on foot.

LEIA: Yes, I can well believe that.

ARTOO: HOOTS MOURNFULLY.

THREEPIO: Don't say that, Artoo! Don't even think it! Of course we'll see Master Luke again.

ARTOO: CHIRPS SADLY.

LEIA: Now what's he saying, Threepio?

THREEPIO: Artoo was unable to pick up any signals from them; but his range is far too small for us to abandon all hope!

DECK OFFICER: *(APPROACHING)* Princess Leia, there's nothing more that any of us can do tonight. The shield door must be closed.

LEIA: Just a few more minutes, Lieutenant?

DECK OFFICER: Our life-support system can't take any more cold; we've lost heat all through the base. And, there's a danger of the door freezing up and jamming in the open position.

LEIA: Then we have no choice.

DECK OFFICER: *(TO OFF)* Stand clear of the shield doors! Prepare to close!

Sound: Men hop to it. Chewbacca roars angrily, off. Artoo chatters sadly.

LEIA: What was that, Artoo?

THREEPIO: Your Highness, he says that their chances of survival out there are 725 . . . to 1.

ARTOO: MOANS CONFIRMATION.

THREEPIO: Actually, Artoo has been known to make mistakes.

CHEWBACCA: SNARLING, COMING CLOSER.

THREEPIO: From time to time.

DECK OFFICER: *(TO OFF)* Prepare to close and seal—

CHEWBACCA: ROARING, ACCOSTING THE DECK OFFICER.

DECK OFFICER: Get back! No!

LEIA: Chewbacca!

THREEPIO: Look out!

DECK OFFICER: Let go!

LEIA: Chewbacca, stop! Leave him alone! Please, Chewbacca!

CHEWBACCA: QUIETS DOWN, BUT STILL SNARLS.

DECK OFFICER: *(PANTING, AS HE'S RELEASED)* I've never given . . . an order that . . . I've regretted more, Chewbacca!

LEIA: If we leave the door open any longer, the whole base will be in danger.

CHEWBACCA: GROWLS AT HER.

LEIA: Do you think we want to do this? But if we don't close that door, everybody in this base will die. Is that what you want?

CHEWBACCA: MOANS.

LEIA: I know, I know, Chewbacca. We just have to hope. Lieutenant?

DECK OFFICER: Yes, Your Highness. *(TO OFF)* Close the shield doors!

Sound: Heavy servomotors grind. The huge door creaks and slides.

DECK OFFICER: I'm sorry, Your Highness. I'm sorry, Chewbacca.

CHEWBACCA: MOANS.

THREEPIO: *(WITHOUT CONVICTION)* Don't worry about Master Luke, Artoo. I'm positive that he'll be all right. He's quite clever, you know—for a human, that is. And so is Captain Solo.

ARTOO: BEEPS SADLY.

Sound: Grinding of doors and thrumming of motors quicken and grow louder.

THREEPIO: They must come back, or . . . Whatever should we do then? What would become of us?

LEIA: I don't know, Threepio. I don't know what would become of us.

Sound: The door rises to a crescendo as Chewbacca looses a long wail of agony, which ends as the shield door shuts with a stupendous clang, reverberating, leaving only the winds of Hoth.

NARRATOR: Though the Empire pursues them, it is not their only enemy. The planet itself can take lives. And now these six can only hope, and await the verdict of the long and deadly night of Hoth.

Music: Up under closing credits.

NARRATOR: CLOSING CREDITS.

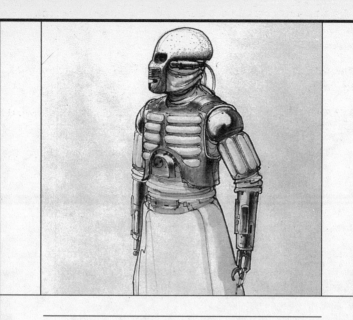

EPISODE THREE:

"A QUESTION OF SURVIVAL"

CHARACTERS:

ANNOUNCER: OPENING CREDITS.

Music: Opening theme.

NARRATOR: A long time ago in a galaxy far, far away, there came a time of revolution, when Rebels united to challenge a tyrannical Empire.

Sound: Hoth winds.

NARRATOR: Now, it is a dark time for the Rebellion. At bay on the ice planet of Hoth, the Rebels are attempting to reorganize their harried, scattered forces. And somewhere out on the frozen landscape, Luke Skywalker and Han Solo have been stranded in an emergency shelter through the long and bitter Hoth night.

Sound: Winds begin to fade.

SCENE 3-1   REBEL HANGAR

Sound: Hangar noises rise.

NARRATOR: Now, sunrise is near. Within the ice caverns of the Rebel base, the Princess Leia Organa watches preparations for the effort to rescue the two men who are her allies, and more.

Sound: Base noises louder.

LEIA: General Rieekan, what's the status of the snowspeeders?

RIEEKAN: The techs have fitted them out for the Hoth climate, Your Highness. The last modifications have been made.

LEIA: Has there been any contact with Luke or Han?

RIEEKAN: No, Princess Leia. But the outside temperature is beginning to rise. We're going to open the shield door and launch as soon as we can.

LEIA: What do you think their chances are? Truly?

RIEEKAN: Solo had survival gear with him, Your Highness. But if he didn't manage to find Commander Skywalker—we can only hope for the best.

LEIA: We must find them, General Rieekan. We must find them both. We've all come through too much together.

RIEEKAN: We're going to try, Leia. Everyone in those speeders has served with Han and Luke.

LEIA: Those two saved my life, did you know that? I was in a cell on the Death Star, and they burst through a door and set me free. I thought I was about to die, and they saved me.

RIEEKAN: That raid is something of a legend in the Rebellion by now, Your Highness.

LEIA: *(QUIETLY)* What if we don't find them?

RIEEKAN: With all respect, Leia, you know the answer to that.

DECK OFFICER: *(APPROACHING)* General Rieekan! The techs say that the outside temperature is within operational limits for the snowspeeders. We're ready to open the main shield door and launch. Everybody's itching to get out there and start looking, sir.

RIEEKAN: Open and launch, Lieutenant. Right now.

DECK OFFICER: Yessir! Thank you, sir! *(TO OFF)* Open main shield door!

CREWMAN: *(FROM OFF)* Open main shield door!

Sound: Main shield door grinds and creaks open, under following.

LEIA: Do you ever have doubts, General? About what we are doing? The Rebellion has cost us so many lives.

RIEEKAN: I was a line officer, Your Highness; I'm a general in the Rebel Alliance by necessity. I've never gotten used to losing people under my command, and I hope I never do. But I believed in the Old Republic. I will never be a subject of the Empire. Never.

DECK OFFICER: *(TO OFF)* Prepare to launch snowspeeders!

CREWMAN: *(FROM OFF)* Rogue Flight, prepare to launch!

Sound: Snowspeeders fire up as techs wild-line to each other.

DECK OFFICER: Stand clear of the shield door!

Sound: Shield door grinds to a halt, open.

CREWMAN: *(FROM OFF)* Shield door open, sir! All clear! Rogue Flight ready to launch!

RIEEKAN: Strange, to see them without Luke flying the lead.

DECK OFFICER: Rogue Two, go!

Sound: A snowspeeder's engine revs, then blares as it blasts off out of the ice cavern.

RIEEKAN: Yes, Rogue Flight; go!

DECK OFFICER: Rogue Three, go!

Sound: A second snowspeeder launches, with others' engines still under in background.

LEIA: Yes, Rogue Flight. Go. And—come back to us.

DECK OFFICER: Rogue Four, go!

Sound: The third speeder launches, as it and base sounds fade.

SCENE 3-2   HOTH SHELTER

Sound: Muted Hoth winds come up. Point of view is inside the emergency shelter.

HAN: Repeat, Hoth Base, this is Solo. Hoth Base, this is Solo! What, is everybody takin' a nap back there?

LUKE: *(WEAK, WEARY)* Yelling into the comlink isn't going to help, Han. Why don't you just try choking it?

HAN: Why don't you just put a plug in it and leave me alone? I'm trying to hitch us a ride, here.

LUKE: What's it like outside?

HAN: The door sensor says it's gettin' lighter and gettin' warmer.

LUKE: Maybe we should send out for room service, get some breakfast.

HAN: Stay still; those injuries won't get any better with you jumpin' all over the place.

Sound: The shelter creaks.

LUKE: Right; I'll need all my strength when this shelter caves in on us from the weight of all that ice.

HAN: Look, I don't need you to depress me. I can depress myself. At least the door's still clear. *(TO COMLINK)* Solo to base. Are you guys really lookin' for us, or are we just kind of a hobby?

LUKE: You should've been a salesman, Solo. *(GROANS WITH PAIN)*

HAN: Luke, you all right?

LUKE: After a fight with a wampa ice beast and a stroll through a Hoth blizzard? No, buddy, I'm not all right at all. I think I'll ask the Rebellion for a raise.

HAN: Well, shut up and keep still! I can't give you another stim-shot; the medi-kit says you're right at the limit now.

LUKE: That's a nice place for me. I'll take a Tatooine sandstorm over a Hoth blizzard, any day. It's a cold way to go.

HAN: Nobody's goin' anyplace but home! If you'd just quit jostlin' my elbow, here, I could get us a little aid and assistance.

LUKE: You were always terrible at rescues, Han.

HAN: Oh, yeah? You could do it better?

LUKE: Couldn't anybody?

HAN: How'd you like me to stick a gag on you?

LUKE: What, without Chewie to help?

HAN: That does it, sonny! You don't think I've got better things to do than mess around out here with you? I don't need—

ROGUE TWO: *(OVER COMLINK)* Echo Base, Echo Base, this is Rogue Two. I think I've got something! Not much, but it could be a life-form; it could be them.

HAN: "Not much"?

LUKE: Don't knock it.

HAN: *(TO COMLINK)* Hey, Rogue Two, Rogue Two! Do you copy? This is Solo!

ROGUE TWO: This is Rogue Two. I hear you. Do you copy?

HAN: Yeah, Zev! Gotcha loud and clear. Good morning! Nice of you guys to drop by; why don't you come down and pay us a call?

ROGUE TWO: *(LAUGHS)* It's a date! I've got your homing beacon on my screen. Be right with you!

LUKE: Then again, Solo, maybe you're not so bad at this rescue stuff after all.

HAN: That's more like it. Practice; the secret is practice, my friend.

LUKE: Crack the door seal, Han. I want to hear.

HAN: Okay, Luke.

Sound: Han breaks the weathertight seal on the shelter door.

HAN: I'm gonna play you—

Sound: Han shoves the door open.

HAN: —some of the sweetest music that—

Sound: Snowspeeders sweep by overhead in a close flyby, with Hoth winds in background.

HAN: —you're ever gonna hear. *(LAUGHS)*

LUKE: LAUGHS.

Sound: Another snowspeeder thunders past as their laughter fades. Hoth winds fade.

SCENE 3-3   MEDICAL CENTER

Sound: Medical center sounds come up.

TOO-ONEBEE: *(DROID VOICE, NOT AS LIVELY AS THREEPIO'S, BUT UNDERSTANDING AND CALM, WITH GOOD BEDSIDE MANNER)* How are you feeling now, Commander Skywalker?

LUKE: I feel fine, Too-Onebee. Just like new. Hoth base may need a lot of other things, but it's got a first class medi-center, I'll say that for it.

TOO-ONEBEE: The latest workups on your condition indicate that all damage has been reversed. Recovery is total. I believe you have been quite fortunate.

LUKE: Yeah, in a lot of ways. I'm not sure I can thank you enough for pulling me through.

TOO-ONEBEE: No further thanks are necessary, Commander, but you are most welcome. It is my function and pleasure as a medical droid to help and heal human beings.

LUKE: When can I leave?

TOO-ONEBEE: I would like to keep you here in the medical center for observation for a short period longer, to make absolutely certain that you're fully recovered. Then you will be able to return to active duty.

LUKE: You're the doctor, Too-Onebee.

TOO-ONEBEE: You may also have visitors now, Commander Skywalker. There have been numerous inquiries about your condition. *(MOVING OFF)* I have to make my rounds now. I shall be back to check on you shortly.

THREEPIO: *(OFF, TO TOO-ONEBEE)* May Artoo and I see him now, Too-Onebee?

TOO-ONEBEE: *(OFF, TO THREEPIO)* Yes, of course, See-Threepio.

THREEPIO: Thank you. You're a credit to all droids, Onebee.

TOO-ONEBEE: You're very kind, See-Threepio. *(MOVING FURTHER OFF)* And now, if you and Artoo will excuse me . . .

THREEPIO: *(APPROACHING)* Master Luke, sir! How wonderful to have you back!

ARTOO: SIGNALS HELLO.

LUKE: Hi, Threepio; Artoo.

THREEPIO: Oh, it's so good to see you functional again, sir!

ARTOO: CHIRPS AND BEEPS.

THREEPIO: And Artoo-Detoo expresses his relief at your rapid convalescence as well.

LUKE: Thanks, Artoo. They're supposed to let me out of sickbay any time now. *(CALLS OFF)* Han! Chewie!

HAN: *(FROM OFF)* Hey, Chewie! Here he is, over here!

THREEPIO: But please don't overexert yourself, Master Luke.

Artoo and I simply couldn't bear it if anything were to happen to you.

CHEWBACCA: HOOTS, APPROACHING.

LUKE: Thanks, you two.

HAN: *(APPROACHING)* What d'ya say, kid? How ya feelin'?

LUKE: A lot better than I did a couple of hours ago. Hi, Chewie.

CHEWBACCA: GREETS HIM.

HAN: You don't look too bad to me. A little nerve therapy, an hour or two in that regeneration tank—what'd I tell you? You're practically back on the duty roster.

CHEWBACCA: COMMENTS.

LUKE: What'd Chewbacca say?

HAN: He says you wouldn't get so cold if you had the sense to grow yourself a decent pelt like his.

LUKE: Oh, I'll make a note of that.

HAN: Don't worry about him, Chewie. He looks strong enough to pull the ears off a gundark.

CHEWBACCA: GROWLS.

LUKE: Thanks to you, Han.

HAN: That's two you owe me now, Junior; twice I've saved your hide. You gotta start bein' more careful.

LUKE: Well, until I can pay you back, you can charge me interest.

HAN: Don't tempt me. *(PAUSE)*

LUKE: I guess I really messed up your departure.

HAN: It's worse than that: They've grounded all ships. Anyway, we're still workin' on the *Millennium Falcon*—almost done.

THREEPIO: An energy source has been reported by the warning sensors you and Master Luke set out, Captain Solo. The monitors think it's moving back and forth on the snowfields, transmitting. They're trying to get a fix on it now.

LUKE: Imperials, Threepio?

THREEPIO: No one knows, sir. But the princess and General Rieekan are very worried.

HAN: And speaking of Her Wonderfulness, it looks like visitors' hours are gettin' pretty busy around here.

LEIA: *(APPROACHING)* Hello, Luke; I came as soon as Too-Onebee told me you were awake.

LUKE: Thank you, Leia. I'm fine; wouldn't want to make a habit of it, though.

THREEPIO: I should certainly hope not, sir!

HAN: Well, Your Worship, it looks like you managed to keep me around for a little while longer.

LEIA: Han, I had nothing to do with it. General Rieekan thinks it's too dangerous for any ship to leave this system until we've activated the base's defensive shield.

HAN: That's a great story. *I* think you just can't bear to let a gorgeous guy like me out of your sight.

LEIA: I don't know where you get your ideas, laser-brain!

CHEWBACCA: GUFFAWING IN A BARKING, SNORTING WAY.

LUKE: LAUGHS.

HAN: Oh, sure, laugh it up, everyone. But you boys didn't see us alone yesterday. Her Highness finally expressed her true feelings for me.

LEIA: My true feelings—

HAN: You don't have to be shy, Leia.

LEIA: Why . . . you stuck-up, half-witted, scruffy-looking *nerf herder*!

HAN: Wait a second, wait a second; *who's* "scruffy-lookin' "?

ARTOO: BEEPS THE ANSWER.

THREEPIO: I don't think the question was addressed to you, Artoo. In any case, he wouldn't like your answer.

HAN: Watch it, Artoo. Well, Luke, I guess I must've hit pretty close to the mark to get her all riled up like that, huh?

LEIA: Han, I guess you just don't know everything there is to know about women yet. The reason I came down here was to welcome Luke back—with a kiss. Hold still, Commander Skywalker . . .

Sound: They kiss.

LUKE: MAKES SURPRISED NOISE, WHICH QUICKLY BECOMES A DISTINCTLY HAPPY MODULATION.

P.A. SYSTEM: *(OVER KISS)* Headquarters personnel, report to the command center.

HAN: Uh, hey, you two . . .

ARTOO: WHISTLES IN ADMIRATION.

LEIA: *(KISSING)* Hmm?

LUKE: *(DITTO)* Hmmmmm?

P.A. SYSTEM: Headquarters personnel, report to the command center.

HAN: You two feel like breathin' for a second, there?

LEIA: Welcome back, Luke.

LUKE: Thanks, Leia. This could make getting injured very popular.

HAN: 'Scuse me, Princess; you've decided to put the Rebellion on hold, is that it?

LEIA: Oh; I have to go. *(MOVING OFF)* I'll see you later, Luke.

LUKE: Good-bye.

CHEWBACCA: WOOPS.

HAN: Aw, shuddup, furball! Luke, if you don't get that smirk off your face . . .

LUKE: I guess it's just my day, huh? When did you say you were leaving, Han?

HAN: Do you have any idea how stupid you look with your eyes crossed like that?

LUKE: LAUGHS.

HAN: Yeah. Well, take it easy, kid. *(MOVING OFF)* I'll see you later. C'mon, Chewie.

ARTOO: BEEPS.

LUKE: What now, Artoo?

THREEPIO: Artoo noticed that the medical scanners registered a flux in your vital signs, sir, but it seems to be stabilizing.

ARTOO: SIGNALS AGAIN.

THREEPIO: Artoo says that he and I should report to the command center, too, sir. We'll look in on you again just as soon as we can. *(MOVING OFF)* We hope you're feeling better, Master Luke!

ARTOO: WHISTLES, MOVING OFF.

LUKE: I'm pretty sure I'll pull through, Threepio! I never felt better in my life.

Sound: Medi-center sounds fade.

SCENE 3-4 REBEL COMMAND CENTER

Sound: Command center sounds come up.

RIEEKAN: Sensors have a fix on that unidentified blip, Princess. We have a visitor.

LEIA: What is it, General?

RIEEKAN: We picked up something outside the base, in Zone Twelve, moving east. It's definitely metallic, and it's transmitting. It contains a powerful energy source, too.

LEIA: You're sure it's not a life-form? One of those wampa ice creatures?

HAN: Maybe it's a snowspeeder, General; one of ours.

RIEEKAN: It is neither, we're certain.

CONTROLLER: *(FROM OFF)* General Rieekan, we've got it pinpointed. There's something very weak coming through.

RIEEKAN: *(TO OFF)* Let's hear it, Controller.

CONTROLLER: Yes, sir. *(TO TECHS)* Patch it in over the speakers!

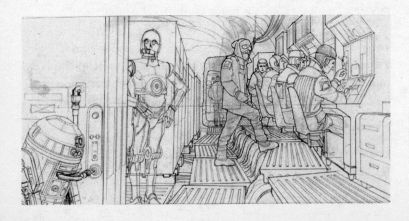

Sound: Switches being thrown. Sounds of the probe droid are heard in the command center.

THREEPIO: Pardon me, General Rieekan, Princess Leia—but I am fluent in six million forms of communication. This signal is not used by the Rebel Alliance.

LEIA: What do you think it is, Threepio?

THREEPIO: It is on a high order of probability that that is an Imperial code, Your Highness.

HAN: Well, it isn't friendly, whatever it is. General, Chewie and me'll go and check it out for you.

CHEWBACCA: GRUNTS AGREEMENT.

RIEEKAN: All right, Solo. You know that zone better than anyone else. But I want you two to be extremely careful. We don't know what it is that you're going up against. Make sure you see it before it sees you.

LEIA: Han, first you ride out to look for Luke and now you volunteer for a recon mission. You're going to ruin your reputation.

HAN: Listen, it's strictly self-interest. As long as me and the Wook and the *Falcon* are stuck here, I want to know what's going on.

LEIA: Uh-huh. Well, just to make you feel better, I'll pretend I believe you.

HAN: I'll be on comlink band alpha, General. *(MOVING OFF)* C'mon, Chewie; let's get this over with.

CHEWBACCA: MOVING OFF WITH HIM, HOOTING.

RIEEKAN: *(TO OFF)* Controller!

CONTROLLER: Yes, sir!

RIEEKAN: Send Rogue Ten and Rogue Eleven to station three-eight and have them fly a holding pattern there at low altitude.

CONTROLLER: Will do, sir.

RIEEKAN: And tell them to expect trouble.

Sound: Command center fades.

SCENE 3-5 HOTH EXTERIOR

Sound: Hoth winds come up.

HAN: You see anything, Chewie?

CHEWBACCA: WOOPS.

HAN: Where? Gimme the macrobinoculars.

Sound: Macros focusing.

HAN: You hit it, partner. There's somethin' or other down there, comin' this way.

Sound: Comlink activating.

HAN: General Rieekan, this is Solo.

RIEEKAN: *(OVER COMLINK)* I copy, Solo. Anything to report?

HAN: We have a visual on your blip, General. It's coming up the canyon towards us, moving slowly, sniffin' around.

RIEEKAN: Can you identify it?

HAN: Made out of metal, right enough. It's too small to be a ship. Looks like a flying spider; some kinda droid.

RIEEKAN: Does it appear to be armed?

HAN: Uh, I think so, yeah. Looks like it's got a bunch of sensor and scanning gear, too.

RIEEKAN: In that case, I want you two to stay clear of it.

HAN: Negative, General. This thing's headed straight for the base. It may already have spotted your defensive generator. We're gonna have to take a crack at it.

RIEEKAN: It sounds like we have no other option. I'll have Rogue Ten and Rogue Eleven make an attack run. You and Chewbacca get out of the target area.

HAN: No, General. There's no time for that. Besides, if it sees the snowspeeders it'll know we're here for sure. Chewie and me'll have to take it on our own way.

RIEEKAN: I'll trust your judgment, Han, but be careful. Good luck.

HAN: Solo, out.

Sound: Comlink deactivating.

HAN: Chewie.

CHEWBACCA: RESPONDS.

HAN: Make your way over to that other snowbank over there, and try to distract it when it floats by. We'll find out what a little blaster fire can do to that gizmo. Keep your bowcaster handy; whatever that thing is, it looks nasty.

Sound: Chewbacca howls affirmation as he hurries off, making footfalls in the crusty snow. Winds come up.

SCENE 3-5A HOTH EXTERIOR

Sound: Probe droid sounds come nearer, slowly, from distance.

HAN: *(UNDER HIS BREATH)* That's it, you nosey scrap heap . . . just keep comin' . . . c'mon, Chewie; careful, now . . .

CHEWBACCA: HOWLS IN DISTANCE.

Sound: Probe droid makes agitated, angry noises. There is a distant hissing of the probe droid's beam weapon.

HAN: Chewie! Get down!

Sound: Han fires his blaster twice. The probe droid makes an electronic shrieking as the second shot scores, exploding against it. The damaged droid rumbles ominously.

HAN: Duck, Chewie! It's gonna blow!

Sound: There is an explosion from the probe droid, then the Hoth winds come up. Winds fade.

SCENE 3-6   REBEL COMMAND CENTER

Sound: Command center rises.

CONTROLLER: *(FROM OFF)* General Rieekan, sensors report energy-weapons fire at Captain Solo's location, followed by an explosion. We've lost the blip.

LEIA: And Captain Solo?

CONTROLLER: We haven't been able to raise him yet, Your Highness.

LEIA: General, I think we should send in the snowspeeders. Han and Chewbacca may have been hurt.

RIEEKAN: I agree, if we don't hear from them soon.

CONTROLLER: *(FROM OFF)* Comlink signal coming through on alpha band, sir!

HAN: *(OVER COMLINK)* Solo to base, d'you read me? What do we haveta do, write you a letter?

LEIA: He's alive! That numbskull . . .

RIEEKAN: *(TO COMLINK)* Base here. What happened, Solo? Are you two all right?

HAN: Not a scratch, General. Chewie did a little decoy work and I got a shot straight into it. I'm afraid there's not much left of it, though.

LEIA: *(TO COMLINK)* What exactly was it, Han?

HAN: Tough to tell; a droid of some kind, is all I can say for sure. I didn't hit it that hard, but it blew up anyway. It must've had a self-destruct mechanism.

LEIA: It sounds like an Imperial probe droid, all right.

HAN: Well, then, it's a pretty good bet the Empire knows we're here. I think it got a peek at the defensive generator.

RIEEKAN: We'd better start an evacuation, Leia, much as I hate to say it.

LEIA: We have no other option. Put our contingency plans into effect.

RIEEKAN: Yes, Your Highness.

LEIA: *(TO COMLINK)* Han, you and Chewbacca get back here right now.

HAN: Best advice I've heard all day! We'll be right there!

RIEEKAN: *(OVER P.A. SYSTEM)* Attention all personnel, attention. Prepare to evacuate the base. Repeat, prepare to evacuate Hoth Base.

LUKE: *(APPROACHING)* Leia! Leia, what's going on? What's happened?

LEIA: An Imperial probe droid has located the base.

LUKE: *That*'s gonna change things.

RIEEKAN: *(OVER P.A.)* All ground troops and evac crews report to assigned posts. Snowspeeder squadrons report to your hangar for briefing and prepare for launch.

LUKE: At least the waiting's over. I'd better go look after Rogue Flight.

LEIA: Luke, are you sure you're feeling well enough?

LUKE: Too-Onebee says I'm fine. It wouldn't matter, anyway; we're going to need everybody we've got.

THREEPIO: Oh, Master Luke, there you are! Does this latest news mean we are leaving?

LUKE: Eventually, Threepio, when the evacuation's organized. I'll be in a snowspeeder until then. Artoo, you'd better get over to the fighter hangar. We're gonna need you in my X-wing.

ARTOO: WHISTLES AGREEMENT, MOVING OFF.

THREEPIO: And what about me, Master Luke?

LUKE: I want you to stay here with the princess. If I don't see you here, I'll meet you at the fleet rendezvous point.

THREEPIO: Very well. Do take good care of yourself and Artoo, Master Luke!

LEIA: Yes, Luke; be careful.

LUKE: *(LAUGHS)* I could say the same thing to you two. Watch out for yourselves, both of you. Good-bye, Leia.

LEIA: Good-bye, Luke; good luck.

LUKE: *(MOVING OFF)* Don't worry. I'll be fine. See you at rendezvous!

THREEPIO: How may I be of service, Your Highness?

LEIA: Just stand by for now, Threepio. We're undermanned at the communications consoles; we may need you there later.

THREEPIO: How do you evaluate our situation?

LEIA: I can't. Too many unknowns in the equation. What's important now is to get our personnel and the critical equipment away from Hoth. The rest of the Alliance is scattered. If the Empire manages to destroy us, it would mean the loss of the Alliance's main organized resistance.

THREEPIO: Can we evacuate quickly enough, Your Highness?

LEIA: We have to, Threepio. If the Empire succeeds in trapping us here, it could be the end.

Sound: Base sounds fade.

SCENE 3-7   STAR DESTROYER BRIDGE

Sound: Sounds of Star Destroyer bridge come up, with wild lines, reports, etc., and the mask-breathing of Darth Vader.

VADER: What is the status of search operations, Admiral Ozzel?

OZZEL: We're ahead of schedule on probe droid deployment, Lord Vader. The starfleet's capital ships are making their assigned sweeps. Our TIE fighters are dispersed according to plan.

VADER: Without having found anything—is that what you are telling me, Admiral?

OZZEL: Lord Vader, we have a huge volume of space to search, but we've worked our way through much of it already. In time, we will root the Rebels out.

VADER: I grow impatient. I expect results, Admiral. And so does the Emperor.

OZZEL: No one knows that better than I, My Lord. Perhaps if more units were assigned to the fleet, we could saturate the region, and then—

VADER: The Empire must be kept in good order, Admiral, and its planets kept . . . pacified. There are no units to spare. If you cannot perform your mission with a starfleet, perhaps someone else can.

OZZEL: I can do it, Lord Vader. We shall find them; you'll see.

PIETT: *(APPROACHING)* Admiral Ozzel, have you a moment?

VADER: Yes, Admiral; I *will* see.

PIETT: Admiral Ozzel, I thought you'd like to know that we have—

OZZEL: Captain Piett, can't you see that you're interrupting Lord Vader and myself? Until we are finished, you will stand by and await my—

VADER: Admiral, I think I should like to hear this interesting news of Captain Piett's.

OZZEL: As you say, Lord Vader. You may continue, Captain.

PIETT: Er, I think we may have something, Admiral. The report is only a fragment, transmitted by a probe droid in the Hoth system, but it's the best lead we've had yet.

OZZEL: You interrupt me for this? We have thousands of probe droids in this region. I want proof, not leads! Return to your duties!

VADER: Just a moment, Admiral. Captain Piett, what have you found?

PIETT: It's up there on the screen, Lord Vader; Admiral. We have a long-range sighting of what appears to be a piece of heavy equipment.

OZZEL: Ridiculous; that could mean anything!

PIETT: But, sir—and, My Lord—the Hoth system is supposed to be devoid of human forms, and the visuals indicate life readings. In addition, the probe ceased transmissions very suddenly. We're not sure how, but we think it may have been destroyed.

VADER: That is it. The Rebels are there.

OZZEL: But, Lord Vader—there are so many uncharted settlements, so many fly-by-night mining operations. This is barely any indication of anything. We would fall seriously behind schedule if we investigated it.

VADER: That is the star system we're searching for.

OZZEL: Piett, what do the intelligence evaluation computers say?

PIETT: Well, the source/data index on this one *is* rather low, but it's the first solid piece of—

OZZEL: There, you see, Lord Vader? The intel computers have been programmed—

VADER: *That is the star system!* The Force tells me so. The Rebels are there, and Skywalker is with them. *(TO OFF)* General Veers!

VEERS: *(FROM OFF)* Yes, Lord Vader?

VADER: Prepare your combat-landing and ground-assault units. Have all Imperial stormtroopers equipped for cold-weather warfare.

VEERS: At once, Lord Vader!

VADER: Admiral Ozzel.

OZZEL: What is your wish, Lord Vader?

VADER: Regroup the starfleet and assume battle formation. Set your course for the Hoth system!

NARRATOR: Darth Vader, betrayer of the Jedi, assembles the might of the Empire, while Rebel forces brace themselves for an uneven battle. New patterns begin to emerge from the Force. And the ice world of Hoth, a planet of frozen wastes, is about to be seared by the fire of war.

Music: Closing theme up under credits.

NARRATOR: CLOSING CREDITS.

EPISODE FOUR:

"FIRE AND ICE"

CHARACTERS:

Luke	First Rebel	Janson
Han	P.A. System	Zev (Rogue Two)
Chewbacca	Second Rebel	Dak
Leia	Hobbie	Veers
Threepio	Wedge	Piett
Artoo	Third Rebel	Ozzel
Vader	Controller	Imperial Technician
Rieekan	Beta	Imperial Pilot
Too-Onebee	Technician	

ANNOUNCER: OPENING CREDITS.

Music: Opening theme.

NARRATOR: A long time ago in a galaxy far, far away, there came a time of revolution, when Rebels united to challenge a tyrannical Empire. Now, it is a dark time for the Rebellion. Its one major base, on the ice planet Hoth, has been located by an Imperial starfleet commanded by Darth Vader.

SCENE 4-1 DESTROYER BRIDGE

Sound: The bridge of Vader's mega-dreadnaught Star Destroyer. WILD LINES: BATTLE STATIONS, ETC. Vader's mask-breathing sounds come up.

VADER: General Veers, what has happened? Something is wrong. *Answer me!*

VEERS: Lord Vader, the starfleet has moved out of lightspeed. All our ships made the transition without incident, but—that is . . .

VADER: *You will pay a terrible price for your next hesitation, General!*

VEERS: Com-scan has detected an energy field protecting Hoth, where our probe droid was destroyed. It is a defensive shield, strong enough to deflect any bombardment the starfleet can deliver.

VADER: Such a shield demands huge amounts of raw power. The Rebels can't possibly operate it constantly. So: They are now alerted to our arrival. Admiral Ozzel has brought the starfleet out of lightspeed too close to Hoth.

VEERS: He—he felt that the advantages of surprise and a close striking distance were more vital. There is a give and take in any battle plan, My Lord, and—

VADER: Admiral Ozzel is as clumsy as he is stupid! This will be no easy victory.

VEERS: No, Lord Vader. The Rebels are well entrenched—in ice caverns; they've turned that part of Hoth into a fortress. But we have the troops and the ships. In the end, we will crush them.

VADER: But at what idiotic waste of Imperial resources! A simple act of conquest now becomes a needless and costly battle. And tell me, Veers, do *you* regard that as *wisdom*?

VEERS: My Lord, Admiral Ozzel is my superior. Admiral Ozzel is—

VADER: *Finished,* General! Have him and Captain Piett contacted instantly. I wish to see their faces on the main communication screen.

VEERS: Very good, sir! *(TO OFF)* Communications section! Lord Vader will speak to Admiral Ozzel and Captain Piett at once!

Sound: WILD LINES, ETC., as commo section works, under next lines. Viewscreen comes on.

VADER: And General Veers . . .

VEERS: What is your command, Lord Vader?

VADER: Prepare your men for a surface attack. We shall have to go in and dig these Rebels out. Our Imperial stormtroopers will land outside the range of the Rebels' shield and fight their way in.

VEERS: Yes, My Lord. All stormtroopers have been equipped for cold-weather warfare, as per your orders. Our All Terrain Armored Transports are ready.

VADER: This is your opportunity to prove your value to me, Veers.

IMPERIAL TECHNICIAN: *(FROM OFF)* Lord Vader, Admiral Ozzel and Captain Piett await your pleasure!

VADER: Watch the main viewscreen, General. What you will see there, you would be well advised to remember.

Sound: As Ozzel and Piett's images appear on the screen.

OZZEL: *(ON SCREEN, OVER COMLINK)* Greetings, Lord Vader.

PIETT: *(ON SCREEN, OVER COMLINK)* I salute you, My Lord Vader.

OZZEL: My Lord, the starfleet has moved out of lightspeed, as I'm sure you're aware. Tactically, we are now in a good— *(BEGINS TO CHOKE)*

PIETT: Admiral Ozzel!

VADER: Stand where you are, Captain Piett! Admiral Ozzel, the power that closes in about your throat is the Force. It is my anger, reaching forth to end your life.

OZZEL: *(CHOKING)* Lord Vader—please! No . . .

VADER: It is pointless to merely punish someone so useless. You have failed me for the last time, Admiral!

OZZEL: UNINTELLIGIBLE, AS OZZEL CHOKES

VADER: Captain Piett!

PIETT: Yes! Yes, My Lord?

VADER: Make ready for an assault landing beyond the Rebels' energy field, and deploy the fleet so that nothing gets off the planet Hoth.

PIETT: I—I—as you command, Lord Vader.

Sound: Ozzel hits the deck, still choking out his last moments.

VADER: You are in command now, *Admiral* Piett.

PIETT: Thank you, My, My Lord. I won't fail you.

Sound: Ozzel expires.

VADER: Excellent, Piett! For, if you should . . . you know the consequences!

Sound: Bridge fades.

SCENE 4-2   REBEL HANGAR

Sound: Rebel hangar sounds come up in background.

FIRST REBEL: *(FROM OFF)* Is that Artoo unit ready? Let's get him up here.

THREEPIO: *(TO OFF)* Just a moment longer, please! *(TO ARTOO-DETOO)* Now pay attention, Artoo-Detoo. Just because you're going to be flying in Master Luke's X-wing fighter is no reason to—to "get cocky," as Captain Solo might put it!

ARTOO: POOH-POOH'S HIM.

THREEPIO: Just you listen to me! I don't want you getting our Master into trouble, something for which you have an almost-uncanny gift!

ARTOO: STILL UNCONCERNED.

THREEPIO: Just take good care of him, do you understand?

ARTOO: BEEPS.

FIRST REBEL: *(FROM OFF)* Okay; hoist that Artoo unit up here!

Sound: Hoist lifting Artoo.

THREEPIO: And . . . do take good care of yourself, too, you . . . you silly little *plumber*!

ARTOO: *(MOVING OFF—UPWARD)* WHISTLES GOOD-BYE.

THREEPIO: Oh dear, oh dear; it's begun again . . .

Sound: Hangar fades.

SCENE 4-3   LUKE'S QUARTERS

Sound: Luke's quarters come up.

TOO-ONEBEE: *(APPROACHING)* I am glad that you're well enough to have left the medical center, Commander Skywalker, but saddened by the circumstances.

LUKE: *(APPROACHING)* You and me both. But thanks for pulling me through, Too-Onebee.

TOO-ONEBEE: Again, you are most welcome. I was told to consult you, sir. My medical center is being evacuated insofar as is possible, but it will take considerable time and effort to evacuate the T-47's.

LUKE: I'm really sorry, Onebee, but we'll have to forget the heavy equipment. There's plenty of time to get the smaller modules onboard the transports, though.

TOO-ONEBEE: Yes, sir. It seems wasteful that the T-47's must be scheduled for demolition. They are useful machines.

LUKE: Would you rather have the Empire use them?

TOO-ONEBEE: I am a medical droid, sir. My political programming is limited.

LUKE: Then take it from me, Onebee: You wouldn't.

TOO-ONEBEE: I once practiced medicine in an Imperial clinic. I take your meaning, Commander.

LUKE: Did you see my comlink around the medical center?

TOO-ONEBEE: The techs are repairing it. Like yourself, it underwent some very unhealthy usage.

LUKE: *(MOVING OFF)* Well, if anybody's trying to get in touch with me, tell 'em I'm on my way to the snowspeeder hangar, with a stop at the *Millennium Falcon*'s hangar bay.

TOO-ONEBEE: It is my hope that you continue in health, working to the good, Commander Luke Skywalker.

Sound: Quarters fade.

SCENE 4-4   REBEL HANGAR

Sound: Hangar comes up. Wild lines, repairs, engines, etc., in background.

HAN: Give it a quarter turn, Chewie. *Quarter turn,* hear me? Any more'n that and they'll be picking up pieces of us!

CHEWBACCA: *(OFF)* ACKNOWLEDGES ANGRILY.

Sound: Power systems hum.

HAN: Okay, that's it! Give 'er a try!

Sound: Power systems overload, spitting sparks, burning.

HAN: Off! Turn it off! It's overloadin', Chewie! *Turn it off!*

CHEWBACCA: HOWLS.

HAN: Now don't start in! Let's just fix the ship, huh?

Sound: Tool sounds as Han works.

HAN: *(MUTTERING TO HIMSELF AS HE WORKS)* "Evacuation," they call it? "Run for your life," is more like it! *(TO CHEWIE)* Now, do it right this time, Chewie! I'd like to leave some empty air where the *Falcon* used to be!

CHEWBACCA: *(OFF)* AGREES.

LUKE: *(APPROACHING)* Well, well, well; so ya haven't gotten around to junking this bucket yet, huh?

HAN: That's gonna cost you, next time you want a joyride, Junior.

CHEWBACCA: *(APPROACHING)* IS ALSO HIGHLY INSULTED.

HAN: And Chewie says you ride with the ballast from here on in.

LUKE: LAUGHS

HAN: Where ya goin' in the funny suit, Commander?

LUKE: Snowspeeder. You heard about the Imperials?

HAN: Why else would we have four tools in each hand? This one's gonna be rough, pal.

LUKE: The command center says we've got a whole starfleet on our hands.

HAN: *Starfleet?*

CHEWBACCA: WOOFS.

HAN: Got any more good news?

LUKE: Kinda short on that right now. I've got a bad feeling I know who it is out there.

HAN: What d'ya think, Vader'd send in the second team? You always say the Force favors freedom. We got a final exam, here.

LUKE: It doesn't necessarily work that way, Han.

HAN: I thought Ben Kenobi had a corner on that kind of talk. By the way, Luke: You probably know by now, but those X-wings of yours have a blind spot, just aft and underneath, very narrow. But if a TIE fighter makes a long approach—it could happen, so keep an eye on it and keep movin'—

LUKE: You wanna wipe my nose, too?

HAN: *(LAUGHS)* Y'know, you looked a lot better when you used to wear your blast shield down over your face?

LUKE: *(LAUGHS)* Chewie, don't let Han wreck this crate, all right?

CHEWBACCA: GROWLS.

LUKE: And I'll see you both—ooof! Chewie! Put me down! *(LAUGHS)*

CHEWBACCA: HOOTS SADLY AS HE LIFTS LUKE UP, HUGGING HIM GOOD-BYE.

HAN: Look, if you two wanna be alone, I could go—

CHEWBACCA: HE RELEASES LUKE.

LUKE: Ooouch! Wookiee good-byes are pretty impressive.

HAN: What's the evacuation plan?

LUKE: We go in groups, one transport and two fighters at a time.

HAN: So everybody's scheduled for an evacuation ship? The command center people, too?

LUKE: Yeah—her, too, Han.

HAN: "Her" who?

LUKE: Why don't you try and guess? The Wookiee'll tell you when you hit it, right, Chewie?

CHEWBACCA: SAYS YES.

HAN: Why do I get the sudden urge to put you back in that medical center?

P.A. SYSTEM: Rogue Flight, briefing begins in one minute.

LUKE: That's me. Watch out for yourselves, you two.

HAN: That's our life's work. And don't forget: No heroics, just—

HAN AND LUKE: "Fly it out and bring it back."

LUKE: I know.

HAN: So, I finally taught you somethin'.

LUKE: "Just 'cause you're *good* at it doesn't mean you're gonna make any *money*!" Recognize the quote, Solo?

HAN: Quit throwin' it in my face.

LUKE: *(MOVING OFF)* See you later, you crook!

HAN: Stay sharp!

LUKE: Bye, Chewie!

CHEWBACCA: SAYS SO LONG.

Sound: Hangar sounds fade.

SCENE 4-5   REBEL HANGAR

Sound: Brief transition to another part of the hangar complex.

P.A. SYSTEM: Ground troops to the perimeter. All ground troops to the perimeter. Stand clear of the ion cannon; stand clear of the ion cannon.

LEIA: Is everyone here?

SECOND REBEL: Commander Skywalker's on his way, Princess Leia.

LEIA: Now, the transport ships will leave, one at a time, as soon as they're loaded. We can only afford two X-wing fighter escorts per transport.

Sound: GENERAL DUBIOUS WILD LINES.

LEIA: We can't keep our defensive shield open for long, or the starfleet will breach it. Each flight will have to squeak through, so, you fighter pilots, stick close to your transports.

HOBBIE: And if they're waiting for us? Two snub fighters are supposed to go up against a star destroyer?

LEIA: We have the ion cannon trained on the escape corridors up there. When the shield opens, it will fire several rounds, to make sure that any Imperial warships will be out of your flight path. When you've gotten past the energy shield, proceed directly to the rendezvous point. Understood?

Sound: General affirmation.

HOBBIE: What about the ground troops, Your Highness?

LEIA: They pull back as we evacuate.

WEDGE: Things're gonna get pretty grim towards the end. How's the last ship gonna get out?

LEIA: We'll set the ion cannon to fire on automatic, and run for it. For what it's worth, that's the ship I'm riding. Any questions?

Sound: General murmuring, "No."

LEIA: I won't pretend that this retreat is a victory. Our mission today is *not* to defeat the Empire. What we *must* do is to *keep the Rebel Alliance alive*! Understood, everyone?

Sound: General murmuring, "Yes."

FIRST REBEL: Okay, everybody to your stations! Rogue Flight, get ready to launch.

Sound: WILD LINES and chatter as pilots shuffle off, under P.A.

P.A. SYSTEM: All positions manned. All crew-served weapons ready. Snowspeeders prepare to launch.

LUKE: *(APPROACHING)* Y'know, Leia, you're developing a real Command Presence?

LEIA: Matter of necessity. I'd meant to speak to you, Luke, but there was so much to do that I never—

LUKE: I know; we've all been rushed. Thought I'd stop off before I get Rogue Flight into the air. I need a favor.

LEIA: Of course, Luke—if I can.

LUKE: Artoo'll be leaving with me, in my X-wing, but I'd be grateful if you'd keep Threepio with you.

LEIA: Didn't you know that I would, Luke? Even though Artoo and Threepio think *they're* looking out for *us*?

LUKE: Yes; I guess I did know.

LEIA: You're in the last flight out, too.

LUKE: Yes; my choice. That's the way the boss would've done it, if he was still around. Besides, I'll be escorting your ship.

P.A. SYSTEM: All defensive zones ready. First transport, prepare for liftoff. Commander Skywalker, report to Rogue Flight hangar bay.

LEIA: So you came to say good-bye—until the rendezvous, Luke—

LUKE: No! I came to say . . . I'll see you later, Leia. Just . . . that I *will* see you later.

LEIA: Later? Luke, what are you talking about? Are you feeling all right—

P.A. SYSTEM: Commander Skywalker, report to snowspeeder hangar bay at once!

LUKE: I meant just what I said, Leia.

LEIA: Luke, we'll all make it; you'll see.

LUKE: Yes, we will. *(MOVING OFF)* In the meantime . . . may the Force be with you, Leia.

LEIA: May it be with us all, Luke.

Sound: Hangar fades.

SCENE 4-6 REBEL COMMAND CENTER

Sound: Command center comes up.

RIEEKAN: *(APPROACHING)* Your Highness, won't you reconsider? You should be evacuated from Hoth Base under the safest possible circumstances!

LEIA: No one is safe on Hoth anymore, General Rieekan!

RIEEKAN: Think what the Alliance loses if you're caught or killed during the evacuation!

CONTROLLER: *(FROM OFF)* General Rieekan, sensors indicate Imperial landings in Zone Twelve.

LEIA: Which flight are you going out on, General?

RIEEKAN: You already know that, Princess Leia: the last.

LEIA: I hope we've got that settled.

RIEEKAN: *(SIGHS)* I suppose we have, Leia. *(TO OFF)* I want ground positions and monitoring techs to stay alert! The Imperials' primary target will be our power generators. Make ready to open the shields for the first transport.

THREEPIO: Excuse me, Your Highness, but how may I be of assistance?

LEIA: I'm not sure, Threepio; just stay ready.

THREEPIO: As you say, Princess Leia.

P.A. SYSTEM: Hoth Base is now at full alert status. Snowspeeders launching now. Repeat, Rogue Flight launching now.

CONTROLLER: *(FROM OFF)* General, message for you, coming in now.

RIEEKAN: Let's hear it.

THIRD REBEL: *(OVER COMLINK)* Command Center, this is Echo

Station 3–T–8. We have a sensor report on something approaching the base, nothing clear. Reported by Outpost Beta.

RIEEKAN: *(TO OFF)* Controller, get me Outpost Beta!

CONTROLLER: *(FROM OFF)* Yes, sir.

Sound: Commo channel opening.

BETA: *(OVER COMLINK) (YOUNG, SCARED)* Outpost Beta here. I have a visual now. These things look like . . . animals. They're huge, maybe twenty, twenty-five meters high, four-legged, and their heads move. But they're made out of metal. They have extremely heavy armor and armament. I count six of 'em so far.

LEIA: Walkers!

RIEEKAN: Yes, Your Highness. Walkers. *(TO COMLINK)* You've got Imperial All Terrain Armored Transports out there, Lieutenant. What is their speed?

CONTROLLER: *(FROM OFF)* We have Imperial walkers on the north ridge.

BETA: They'll be within firing range of the perimeter in another minute or so.

THREEPIO: Hoth Base must be most important, Your Highness; the Empire is employing its most powerful ground weapons today. I imagine they intend for this to be the final battle.

LEIA: Then I'm afraid the Empire's in for a disappointment.

RIEEKAN: *(TO COMLINK)* Outpost Beta.

BETA: *(OVER COMLINK)* Yes, sir?

RIEEKAN: Those walkers will pick up your presence any time now. You and your men get out of there on the double, understand me, son?

BETA: Halfway home, General! Outpost Beta, out.

CONTROLLER: *(FROM OFF)* Rogue Flight launched, General; Commander Skywalker's forming them for attack.

RIEEKAN: Patch him in over the communications net. Tell everyone on the perimeter to get set.

CONTROLLER: The walkers have opened fire on Echo Station 5–7, sir.

RIEEKAN: Open fire, Controller.

CONTROLLER: Open fire!

LUKE: *(OVER COMLINK)* Echo Station 5–7, this is Rogue Flight. We're on our way.

THREEPIO: Master Luke!

Sound: Burst of static, weapons fire, explosions, etc. Ceases abruptly.

CONTROLLER: The Imperial walkers are firing on Outpost Beta, sir. We think most of our men got clear.

THIRD REBEL: *(OVER COMLINK)* We have the walkers in sight now. They've slowed to combat mode.

LEIA: Remind everyone that we're short on ammunition and power. *Don't waste it!*

CONTROLLER: Yes, Your Highness!

RIEEKAN: What's the status on the snowspeeders?

Sound: Background cries, firefighting, etc.

CONTROLLER: *(FROM OFF)* They're nearly at Echo Station 5–7, sir. The walkers have knocked out two of our gun emplacements with long-range fire.

LEIA: General, those snowspeeders are flying into a pretty uneven fight.

RIEEKAN: Someone's got to engage the walkers. We need time!

CONTROLLER: The first transport ship is off! Prepare to fire ion cannon!

TECHNICIAN: *(FROM OFF)* Transport approaching the defensive shield, sir!

RIEEKAN: Open the shield! Fire ion cannon, two rounds!

Sound: Orders repeated. The base reverberates to the discharges of the ion cannon.

CONTROLLER: Imperial Star Destroyer on intercept course. First-round miss . . . second-round hit!

THREEPIO: But will that suffice?

CONTROLLER: Destroyer's shields overloading; she's losing her helm. Transport and escorts are in the clear! *They're clear!*

Sound: Background cheering from command center personnel.

THREEPIO: That's one, Your Highness.

LEIA: That's one—a part of the Rebellion has survived.

P.A. SYSTEM: Attention, Hoth Base. The first transport has gotten clear of the Imperial blockade.

Sound: Distant cheers, etc.

CONTROLLER: Walkers are breaking through the outer defenses.

RIEEKAN: What about Rogue Flight?

CONTROLLER: Signal from Commander Skywalker. He's sighted the walkers. *Rogue Flight is attacking.*

Sound: Base fades.

SCENE 4-7 SNOWSPEEDER COCKPIT

Sound: Luke's snowspeeder cockpit comes up. Swooping, etc., under.

THIRD REBEL: *(OVER COMLINK)* Rogue Flight, the walkers are breaking through! We're taking heavy losses! *Where are you?*

LUKE: Right overhead. Just stay out of our way. Hey, Dak, you all right back there?

DAK: *(SLIGHTLY OFF, AT TAIL GUN POSITION)* I feel like I could take on the Empire by myself, Luke!

LUKE: *(WEARY, IRONIC)* I guess I know what you mean, but you won't have to. Bear a hand on that gun and we'll be all right.

DAK: What about you, Luke? You're the one who just got out of the medi-center.

LUKE: I hear it's part of the job. *(TO COMLINK)* Rogue Flight, take up positions. Wing leaders, form up on me.

ZEV: Lookit 'em, boss! Great, big, fat gray targets!

LUKE: Yeah, Zev, but they've got a long reach. Stand ready, all wings. Prepare for attack run. We're open for business, Dak!

DAK: 'Bout time! Let's hit 'em, then open a scrapyard!

LUKE: You gotta stop being so pessimistic, Dak. *(TO COMLINK)* Rogue Leader to Rogue Flight. Form for attack pattern delta.

DAK: Will you look at those walkers? Has there ever been anything so big and gray and ugly, Luke?

LUKE: Dak, if you don't like 'em, I'll take you down where you can do something about it. *(TO COMLINK)* This is for the money, Rogue Flight! All right, boys; keep tight now!

Sound: Snowspeeders zoom.

LUKE: I have gunlock on the walkers, Dak. How're you doing?

DAK: Luke, my screen's a blank! I have no approach vector! I'm not set!

LUKE: Steady, Dak. Forget the screen. Eyeball it.

Sound: The speeder swoops.

LUKE: Okay, Rogue Flight: attack pattern delta. Go now!

Sound: They attack-dive.

LUKE: All right—I'm coming in. Hobbie, you still with me?

HOBBIE: Right on your elbow, boss!

LUKE: We're going in between the legs of the first one, then over the back of the second.

HOBBIE: Got it.

LUKE: Watch out for the heavy guns in those head-turrets; keep an eye on which way the heads swing.

Sound: Snowspeeders roar, attacking, firing.

LUKE: I'm on approach vector four, Dak; pick 'em up in your eight.

Sound: Luke, then Dak, fires.

HOBBIE: Luke, they got Rogue Six!

LUKE: Careful—*everybody*! Dak, give 'em everything you've got!

DAK: I'm trying! It has no effect!

WEDGE: Watch that counterfire, you guys!

Sound: The snowspeeders swoop up from their run.

DAK: The walkers just shrugged it off, Luke! We didn't even dent 'em!

LUKE: I know; be quiet a second, Dak. *(TO COMLINK)* Rogue Flight, that armor's too strong for our blaster cannon.

WEDGE: I hope that's not all you have to say about this little problem, boss!

LUKE: We're gonna have to use our harpoons and tow cables. Go for their legs; it's our only chance of stopping them.

WEDGE: Luke, you think we've got a chance?

LUKE: Just watch. Dak!

DAK: Tell me what you want, Luke.

LUKE: We're gonna haveta improvise, here. Stand by the harpoon gun!

DAK: Wait! Luke! We've got a malfunction in the fire-control computer! I'll have to cut in the auxiliary.

Sound: Snowspeeder maneuvering.

LUKE: Never mind that! Just hang on; hang on, Dak! And get ready to fire that tow cable!

Sound: Speeder attacks, buffetted by walker antiaircraft fire.

DAK: Just gimme a target; I'll hit it. There's nothin' I can't skewer with this thing—

Sound: Explosion within the snowspeeder as it's hit by AA fire. Bursting tail canopy.

DAK: DEATH SCREAM

LUKE: Dak? *Dak?* No; Dak . . .

WEDGE: The walkers are moving in on the power generators, Luke. What's wrong?

LUKE: Wedge, I've lost my gunner. You'll have to make this harpoon shot.

WEDGE: I copy, Rogue Leader.

LUKE: I'll fly cover for you and draw the walkers' fire.

Sound: Walkers swoosh.

LUKE: Have your gunner set his harpoon. Follow me on the next pass.

WEDGE: Comin' around, Rogue Leader. Lead me to 'em, Luke!

Sound: More fire. Speeders knocked around.

LUKE: Steady, Rogue Three. It's your show, Wedge!

WEDGE: Gunner ready? Activate harpoon! Fire!

Sound: More zooming. Harpoon gun over comlink.

WEDGE: Good shot, Janson! Luke, the cable's secured to the walker's leg!

LUKE: Wind that cable right around its legs! The only way we can stop the walker is to trip it!

WEDGE: Keep up the slack on that line, Janson!

LUKE: That's it, Wedge! You're doing it!

Sound: Speeders circling.

WEDGE: One more pass! How's it goin' back there, Janson?

JANSON: *(OVER COMLINK)* Come around once more, Wedge! Once more!

LUKE: Careful, Wedge! Pay the cable out and get clear!

JANSON: The cable's out! Let 'er go!

WEDGE: Detach cable!

JANSON: Cable detached, Wedge! Get us outta here!

Sound: Zooming, firing, etc.

LUKE: It's working! The walker's legs are tangled in the cable!

WEDGE: It's falling!

Sound: Walker's fall, crash.

LUKE: It's down! The walker's down, command center!

WEDGE: I think its power plant is ruptured, Luke; I see smoke coming from—it's gonna blow!

Sound: Distant explosion of the Imperial walker.

WEDGE: Whoooo-ha!

LUKE: LAUGHS

WEDGE: That got him! Nothin' left of that walker but odds 'n' ends!

LUKE: I see it, Wedge. Good work!

Sound: Speeders swoop.

LUKE: All right, let's tackle the next one. Rogue Two, you all right?

ZEV: Yeah, I'm with you, Rogue Leader.

LUKE: Set your harpoon, Zev. I'll cover for you.

ROGUE TWO: Coming around, Luke.

LUKE: Watch that crossfire when you're down in the middle of their formation, boys!

Sound: Zooming. Imperial antiaircraft fire coming toward Luke's point of view.

ZEV: I'm set for position three, Rogue Leader. Steady back there, gunner!

Sound: Attack dive.

LUKE: Stay tight and low!

WEDGE: Zev, look out! Break left! Break left!

Sound: Fire hits Zev's speeder.

ZEV: Aaaah! *We're hit!* They got our power—

Sound: Explosion of Zev's speeder.

HOBBIE: Zev's gone, Luke.

LUKE: Hobbie, the crossfire's murder down here . . .

Sound: Walker fire hits Luke's ship, cockpit.

LUKE: *(REACTS, MOANS)* Hobbie, I'm hit! Goin' down!

Sound: Luke's snowspeeder goes into a crash dive, landing with tremendous impact as the scene fades.

SCENE 4-8 REBEL COMMAND CENTER

Sound: Command center comes up underneath. Wild lines: casualties, third transport's made it through, etc.

CONTROLLER: *(FROM OFF)* General Rieekan, Rogue Leader's gone down. He crash-landed.

THREEPIO: Master Luke! It can't be! It mustn't! *It mustn't be!*

LEIA: Is Luke all right? Did he get out?

CONTROLLER: Nobody in Rogue Flight is sure. They're trying to find out.

RIEEKAN: Let me talk to them, Controller.

Sound: Comlink crackles.

RIEEKAN: Rogue Three, this is Rieekan.

WEDGE: I copy, General.

RIEEKAN: You're in charge now, Wedge. Can you see Luke?

WEDGE: No, I—wait! Yes!

THREEPIO: I knew it! Oh, Master Luke, I never doubted it!

LEIA: Threepio, sshhhh!

WEDGE: He got clear of his ship just before a walker crushed it. I'm gonna try for a pickup.

RIEEKAN: Negative, Wedge! You'd only throw your life away, and I can't spare you. Luke can make it out of the area on his own.

THREEPIO: But someone must go to his rescue!

LEIA: Threepio . . . General Rieekan is right.

WEDGE: I don't believe this! Luke's going after the walker!

THREEPIO: No! Master Luke, don't do it!

WEDGE: He's got a hoist cable attached to its underside, and he's hauling himself up! We can't even give him covering fire; he's too close!

LEIA: What can he be doing?

WEDGE: I can't see him—don't think the Imperials can, either. He must be hanging onto the walker's underbelly.

THREEPIO: My poor, poor master has gone mad!

WEDGE: Luke's dropping clear! He looks like he's okay!

LEIA: Ohh! Luke, what are you doing?

WEDGE: There was an explosion inside the walker! I think Luke got a sapper charge into it. I see secondary explosions! The control turret just blew, and *the walker's going down*!

LEIA: Rogue Three, can you see Luke?

WEDGE: He's headed for the transports!

THREEPIO: Hurry, Master Luke, hurry!

WEDGE: He's out of the line of fire. I'm taking Rogue Flight in for another attack.

RIEEKAN: Play it carefully, Wedge. Just buy us as much time as you can, then get back here for the final evacuation.

WEDGE: You don't have to tell me twice. But the walkers are still advancing. Rogue Flight, form up on me. Time to earn your pay!

Sound: Comlink zooming and command center sounds fade.

SCENE 4-9   WALKER COCKPIT

Sound: Inside of the command-module head of the lead walker comes up, with the machine's grinding sounds of movement.

VEERS: This is General Veers to Starfleet. Inform Lord Vader that Rebel resistance is beginning to crumble. My walkers will be inside their outer defenses momentarily.

IMPERIAL PILOT: General Veers, all remaining walkers are advancing according to plan.

VEERS: Very good. And our stormtroopers?

IMPERIAL PILOT: They're ready to debark for ground assault as soon as we've passed the base's outer defenses.

VEERS: Concentrate all fire on their defenses for now, but have all walkers fire on the Rebel power generators when they're within range. *They* are our key to victory!

Sound: Walker's movement, firing, etc., fades.

SCENE 4-10   REBEL COMMAND CENTER

Sound: Rebel command center comes up. Wild lines, confusion, etc.

CONTROLLER: *(FROM OFF)* Princess Leia, our ground troops are pulling back from the second defensive ring. We're taking heavy casualties in all zones.

LEIA: Get the wounded aboard the evacuation transports. Consolidate all remaining units in the central defensive arc.

CONTROLLER: Yes, Your Highness!

LEIA: Can we bring the ion cannon to bear on the walkers?

CONTROLLER: It won't fire at that low an angle, Princess Leia. And, we're using it to cover the transports' escape.

LEIA: Tell the ground officers to hurry, Controller; we haven't much time.

CONTROLLER: *(UNDER THREEPIO)* Yes, Princess Leia!

THREEPIO: *(APPROACHING)* Your Highness! Princess Leia! Has anything more been heard with regard to Master Luke?

LEIA: After he was shot down, he was seen making his way toward the transport site on foot.

THREEPIO: He must make it! He simply has to get there!

CONTROLLER: *(FROM OFF)* We've lost two more snowspeeders, Your Highness!

LEIA: Recall them, Controller; have the pilots get to their fighters.

P.A. SYSTEM: Prepare for evacuation phase three. All personnel, evacuation phase three.

RIEEKAN: *(APPROACHING)* Shift all command channels over to my transport! Then get your team over there, Controller, right away!

CONTROLLER: Yes, General Rieekan!

LEIA: Threepio, maybe you'd better start for the evacuation ship now.

THREEPIO: With all due respect, Your Highness, Master Luke was quite definite in ordering me to remain with you.

HAN: *(APPROACHING)* Hey, d'anybody see Her Royalness around here?

LEIA: Thank you, Threepio. I'm very grateful.

HAN: *(MOVING ON)* Leia! Are you okay? You all right?

LEIA: Han, why are you still here?

HAN: Uh, I heard the command center'd been hit.

LEIA: The shields held. I thought you'd gotten your clearance to leave.

HAN: Don't worry, don't worry, I'll leave! First, I'm gonna get you to your evacuation ship.

LEIA: You mean you and the Wookiee actually fixed the *Falcon*? Miracles will never cease!

Sound: A blast shakes the caverns.

HAN: Save the humor, all right?

THREEPIO: Your Highness, we absolutely must take that last transport ship. It's our only hope of surviving!

CONTROLLER: *(FROM OFF)* Imperial walkers closing on the defensive generators! Stormtroopers have debarked, all along the inner defensive arc!

LEIA: *(TO OFF)* Send all troops in Zone Twelve to the takeoff site, to protect the transports and fighters!

Sound: Another blast. Debris falls, and ice shards. Techs cry out, etc.

HAN: C'mon, Leia; that's walker-fire, close-range. The clock's run out.

LEIA: Leave me alone! Controller, see if you can contact the outer—

Sound: Another impact, closer.

HAN: *Leia, you run and you live, or you die right here! Decide!*

P.A. SYSTEM: Imperial stormtroopers have entered the base. Repeat, Imperial—

Sound: P.A. dissolves in a burst of static.

HAN: Leia . . . that's *it*, don't you understand?

LEIA: *(BEAT)* Controller, give the evacuation signal. Then get to the transport, all of you! See if you can't get—

HAN: *Come on!*

LEIA: *(BEING LUGGED OFF)* Give the Omega Signal! All troops disengage!

Sound: Siren or loud, whooping alarm begins.

CONTROLLER: Omega Signal! All troops, break contact! Final evacuation beginning now! *Move, everybody! Move!*

Sound: Command center, etc., fades.

NARRATOR: With their last stronghold about to fall, the Rebels must try to escape to the stars. With a terrible determination, Darth Vader throws all his forces against them. The starfleet encircles the planet, and stormtroopers assault Hoth's defenses. And Rebels racing against time and battling against overwhelming odds, seek desperately to keep the light of freedom from permanent extinction.

Music: Up and under closing credits.

NARRATOR: CLOSING CREDITS.

EPISODE FIVE:
"THE MILLENNIUM FALCON
PURSUIT"

CHARACTERS:

Luke	Artoo	Transport
Han	Vader	Piett
Chewbacca	Tarrin	Veers
Leia	Wedge	Imperial Pilot
Threepio		

ANNOUNCER: OPENING CREDITS.

Music: Opening theme.

NARRATOR: A long time ago, in a galaxy far, far away, there came a time of revolution, when Rebels united to challenge a tyrannical Empire.

Sound: Battle, Wild lines, etc.

NARRATOR: Now, it is a dark time for the Rebellion. Darth Vader, with an Imperial starfleet at his command, has attacked the Rebels' fortress-base on the ice planet Hoth. Stormtroopers, assaulting the base in "walkers," enormous, armored war machines, are about to breach their defenses. The Rebels rush to evacuate the base, but within the lead walker, the Imperial ground commander prepares for a final assault.

SCENE 5-1   WALKER COCKPIT

Sound: Walker noises come up.

VEERS: Pilot, what is the distance to the Rebel power generators?

PILOT: One seven, decimal two eight, General Veers.

VEERS: Very good; we're within range. Have all walkers redirect their fire at the generators, maximum power. And open a comlink channel to Lord Vader's ship.

PILOT: Yes, sir.

Sound: Comlink.

VEERS: Lord Vader, General Veers here. The Rebel defensive shields will be down presently. You may begin your landing approach.

Sound: Walker fades.

SCENE 5-2   HOTH CAVERN TUNNEL

Sound: Hoth cavern tunnel comes up. Distant, muffled explosions. Han and Leia running, approaching.

LEIA: *(APPROACHING)* Han, will you kindly stop trying to yank my arm off? I'm hurrying!

HAN: *(APPROACHING)* Nice, Princess! I just want to get you down this tunnel and outta the base. Try and do somebody a favor, and what d'you get—

Sound: Huge explosion, closer.

LEIA: Ohh!

Sound: The ceiling ice cracking.

HAN: Look out! Get back! Leia!

LEIA: SCREAMS AS THEY BOTH FALL

Sound: Cave-in, as the ice gives way and the tunnel collapses, blocking their way.

HAN: Are you okay? Here, get up—

LEIA: I'm fine—just *let go*! *(BEAT)* Um, are you all right, Han?

HAN: Yeah. The tunnel's never gonna be the same, though. They must've hit the power generators.

Sound: Comlink.

HAN: Transport, this is Solo.

TRANSPORT: *(OVER COMLINK)* Transport here, Solo.

HAN: Y'better take off right away, boys. The south tunnel's collapsed and we can't get to you. I'll get the princess out of here in the *Millennium Falcon*.

TRANSPORT: I copy, Solo! Move fast! You're only one step ahead of the stormtroopers! And good luck!

Sound: Comlink deactivates.

HAN: Always gets me nervous when people start wishin' me luck. Awright; the last bus is loadin' now, Princess.

LEIA: *(SIGHS)* Looks like I'm with you, flyboy.

THREEPIO: *(APPROACHING)* Your Highness, thank you so much for waiting! I—what's happened to the tunnel?

LEIA: *(MOVING OFF)* Threepio, follow us! Hurry! There's no time!

THREEPIO: *(FOLLOWING AFTER)* But, but, but—where are you going? Oh! Come back!

SCENE 5-2A   HANGAR DOOR

Sound: Brief transition to hangar door. Han and Leia, approaching at a run. Power door opens.

HAN: *(APPROACHING, PANTING)* Into the hangar! Maybe the power door'll hold 'em back for a while!

LEIA: *(PANTING)* Han, why is it that life's one big footrace when you're around?

HAN: Get inside!

THREEPIO: *(DISTANT, APPROACHING)* Wait! Oh, wait for me! Captain Solo—

Sound: The power door closes.

THREEPIO: *(APPROACHING)* Your Highness, please! Come back! Stop! *(TSKS)* A power door in my face! How very typical! Abandoned! Left to a cruel fate by the very people for whom I have given my all—

Sound: Power door opens again.

HAN: You too, Threepio. Get in here!

THREEPIO: Sir, may I say how—*urrrk*! *(AS HE'S PULLED INSIDE BY HAN)*

Sound: Power door closes once more. Point of view is now inside hangar.

HAN: Everybody, into the *Falcon*! *(MOVING OFF)* Hurry up, Goldenrod, or else you're gonna be a permanent resident here!

LEIA: *(MOVING OFF)* Quickly, Threepio!

THREEPIO: *(MOVING OFF AFTER)* I will give it my most diligent effort, Your Highness. Waaiiiiit!

SCENE 5-2B HANGAR BAY

Sound: Brief transition, bringing them to the Falcon's *hangar bay. Footsteps, running, come closer. Point of view is Chewie's.*

HAN: *(PANTING, APPROACHING)* Chewie, hey, partner, is she ready for liftoff?

CHEWBACCA: WOOFS, WITH MISGIVINGS.

LEIA: *(COMING ON, PANTING)* What'd he say, Han?

HAN: He had to close 'er up by himself, and he was rushed.

THREEPIO: *(APPROACHING)* I'm so glad you paused in order to let me catch up!

LEIA: *(TO HAN)* Can't you two even keep that junk heap flying?

HAN: *(TO THREEPIO)* Yer just in time, Shiny; we're raisin' ship. *(TO LEIA)* I notice it's not beneath *you* to ride in 'er now 'n' then, Your Highnesshood!

Sound: Series of distant explosions.

CHEWBACCA: HOWLS.

THREEPIO: May I ask what First Mate Chewbacca's remark meant?

LEIA: Who has to guess? The stormtroopers are coming.

THREEPIO: They're still fighting?

HAN: No. The Imperials're mopping up. Everybody, *inboard*! My solution to all this's to—

LEIA AND HAN: GET THE HELL OUTTA HERE!!

LEIA: —you've mentioned it. Every now and then you use your head, Solo.

HAN: Just move it!

Sound: Brief transition.

SCENE 5-2C *FALCON* COCKPIT

Sound: Falcon *cockpit sounds come up. Switches, controls, etc., being worked furiously.*

HAN: How's this, Chewie?

CHEWBACCA: GRUNTS.

LEIA: Would it help if I got out and pushed?

HAN: It might!

THREEPIO: Sir, might I suggest that you—

HAN: *Don't push it, Smiley!*

THREEPIO: Wouldn't dream of distracting you, sir. It can wait . . .

CHEWBACCA: GROWLS.

HAN: So? Let's lift off.

LEIA: What did he say?

HAN: He says she's not ready. We're still lifting off.

THREEPIO: I am compelled to object, Captain! You will either cause the vessel's power plant to explode or you will—

HAN: Or we'll get captured by the Empire. The *Falcon* won't let me down.

Sound: The ship's consoles sounds suddenly go dead.

HAN: What . . . ?

LEIA: You were saying?

HAN: Minor adjustment, here . . . *(AS HE POUNDS THE CONSOLE WITH HIS FIST)* Ummph!

Sound: Han's fist striking the console.

LEIA: Wonderful finesse there, Solo!

Sound: The instrumentation kicks in again.

HAN: See? Buckle yourself in, sister!

THREEPIO: The stormtroopers! Look, they're burning their way through the power door!

LEIA: This bucket of bolts is never going to get us past that starfleet blockade.

HAN: This baby's still got a few surprises left in 'er, sweetheart!

THREEPIO: The stormtroopers are inside the hangar!

Sound: As the engines rise.

LEIA: Let's see it! Let's see the famous Han Solo Solution! *Get us out of here!*

Sound: The engines, complaining, stormtroopers firing on the ship.

THREEPIO: They're firing on us!

HAN: The engine's dummyin' out! Open up with the forward gun-pod, Chewie!

CHEWBACCA: HOOTS.

Sound: Chewbacca throwing a switch. Servos whine as the gun lowers from its pod and opens up with rapid laser shots.

THREEPIO: The stormtroopers are falling back, Captain.

HAN: Prepare to switch over power systems, Chewie! Let's just hope we don't have a burnout! *(MUTTERS)* That could really get embarrassing, right about now . . .

THREEPIO: The stormtroopers are setting up a cannon!

HAN: Aw, quit worryin'; the shields'll hold. Bring up the engines, Chewie!

Sound: The engines blare to full power.

HAN: What'd I tell ya, Princess?

LEIA: Someday you're going to be wrong, Han, and I just hope I'm there to see it.

HAN: Blast those stormtroopies, partner! And let's make our exit.

CHEWBACCA: HOWLS.

Sound: Pod-gun fires.

HAN: Nice shootin'!

LEIA: Look! By the power door! Darth Vader!

THREEPIO: All is lost! We're finished!

HAN: *Shut up!* Punch it, Chewie!

Sound: The Falcon*'s engines blast, indicating rapid exit, out of hangar and into the Hoth sky.*

LEIA: Han, you idiot, *you did it!*

HAN: Was it my imagination, or did Vader have a sort of a dumb look on his mask as we left?

Sound: Engines blare. Alarms beep.

LEIA: What's that alarm flasher?

HAN: Of all the—TIE fighters, right on our tail.

Sound: Ship jolts as she's fired upon.

HAN: What a life! Charge main gun batteries, Chewie!

Sound: Falcon fades.

SCENE 5-3   HOTH EXTERIOR

Sound: Transport site, exterior Hoth, comes up. Wild lines, etc., as the transports are loaded, X-wings warm up in background.

TARRIN: Hey, Wedge, will you look at what's coming?

WEDGE: Phew! Finally! *(TO OFF)* Hey, Luke! *Luke!* (LAUGHS)

LUKE: *(APPROACHING)* Glad you guys are still here, Wedge, Tarrin!

TARRIN: You made it just in time, Luke. We tried to find you, but we couldn't.

WEDGE: This is the last evacuation group.

LUKE: You should be gone already. How come you're still hanging around?

WEDGE: Well, we sort of got delayed—a little of this, a little of that, while we were, uh—

LUKE: While you were waiting for me. Thanks, boys. What about the base?

WEDGE: The stormtroopers are already inside. Everybody who still could, got clear.

LUKE: What about the princess?

TARRIN: She got out with Solo in the *Millennium Falcon*.

LUKE: Then they're safe. Good. I saw the *Falcon* take off before.

WEDGE: There's no time left, Luke. Your X-wing's ready.

Sound: Explosions, distance.

LUKE: Okay, I'm with you. *(TO OFF)* Everything set, Artoo?

Sound: Artoo, from off, beeps a greeting and reassures him.

LUKE: Don't worry, Artoo; we're going, we're going!

WEDGE: Artoo's got the coordinates for the rendezvous. The Alliance is gonna regroup out beyond the galactic rim.

Sound: Explosion, closer.

LUKE: Uh-oh. Get to your ships; let's lift off!

WEDGE: Listen, Luke, the Imperials destroyed—

Sound: More explosions.

LUKE: No time, Wedge! Get upstairs! *(TO OFF)* Artoo, get 'er ready to go!

Sound: Artoo responds, and the X-wing's engines whine, under next lines.

TARRIN: Luke, will you listen—

LUKE: Get that transport up *now*, Tarrin!

TARRIN: *(MOVING OFF)* I'll tell you about it upstairs, Luke . . .

WEDGE: Get to your fighter, Luke; the stormtroopers'll be all over us in another minute!

Sound: Hoth fades.

SCENE 5-4 *FALCON* COCKPIT

Sound: Falcon comes up—alarms, etc.

LEIA: Han, there's something new on the sensors!

CHEWBACCA: HOOTS.

HAN: I know, I see 'em, Chewie!

LEIA: See what?

HAN: Star Destroyers, two of 'em, comin' right at us.

THREEPIO: Sir? Captain Solo, sir?

HAN: *(REGARDING THREEPIO)* Leia . . .

LEIA: *Threepio . . .*

THREEPIO: Captain Solo, would you be so kind as to take under consideration the possibility that—

CHEWBACCA: GROWLS.

HAN: Leia, shut him up or shut 'im down!

THREEPIO: Indeed! I was merely attempting to be of assistance, I'm sure, Captain Solo—*ah*!

Sound: Falcon *screams as Han puts on an aerobatic display.* Falcon*'s hit by TIE fire.*

HAN: They're on us! Chewie, check the deflector shields; she can't take much more of this!

CHEWBACCA: ACKNOWLEDGES.

HAN: Well, we can still out-maneuver 'em!

Sound: Frantic flying. TIE fighter wailings.

LEIA: The Star Destroyers are converging on us!

HAN: Yeah; let's hope they're watchin' us and not each other!

THREEPIO: Captain Solo, have you gone mad? They are practically upon us!

HAN: *Just stay gripped!*

THREEPIO: Ah! Nooooo!

Sound: The Falcon *banks, rolls, and dives. TIEs pursue.*

LEIA: The destroyers collided!

HAN: That's kinda what I had in mind.

THREEPIO: But the TIE fighters haven't abandoned the chase!

HAN: Prepare to make the jump to lightspeed, Chewie!

CHEWBACCA: ANSWERS.

THREEPIO: But, Captain Solo—

LEIA: Those TIE fighters are getting closer in a big hurry, hotshot!

HAN: Oh yeah, Your Wonderfulness? Well watch this! S'long, you Imperial suckers!

Sound: Hyperdrive builds, but then dies away to a sickly cough.

LEIA: Watch what, Han? What happened to the famous Solo disappearing act?

CHEWBACCA: BARKS.

HAN: I think we're in trouble . . .

THREEPIO: *If I may say so, sir:* I was trying to tell you earlier that I'd noticed that the hyper/drive motivator has been damaged. It's impossible to go to light speed.

HAN: *(DEADPAN)* We're in trouble.

LEIA: The TIE fighters are coming in again! Break right! *Break right*, Han!

Sound: The Falcon *breaks right. TIEs scream. Cannonfire slams the ship.*

HAN: Umm, this's gonna be a little tougher than I figured, here . . .

LEIA: You were always terrible at this kind of thing, Han. What d'we do *now*?

Sound: Falcon, TIEs following. Firing. Falcon *shudders to hits.*

HAN: You and Threepio fly this thing. Me 'n' Chewie'll have to repair her.

THREEPIO: But, Captain! The optimal projections give you a margin of time that can barely allow for favorable resolution even if—

HAN: Co-pilot's seat or airlock, Threepio: Which is it gonna be?

THREEPIO: Co-pilot's seat, if you please!

HAN: C'mon aft, Chewie. *(MOVING OFF)* Just keep this thing headed in one direction, Leia; me 'n' the Wookiee'll do the rest!

Sound: Chewie follows Han. Brief transition.

SCENE 5-5 LUKE'S COCKPIT

Sound: X-wing noises, Luke's cockpit, come up, engines roaring, and so forth.

LUKE: Everything okay back there, Artoo?

ARTOO: BURBLES AN ANSWER.

LUKE: Good. Gimme all the power you can. Transport, this is Skywalker.

TARRIN: I copy, Luke.

LUKE: Tarrin, my instruments say the base's generators are gone.

TARRIN: We were trying to tell you. The walkers destroyed the generators. That means no covering fire from the ion cannon.

LUKE: *Ooo.* Well, at least the starfleet's scattered from all the fighting. Maybe we can slip through the blockade—

WEDGE: No such luck, boss! I've got a Star Destroyer on my scope!

LUKE: I see him, Wedge. All right: Pull in close to me and stay up tight underneath the transport ship, so they won't see us. All power to forward shields, everybody!

WEDGE: Gotcha, Luke!

Sound: X-wing maneuvering.

LUKE: This close together, we'll all make one blip on their sensors. They'll think they've got an unarmed transport coming. We're gonna give 'em a little surprise.

WEDGE: Suits me fine, boss!

TARRIN: The destroyer's converging with us!

LUKE: Arm your proton torpedoes, Wedge. When I give the word, let go with everything you've got.

WEDGE: Just say when.

TARRIN: Got a visual on the destroyer—closing fast! They're reducing their shields, so they can board me!

LUKE: Wedge! Go now!

Sound: X-wing banks, accelerates.

LUKE: Launch torpedoes!

Sound: Torpedoes away.

WEDGE: They're away!

LUKE: Open fire, Wedge!

Sound: X-wing cannon.

TARRIN: You hit it! I register damage to the destroyer! It's losing speed!

LUKE: Pour it on! Let's get out of here!

Sound: Engines roar.

TARRIN: The Star Destroyer's dropping back!

WEDGE: We made it!

LUKE: I wish I could see the looks on those Imperials' faces.

WEDGE: We're almost ready for the jump to the rendezvous point, Luke. Just give the word, and we can go to lightspeed as soon as we're out of Hoth's gravity field.

LUKE: Uh, look: That destroyer might still try to catch us. Wedge, you go on ahead with Tarrin. You guys make the jump to light-speed. I'll stay back to screen you, and follow when you're clear.

WEDGE: Luke, are you sure? I don't think that Imperial can catch us now.

ARTOO: OBJECTS.

LUKE: No, Artoo-Detoo; I *don't* want you to program the jump. Not just yet.

WEDGE: Luke, is your Artoo unit okay? What's the problem?

LUKE: There's no problem, Wedge. Just get goin'! And good luck!

WEDGE: I—well, if you say so, Luke. See you at rendezvous, Rogue Leader!

Sound: Comlink off.

LUKE: Artoo, get set to come onto a new course as soon as they're safely away.

ARTOO: ASKS WHAT'S WRONG.

LUKE: *(LAUGHS)* There's nothing wrong, Artoo. I'm just changing our destination. We're not going to regroup with the others. We're going to the Dagobah system.

ARTOO: WHISTLES, OBJECTING, WANTING TO TAKE BACK CONTROL.

LUKE: No, Artoo; that's all right. I'll just keep the ship on manual control for a while, thanks.

ARTOO: BURBLES.

LUKE: I have to go there, Artoo. It's got to do with Ben Kenobi and . . . I just have to do it, that's all. There's something there for me, something important.

ARTOO: COMMENTS.

LUKE: Well, thanks for worrying about me, Artoo, but it'll be all right, I promise. Hold on, little buddy; prepare to accelerate. Course engaged . . . for Dagobah!

Sound: X-wing accelerates, fades.

SCENE 5-6 *FALCON* COCKPIT

Sound: Cockpit comes up again.

THREEPIO: How are repairs proceeding, Princess Leia?

LEIA: I don't know. The two of them are back there yelling at each other about "hydrospanners" and "alluvial dampers."

Sound: The ship jolts to Imperial fire.

LEIA: The TIEs are closing in again, too.

THREEPIO: It was very nearly a successful escape, wasn't it?

LEIA: Don't count us out yet, Threepio. Those two maniacs have a knack for getting out of scrapes like this, and so far they—

Sound: Massive concussion, as asteroid fragment smashes against the Falcon*'s shields, nearly overloading them.*

THREEPIO: Oh dear, the Imperials are upon us again! This is the end, Your Highness!

Sound: Another asteroid.

THREEPIO: I wish I'd gotten to bid Artoo-Detoo a last farewell before we—

LEIA: That isn't cannonfire! Look out there!

THREEPIO: Asteroids! The sky is filled with them! Oh no—

LEIA: Here comes another—

Sound: Collision with the fragment.

THREEPIO: It just doesn't seem fair, what with all the other problems we have. Will our deflector shields hold?

LEIA: *(TO THREEPIO)* Not if we hit one of the big ones, Threepio. *(TO COMLINK)* Han, you and Chewie get up to the cockpit! Now!

CHEWBACCA: HOOTING, APPROACHING.

HAN: *(APPROACHING)* What's goin' on up here? Ah, more good news!

Sound: Another impact.

HAN: Where're the Imperials?

LEIA: The TIE fighters are closing on us. If we swing clear of the asteroid field, we'll run right into a Star Destroyer.

HAN: Hmm. Okay, me and Chewie'll take back the controls.

LEIA: *(AS SHE AND THREEPIO CHANGE PLACES WITH HAN AND CHEWBACCA)* That's fine with me!

THREEPIO: Nor will I object, I assure you!

HAN: *(NOW AT THE CONTROLS)* Okay, partner; set course 2–7–1.

LEIA: Han, what're you doing? You're not actually taking us into that asteroid field?

HAN: *(LAUGHS)* The Imperials'd be crazy to follow us in there, wouldn't they? Hang onto your tiara, Princess!

Sound: Falcon cuts deeper into the asteroid field. Asteroid bits bounce from the shields like marbles, or gravel.

LEIA: Han, you don't have to do this to impress me!

THREEPIO: Sir, the possibility of successfully navigating an asteroid field is—

Sound: A loud collision as Falcon races on.

THREEPIO: —approximately seven hundred and twenty to one!

HAN: Never tell me the odds!

LEIA: Watch out!

Sound: Another collision. Maneuvering.

CHEWBACCA: WAILS.

THREEPIO: Here comes another!

Sound: Impact. Sound of TIE fighters, as Falcon *swoops past. TIEs firing.*

HAN: The TIE fighters are firing on us. They're following us! Those guys *are* crazy!

Sound: Explosion.

HAN: One of 'em hit an asteroid!

Sound: Another impact.

HAN: You said you wanted to be around when I made a mistake. Well, this could be it, sweetheart!

LEIA: I take it back, Han!

Sound: More jolting.

LEIA: We're gonna be pulverized if we stay out here much longer!

HAN: I ain't gonna argue with that.

THREEPIO: *Pulverized?* Surely there's some alternative!

Sound: Distant explosion.

HAN: 'Nother TIE fighter's gone! I'm goin' in closer to that big asteroid!

LEIA AND THREEPIO: *Closer?*

CHEWBACCA: BARKS.

THREEPIO: You'll crash us!

HAN: Nope; I'm just gonna hug the surface. Let's see how good those guys back there can fly.

Sound: Falcon *dives, TIEs scream.*

CHEWBACCA: HOWLS.

LEIA: Look out for that mountain!

HAN: *You* wanna fly, so *I* can sit back there and complain?

LEIA: Han, this canyon's too narrow, and it's getting narrower!

HAN: That's the idea; we've still got those TIEs on us.

THREEPIO: But the *Millennium Falcon* can't fit through that opening.

HAN: She's wide, but she's flat, Threepio! We can make it sideways—I think. Hold on tight!

Sound: Falcon *rolls onto her starboard edge, makes the passage. After she's "past," TIEs wail on, then strike the canyon walls, exploding.*

THREEPIO: We made it! We're alive!

HAN: "Alive"?

LEIA: Traveling with you is never boring, I'll say that for you, Solo. What about the TIE fighters?

HAN: They didn't make it; both of 'em hit the canyon walls. I guess it's time to look around for a landing spot.

THREEPIO: Oh, this is sheer suicide!

HAN: Uh, that cave down there looks pretty good. Yeah; that'll do nicely. Ease 'er down, Chewie.

CHEWBACCA: HOOTS.

Sound: Falcon *slows, descending.*

THREEPIO: But why a cave, Your Highness?

HAN: Gotta make some repairs on the ship, Threepio.

LEIA: I just hope you know what you're doing, for a change.

HAN: Yeah. Me too.

Sound: Falcon *fades.*

SCENE 5-7 VADER'S MEDITATION CHAMBER

Sound: Vader's meditation chamber, inboard his Star Destroyer, comes up.

PIETT: *(APPROACHING)* Lord Vader, we have an urgent signal. I hope this interruption—*(IN SHOCK, REPULSION)* is—is not—

VADER: *(WITHOUT MASK NOISES, ETC.) Remain where you are, Admiral, until my helmet is in place!*

Sound: Vader flicks a switch. Servo apparatus lowers his helmet onto his armor, and it seats and fastens with a click. Mask breathing begins.

VADER: *(NOW WITH MASK SOUNDS)* You may approach me now. You were . . . shocked by what you saw, Piett?

PIETT: *(APPROACHING)* Lord Vader, I, I was behind you. I only saw the back of—

VADER: *I am aware of what you saw!* You know that I am not to be disturbed when I am in my meditation chamber. There had better be an excellent reason for this intrusion!

PIETT: The—the starfleet has sighted the *Millennium Falcon.* We pursued her into the asteroid field, but we lost four TIE fighters in the chase. She's in among the asteroids now—

VADER: Asteroids do not concern me, Admiral! I want that ship, and her crew and passengers, not excuses! Do you recall the fate of Admiral Ozzel?

PIETT: It is—difficult to forget such a sight, Lord Vader.

VADER: As it was meant to be. Now go, *and get me the* Millennium Falcon!

Sound: Meditation chamber fades.

SCENE 5-8 *FALCON* HOLD

Sound: Falcon, *mostly shut down, steam purging, etc., comes up.*

HAN: *(COMING UP WITH SOUND)* . . . and run a check on the vector guides, too; maybe that's where the problem is, Chewie.

CHEWBACCA: HOOTS.

HAN: Leia, how's the transition rig lookin'?

LEIA: It would be fine, if you'd just let me work.

HAN: Don't be so touchy. Looks like I'm gonna have to shut down everything but the emergency power systems.

Sound: Internal noises come down to near silence.

THREEPIO: Er, Captain Solo, I'm almost afraid to ask, but . . . does that include shutting me down, too?

HAN: Naw, Threepio; I need you to talk to the *Falcon*, find out what's wrong with the hyperdrive. You and her speak the same language—

Sound: Rumbling, as the ship rocks, the cave quaking.

THREEPIO: Oh . . . that is the third disturbance we've experienced since landing in the cave, Captain. It's quite possible that this asteroid is not entirely stable.

HAN: "Not entirely stable"? I'm glad yer here t'tell us these things, Threepio. Chewie!

CHEWBACCA: SAYS "WHAT?"

HAN: Take the Professor, here, back to the tech station and plug 'im into the *Falcon*'s systems.

THREEPIO: Well, really! Sometimes I just don't understand human behavior! Oh—

Sound: Chewbacca hauls Threepio off, ululating.

THREEPIO: *(MOVING OFF)* After all, I'm only attempting to perform my function in the most expeditious and efficient manner possible—

LEIA: He *is* doing his best to help, you know. We're lucky he's here.

HAN: Yeah, you're right; he's not too bad, for a piece of machinery who talks back—

Sound: The cave quakes again.

HAN: Ooops! Look out!

LEIA: Hey! Hands off!

Sound: Quake subsides.

HAN: Just lookin' out for my crew, Leia.

LEIA: Han . . . let go. Please.

HAN: Don't get excited!

LEIA: Captain, being held by you isn't quite enough to get me excited.

HAN: Sorry, sweetheart! *(MOVING OFF)* We just haven't got the time for anything else right now!

LEIA: *Don't tempt me when I've got a wrench in my hand, Solo!*

HAN: OFF, LAUGHS

LEIA: *(TO HERSELF)* One of these days, Han . . .

Sound: Reverberation of metal as she hits the bulkhead.

LEIA: . . . *one of these days!*

Sound: Brief transition.

SCENE 5-9 *FALCON* HOLD

Sound: Different ship noises.

THREEPIO: Where, oh where, is Artoo-Detoo when I need him? What an incredible mess!

Sound: Switches, beep tones.

HAN: *(APPROACHING)* How we goin' on the hyperdrive, Three-pio? Fixed yet?

THREEPIO: Captain, I don't know where the *Falcon* learned to communicate, but she has the *most* peculiar dialect! She is very intelligent, but—she can be so very *rude*, at times!

HAN: Comes from hangin' around with me 'n' Chewie. You're liable to start doin' it yourself. What'd she say?

THREEPIO: I believe she says that the power coupling on the negative axis has been polarized, sir. I'm afraid you will have to replace it.

HAN: Well, of course I'll have to replace it.

THREEPIO: *(MOVING OFF)* I'll go and see about the transition apparatus, sir.

HAN: *(TO OFF)* Hey, Chewie!

CHEWBACCA: WOOFS, APPROACHING.

HAN: Here's the core wire you wanted. Look, I been thinkin'; we better replace the negative power coupling.

CHEWBACCA: *(MOVING OFF)* GROWLS.

Sound: Brief transition.

SCENE 5-10 *FALCON* HOLD

Sound: Sounds of Leia, exasperated, repairing the cowling, sticking as she tries to close it.

HAN: *(APPROACHING)* What's the matter, Princess? Need a hand with that? Let's see, here . . .

145

LEIA: *(THROUGH LOCKED TEETH, AS SHE SHAKES HIS ARM OFF)* Uhh!

HAN: Hey!

LEIA: What I *don't* need is your arm around me!

HAN: Look, Your Worship, I'm only tryin' to help, here.

LEIA: And would you please stop calling me that? I didn't ask to be what I am. I'm trying to do the best I can.

HAN: Sure, Leia, sorry. Royalty always throws me.

LEIA: Oh, Han, you make it so difficult to get along, sometimes.

HAN: I do, I really do. I know that, Leia.

LEIA: What's this, *honesty*? Quick, Han; I'm about to faint!

HAN: You could be nicer, too, though. Come on. Admit it: Sometimes you think I'm all right.

LEIA: Occasionally, maybe. When you aren't acting like a scoundrel.

HAN: Scoundrel? *Scoundrel?* I like the sound of that word. C'mere and say it again, Leia . . .

LEIA: Han—stop that! Please let go of my hand.

HAN: Stop what? Looks like you barked your knuckles.

LEIA: Stop rubbing my hand; it's. . . . it's all dirty.

HAN: My hands're dirty, too. What're you afraid of, Leia?

LEIA: "Afraid"?

HAN: Tell me I'm wrong.

LEIA: I—just don't like you holding my hand. I don't like you looking at me like that.

HAN: You're trembling, did you know that?

LEIA: I'm not trembling. Please let me go.

HAN: You like me *because* I'm a scoundrel! There aren't enough scoundrels in your life. *(MOVING)* Wait; where you goin'?

LEIA: I happen to like nice men. Let me by, Han . . .

HAN: I'm a nice man, Leia.

LEIA: No you're not! You're a, a—*(REACTS, AS HE KISSES HER) (IN THE MIDST OF IT)*—you're . . .

HAN: *(ALSO IN THE MIDST OF IT)* Um-hmmm!

THREEPIO: *(OFF)* Captain Solo! Oh, sir, sir! I have been talking with the *Falcon*!

LEIA: *(BREATHLESS, AS THEY PART)* Let me go, Han. Please . . .

HAN: No, Leia.

THREEPIO: *(APPROACHING)* I have isolated the reverse power flux coupling that has been plaguing us, sir!

LEIA: I'll go take a look at it! *(MOVING OFF)* Good work, Threepio! Very good work!

HAN: Yeah. Thank you, Threepio. Thank you very, very much!

THREEPIO: You're perfectly welcome, I'm sure, Captain. Never you mind, sir; we'll get things repaired. *(MOVING OFF)* After all, the *Falcon*'s not all that big a ship, is she, sir?

HAN: *(TO HIMSELF)* No, Threepio. She's not a very big ship at all.

Sound: Brief transition.

Scene 5-11 *FALCON* COCKPIT

Sound: Cockpit sounds come up.

LEIA: EVEN BREATHING INDICATING SLEEP. LOW SOUND, AS SHE HAS A TROUBLED DREAM.

Sound: A mynock flutters against the hull. (Lotsa luck, Voegeli!!!)

LEIA: Hmmm? *(AWAKENING)* What. . . . what was . . .

Sound: The mynock fastens itself to the canopy with a thump, gibbering, then flutters away.

LEIA: *(SCREAMS)* Han! Get up, get up to the cockpit! *Han!*

HAN: *(APPROACHING)* What? What's wrong? What happened?

THREEPIO: *(APPROACHING)* Your Highness, are you all right?

CHEWBACCA: *(APPROACHING)* WOOFS.

LEIA: There's something out there, in the cave. It fastened itself to the canopy for a second, then flew away.

HAN: Easy, easy, Leia. You were dreaming.

LEIA: *I was not dreaming, you simpleton!* See, it left that goop smeared on the canopy.

Sound: More fluttering on the hull.

THREEPIO: Do you hear that? Her Highness is right! Listen, listen!

HAN: I'm goin' out there.

LEIA: Are you out of your mind?

HAN: Look, I just got this bucket back together. I'm not gonna let somethin' tear 'er apart!

LEIA: *(DRAWS A BREATH)* Ohh-kay! Then, I'm going with you.

HAN: Whatever you say. You too, Chewie. Break out the breathing masks. And get your bowcaster!

CHEWBACCA: *(MOVES OFF)* HOOTING.

THREEPIO: Pardon me, sir, but I think it might be better if I remain inside and guard the ship.

HAN: Suit yourself, Threepio. Let's go, Princess!

Sound: Brief transition.

SCENE 5-12 SPACE SLUG INTERIOR

Sound: Dank, echoing cave, squishy footsteps as they leave the ramp.

LEIA: This ground sure feels strange. It doesn't feel like rock, or soil. Ugh! It's too squishy and slick.

HAN: There's an awful lot of moisture in here. Pretty warm for a cave, too.

LEIA: Han, I have a bad feeling about this.

HAN: You're not the only one. Chewie, keep your bowcaster ready.

CHEWBACCA: ACKNOWLEDGES.

HAN: Let's see what it was you heard, Leia.

Sound: Squishy steps.

LEIA: It sounded like it was right up there on the hull—

Sound: The mynock swoops at them, flapping, gibbering.

HAN: Look out!

LEIA: Han!

Sound: Han's blaster, one shot, mynock, expires, thuds to the floor.

HAN: It's all right! I got it! It's all right!

LEIA: What *is* it?

HAN: Just what I thought: a mynock. Chewie, check the rest of the ship and make sure there're no more of 'em attached to 'er.

CHEWBACCA: ANSWERS.

LEIA: "Mynock"?

HAN: Yeah, they stick to a ship and chew on the power cables. Go on back inside. We'll clean 'em off if there're any more.

Sound: Another mynock flies toward them, and hovers nearby, gibbering.

LEIA: Look out! *(BATTING AT IT)* Get away!

HAN: Duck, Leia!

Sound: Han shoots again, twice. Mynock is hit and killed by second shot, dropping. Cave begins to rumble.

CHEWBACCA: YELPS.

LEIA: Ohhh!

HAN: Hold onto me!

Sound: Quake subsides.

LEIA: These quakes are getting worse.

HAN: Wait a minute. That was no quake; it started when my first shot hit the ground . . .

LEIA: Try it again.

Sound: Han fires. Rumbling starts again.

LEIA: Ohh! What's it mean, Han?

HAN: Everybody back into the ship! *Right now!*

Sound: Brief transition.

SCENE 5-13 *FALCON* COCKPIT

Sound: Cockpit up.

THREEPIO: Oh, those ghastly, beastly creatures!

LEIA: *(APPROACHING)* Han, Han, the starfleet's still nearby. I don't think it's wise to try to get past them right—

HAN: *(APPROACHING)* I got no time to discuss this in committee!

LEIA: Ohh! I am *not* a committee!

Sound: The Falcon*'s engines rise as Han works controls.*

LEIA: Han, you can't make the jump to lightspeed in this asteroid field!

Sound: Cave rumbling, quaking.

THREEPIO: *(TOSSED AROUND)* Oooooops!

LEIA: Ah!

Sound: Falcon rises on thrusters.

HAN: Siddown, sweetheart! We're leavin'!

THREEPIO: Look! The cave entrance!

HAN: I see it, I see it . . .

LEIA: The cave is collapsing! The entrance is closing.

HAN: That's no cave entrance. It's a mouth, see?

LEIA: *We're inside of something!*

CHEWBACCA: KEENS.

Sound: The Falcon *blasts forward.*

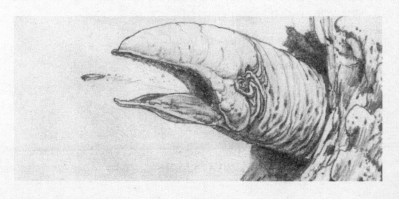

THREEPIO: The mouth is practically closed! We're certain to perish!

HAN: Not if *I* can help it—

Sound: The Falcon *thunders "past," out of the cave.*

LEIA: You can take your hands away from your photoreceptors, Threepio.

THREEPIO: We made it! I can scarcely credit my sensors!

LEIA: With no room to spare. Han, what *was* that thing?

HAN: They call 'em space slugs. Probably dormant when we landed; we woke it up.

LEIA: Only you, Solo, could pick a monster's esophagus to park in!

HAN: Look, I got us out, didn't I?

Sound: Alarm flasher on the console.

HAN: *TIE fighters!* The Imperials've picked us up again!

CHEWBACCA: MOANS.

Sound: Concussions as the TIEs open up.

THREEPIO: They're firing! Why can't I lead the sort of placid existence for which I was designed?

LEIA: We can't go to lightspeed here!

HAN: We're gonna haveta outrun 'em!

Sound: More hits on Falcon.

HAN: Everybody, hold on! *Hit it, Chewie!*

Sound: Falcon*'s engines blare, fade.*

NARRATOR: Unable to escape into hyperspace, the *Millennium*

Falcon is now locked in a desperate race against Imperial warships. Elsewhere, Luke Skywalker is about to enter a new phase of his life as a Jedi Knight. And strands of the future, as woven by the mysterious workings of the Force, draw the Rebels towards new and horrible danger.

Music: Up under credits.

NARRATOR: CLOSING CREDITS.

EPISODE SIX:
"WAY OF THE JEDI"

C H A R A C T E R S :

Luke	Ben
Artoo	Needa
Yoda	Piett
Vader	Emperor

Music: Opening theme.

NARRATOR: A long time ago in a galaxy far, far away, there came a time of revolution, when Rebels united to challenge a tyrannical Empire. Now, it is a dark time for the Rebellion. Their base on the planet Hoth has been destroyed. The surviving Rebel units are scattered among the stars, attempting to elude the Imperial warships that hunt them, and waiting to regroup at a secret rendezvous point.

Sound: Luke's X-wing fighter.

NARRATOR: But one Rebel must follow his own course. Commander Luke Skywalker obeys the instructions given him by the spectral image of his onetime teacher, Obi-Wan Kenobi. With the aid of his astro-droid Artoo-Detoo, Luke is bringing his X-wing fighter on a landing approach to the mysterious planet Dagobah. There, he is to further his training as a Jedi Knight, under the tutelage of the legendary Jedi Master, Yoda.

SCENE 6-1 X-WING COCKPIT

Sound: X-wing cockpit comes up.

LUKE: That's Dagobah, Artoo, I'm sure of it.

ARTOO: WHISTLES AN OBJECTION.

LUKE: I *know* it's not on the charts! I'm not even sure how I found it.

ARTOO: BURBLES A QUESTION.

LUKE: No, Artoo; I'm not gonna change my mind about this. Can you detect any breaks in the cloud cover?

ARTOO: SAYS NO.

LUKE: Neither can I. It's dense, too. Let's check it out with the sensors.

Sound: Sensors hum and beep softly.

LUKE: Mm. I'm not picking up any cities or technology. Massive life-form readings, though. There's something alive down there, all right.

ARTOO: WHISTLES AN ANXIOUS QUESTION.

LUKE: *(CHUCKLES)* Yes, I'm sure Dagobah's perfectly safe for droids, Artoo! Let's go in a little lower, see if we can pick up some terrain features.

Sound: Fighter swoops lower.

LUKE: What the . . .

ARTOO: SIGNALS URGENTLY.

LUKE: I know, I know; I hear ya, Artoo! All my scopes just went dead! I can't see a thing through this cloud layer! And I can't tell what's doin' it.

ARTOO: BEMOANING HIS FATE.

LUKE: Well, we can't turn back now! Just hang on; I'm gonna start the landing cycle.

Sound: Engines whine.

ARTOO: COMPLAINS.

LUKE: Settle down, Artoo! Instruments and visual approaches aren't the only way to land a ship.

Sound: Engines rise, turbulence, as the fighter descends through the atmosphere.

LUKE: *(CALMING, DRAWING ON THE FORCE)* Just be quiet, and let me concentrate. The Force hasn't let me down yet . . .

Sound: Ship bucking.

ARTOO: SQUEAKS.

LUKE: Brace yourself, Artoo, and . . . have a little faith, here . . .

Sound: Impact of swamp tree branch, rattling the ship.

ARTOO: YELPS.

LUKE: Watch out for those branches—we're almost down . . .

Sound: More branches.

LUKE: It's a swamp! The whole planet's a swamp! Get ready; this one's gonna be rough!

Sound: More branches, vines, etc., hissing steam.

ARTOO: SCREAMS IN FEAR.

Music: Music up.

SCENE 6-2   STAR DESTROYER BRIDGE

Sound: Sounds of Vader's destroyer's bridge come up. Vader's mask-breathing.

CAPTAIN NEEDA: *(APPROACHING)* Lord Vader, our TIE fighters have been unable to reestablish contact with the *Millennium Falcon*.

VADER: Well, Captain Needa?

NEEDA: Considering the number of smaller craft we've lost in the asteroid field and the damage to our Star Destroyers, intelligence has concluded that the *Falcon* and her crew have been destroyed.

VADER: No, Captain Needa; they're alive. I want every ship in the fleet to sweep this asteroid field until they are found and captured.

ADMIRAL PIETT: *(APPROACHING)* Lord Vader, we've had a priority signal.

VADER: What is it, Admiral Piett?

PIETT: The Emperor commands you to make contact with him.

VADER: Move my flagship out of the asteroid field at once, so that I may send a clear transmission. Prepare my communications vault.

PIETT: At once, Lord Vader!

SCENE 6-3   VADER'S COMMUNICATIONS VAULT

Sound: Brief transition to the echoing quiet of Vader's communications vault. Vader's steps resound, approaching, then stop. Vader's breathing. The low hum of the special commo equipment.

VADER: Thy servant awaits thee on bended knee, my Emperor. What is thy bidding, Master?

EMPEROR: *(DISEMBODIED, SEPULCHRAL)* There is a great disturbance in the Force, Vader.

VADER: Yes; I have felt it.

EMPEROR: We have a new enemy. Luke Skywalker.

VADER: Yes, my Master.

EMPEROR: He could destroy us.

VADER: He's just a boy. Almost untrained, scarcely tested. And, Obi-Wan can no longer help him.

EMPEROR: The Force is strong within him. *The son of Skywalker must not become a Jedi!*

VADER: If he could be turned, he would become a powerful ally.

EMPEROR: Yes. He would be a great asset. Can it be done?

VADER: He will join us or die, Master!

EMPEROR: How will you find him?

VADER: I shall tempt him with bait he cannot resist. Once I have the *Millennium Falcon* in hand, Luke Skywalker is as good as ours.

EMPEROR: Go forth then, faithful servant, and work my will!

Sound: Commo vault fades.

SCENE 6-4   DAGOBAH SWAMP

Sound: Dagobah swamps come up. Bubbling mire, flying lizards, mutant crickets, dinosaurian hisses, thing-shrieks, creature-whoops, etc. X-wing's engines steaming a little. Artoo, slightly off, whistles worriedly. Suddenly, Luke's canopy pops and lifts on servos.

LUKE: Whew! Glad Han didn't see that landing, Artoo! He'd never let me live it down!

ARTOO: INQUIRES ANXIOUSLY.

LUKE: Yeah, I'm all right. Just jostled around a bit. How're you?

ARTOO: REASSURES HIM.

LUKE: Good. Well, no use sitting here—

Sound: Luke unbuckling his safety belt, etc.

LUKE: *(EFFORT, AS HE DRAWS HIMSELF OUT OF THE COCKPIT)* Oh, terrific landing, Skywalker! Right into a marsh!

ARTOO: WHISTLES.

LUKE: No, you stay in your socket, Artoo. It's only a short wade to shore; *(MOVING OFF)* I'll have a look around.

Sound: Artoo raising himself from the socket.

ARTOO: TWEEDLES, WADDLING CLOSER.

LUKE: *(CALLS)* No, lock yourself back down, Artoo! Look out, *you're gonna lose your balance*!

Sound: Under the above: Artoo beeps in fear, falling. Splash as he hits, water ripples under Luke's next line.

LUKE: *(OFF)* Artoo? Artoo-Detoo! *(MOVING ON)* Where are you? Artoo!

Sound: Water parts as Artoo's periscope breaks the surface.

ARTOO: BUBBLES A SUBMARINE SOUND OF SURPRISE.

LUKE: *(SIGHS IN RELIEF)* Will you be more careful? Lucky the water's only periscope-deep on a short droid! I'll meet you over there, on the shore.

ARTOO: ACKNOWLEDGES, THEN STARTS OFF, HUMMING TO HIMSELF.

Sound: Artoo's periscope cutting a little wake in the water.

LUKE: Artoo-Detoo . . .

ARTOO: RESPONDING, "WHAT?"

LUKE: Artoo, the shore is over *that* way. See it?

ARTOO: REPLIES WITH CONFIDENCE, COMING ABOUT. HE RESUMES HUMMING.

Sound: Luke's footsteps on the hull.

LUKE: *(SIGHS TO HIMSELF)* I don't think I have any more idea of where we are than he does. *(GRUNTS WITH EFFORT AS HE JUMPS INTO THE WATER)*

SCENE 6-4A DAGOBAH EXTERIOR

Sound: Brief transition. Luke's point of view is ashore.

LUKE: *(TO OFF)* Artoo, over this way. The bank isn't as steep here.

ARTOO: ANSWERS, APPROACHING.

Sound: Something large, swimming closer.

LUKE: Artoo, there's something out there in the water! It's coming this way!

ARTOO: FRIGHTENED BEEPS.

Sound: Swimming gets closer.

LUKE: Artoo, get up here! Hurry!

Sound: Monster, yowling, surfaces to gulp.

ARTOO: SCREAMING.

LUKE: *Artoo!*

Sound: Splashing, then wavelets, as monster dives.

LUKE: *Answer me!* Artoo-Detoo! Oh, no . . .

Sound: Turbulence, splashing, as monster surfaces and spits Artoo into the air. Artoo's shriek as he flies through a high trajectory.

LUKE: *Artoo!*

Sound: Thump, as Artoo lands, rolls. His moaning and whimpering grow louder as Luke's point of view moves to him.

LUKE: Hey! Hey! *(AS HIS POINT OF VIEW MOVES TO ARTOO— PANTING)* Are you all right? Say something!

ARTOO: ANSWERS GROGGILY. SOBS.

LUKE: C'mon; stand up, little buddy. *(WITH THE EFFORT OF RIGHTING ARTOO)* C'mon—uh!

Sound: Artoo righted.

ARTOO: WHISTLES UNSTEADILY.

LUKE: Whatever that thing was, it spit you out. You're lucky you don't taste very good.

ARTOO: AGREES DAZEDLY.

LUKE: Anything broken?

ARTOO: SAYS NO, THEN WARBLES INDIGNANTLY.

LUKE: If you're saying that coming here was a bad idea, I'm beginning to agree with you. *(SIGHS)* Oh, Artoo, what are we doing here?

ARTOO: CONFUSED.

LUKE: This is like . . . something out of a dream, or—I don't know. I'm not even sure how I got us here. Maybe I'm just going crazy.

ARTOO: BEEPS, WITH SLUGGISH, CLOGGED NOISES.

LUKE: What'd you, take some mud into you? Better purge your intakes.

Sound: Artoo's purge cover pops open and he disgorges mud all over the place.

LUKE: Hey! Watch where you squirt that stuff, will ya?

ARTOO: APOLOGETIC.

LUKE: Aw, never mind. Night's comin' on; we better set up camp. With the X-wing stuck in the swamp, we're gonna be here for a while. First thing we're gonna need's a log, so I can get to the ship. *(GRUNTS, RISING)* Let's get at it, Artoo . . .

SCENE 6-5 DAGOBAH EXTERIOR

Sound: Brief transition. Night sounds. Luke sets down a metallic box.

LUKE: *(WITH EFFORT)* That's the last of the gear. You ready for a recharge, Artoo?

ARTOO: ACCEPTS EAGERLY.

LUKE: Okay, c'mere by the lamp. Let's hook you up to the fusion furnace.

ARTOO: AGREEING.

LUKE: *(WITH EFFORT, AS HE CONNECTS ARTOO)* Let's see, now: Put that in there . . .

Sound: Hum of fusion power unit. Connecting sounds.

LUKE: There y'go, Artoo.

ARTOO: CONTENTED, BEEPS.

LUKE: You're welcome. What're friends for? *(SIGHS)* Now all I gotta do is find this Yoda, if he even exists. But where?

ARTOO: PROFESSES IGNORANCE OF THE SUBJECT'S WHERE-ABOUTS.

LUKE: I don't know, either. I don't even know where to start. I was expecting a fortress or something. A swamp planet's a strange place to find a Jedi Master.

Sound: The caw of a flying thingie.

ARTOO: EXPRESSES DOUBT.

LUKE: Yeah; this place gives me the creeps, too.

ARTOO: CHIRPS.

LUKE: *(SIGHS)* You're right; I could use a little supper.

Sound: Luke opens and rifles through a canister, extracts a ration bar.

LUKE: *(EATING)* Still—there's something familiar about this place. I dunno; I feel . . . I feel like . . .

YODA: *(SLIGHTLY OFF)* Feel like what, stranger?

LUKE: *(WHIRLING)* Like we're being watched! Don't you move, shorty, or I'll blow you right out of that tree!

YODA: Ooo! *Don't shoot!* Away put your blaster! Only my walking stick have I! No harm to you or the droid I mean!

LUKE: Well, sneaking up on somebody like that's a good way to get yourself roasted, old-timer.

YODA: Merely curious am I! I am wondering: Why are you here? Please slay me not.

LUKE: Listen, you can come down. It's okay. I'm just looking for someone.

YODA: *Looking? (LAUGHS) (AS HE JUMPS, WITH EFFORT) Ummp!*

Sound: Yoda lands with a little thud.

YODA: *(APPROACHING) Found* someone you have, I would say, hmm? *(LAUGHS)*

LUKE: Oh. Right. But a green gnome wasn't what I had in mind, old-timer.

YODA: Help you I can, stranger! Yes, mmm . . .

LUKE: *(LAUGHS)* I don't think so, little fella. I'm looking for a great warrior.

YODA: Ahh! *(LAUGHS)* "A great warrior!" *(LAUGHS) Wars* not make one great! *(HUFFS AND MUMBLES TO HIMSELF)* Aha! In time for eating have I arrived!

Sound: Yoda ransacking the food canister.

YODA: Plenty there is! *(EATING, EVALUATING IT)* Hmm, hmm . . .

LUKE: Put that down! Now, Artoo and I—hey! That's my supper!

ARTOO: OBJECTING, TOO

YODA: *(MUNCHING)* Phuh! *(SPITTING IT OUT)* Awful, it tastes! How you get so big, stranger, eating food of that kind?

LUKE: *(DRAWING A DEEP BREATH)* Listen, friend, I'm not exactly wild about survival rations either. We didn't mean to land in that mud puddle, and if we could get our ship out, we would. But we can't, so why don't you just run along and do whatever it is that you—

YODA: Aww, cannot get your ship out? *(LAUGHS)* What else you have in these metal boxes besides bad food, *hey*?

Sound: Yoda rummaging around in the supply containers. Throwing things in all directions, etc.

LUKE: Hey, leave those alone!

YODA: Ahh, so many useless things you carry around!

LUKE: Hey, look out! You could've broken that power capsule!

Sound: Yoda throwing things over his shoulder as he burrows into the canister.

YODA: Bah! With junk, are your boxes filled!

LUKE: Don't do that . . .

YODA: *(LAUGHING, STILL THROWING THINGS)* Worthless are these gadgets!

ARTOO: BEEPS, ANGRY.

LUKE: *Will you open those big green ears and listen to me? Aw . . .* you're makin' a mess!

YODA: CHORTLES

LUKE: Hey, gimme back the energy lamp, will ya?

ARTOO: YELPS.

Sound: Things scattered as Yoda skitters away from Luke.

YODA: No, stranger! Mine it is! Or I will help you not!

LUKE: Look, peewee, I don't *want* your help. I want my lamp back. I'm gonna need it to get out of this slimy mudhole.

ARTOO: EXPOSTULATES.

Sound: Artoo's arm extending under.

YODA: *"Mudhole?" "Slimy?"* My home, this is! Not for you, to say such things about my—

ARTOO: WHISTLES WITH TRIUMPH.

Sound: Artoo grabbing the lamp.

YODA: *What?* No, droid no! My lamp; mine! Let it go!

Sound: Artoo's servos whining, Artoo's sounds, under tug-o'-war over the lamp.

YODA: Ah! Ah! Ah!

LUKE: Artoo-Detoo . . .

YODA: Let go he must, your droid! Mine is this lamp! Umph!

Sound: Yoda's gimer stick hitting Artoo.

YODA: Mine! Mine! Mine! *(TO LUKE)* Tell him, stranger!

ARTOO: WHISTLES ANGRILY.

LUKE: Oh, let him have the lamp, Artoo. Just so he'll leave . . .

ARTOO: WHISTLES, SURRENDERS.

YODA: *(WRESTING IT AWAY)* Hah! Mine! *Mine!*

LUKE: Sure; yours, yours. Now will ya move along, little fella? Artoo and I have a lot of work to do.

YODA: No, no, generous stranger! Stay and help you, I will! *(LAUGHS)* Find your friend, hmm?

LUKE: *(EFFORT OF PATIENCE)* I am not looking for a friend. I'm looking for a Jedi Master. He's supposed to be here on Dagobah, but I guess I'm—

YODA: Oh-hh! "Jedi Master!" Yoda! You seek *Yoda*!

ARTOO: SURPRISED.

LUKE: Hold it; you know him?

YODA: Mm-hn! Take you to him, I will! *(LAUGHS)* Yes, yes. But now, we must eat. Not this nonsense food of yours. Come. To my house!

LUKE: But—wait a second . . .

YODA: *(MOVING OFF, LAUGHING) Good* food have I there! Sorry you will not be! Come! *(LAUGHS)*

ARTOO: MAKES DUBIOUS SOUNDS.

YODA: *(FROM OFF)* Follow me, big stranger! Come! *(LAUGHS, MOVING OFF)*

LUKE: Oh, brother! Artoo?

ARTOO: ACKNOWLEDGES.

LUKE: Stay here and watch after the camp.

ARTOO: WARBLES CONCERNEDLY.

LUKE: *(MOVING OFF)* I haven't got any choice, Artoo! I have to find this Yoda. I'll be back as soon as I can!

ARTOO: HOOTS MOURNFULLY.

SCENE 6-6   YODA'S HOUSE

Sound: Brief transition to Yoda's house, interior. Crackling, low fire, hiss and slither of snakes, etc. Rain outside.

YODA: *(APPROACHING)* Come in! That's right! Low, keep your head! Careful, careful—

Sound: (OFF) Luke bumps his head on the ceiling.

LUKE: *(OFF)* Ouch! *(APPROACHING)* Whoo! Low is your ceiling—uh, I mean, your ceiling's kinda—

YODA: High enough it is for me! Giants like you must bend! Over there on the floor seat yourself! *(BUSTLING AROUND)* Time now for food.

Sound: Yoda stirring pot, ladling food, etc.

LUKE: *(GRUNTS, SEATING HIMSELF TAILOR-FASHION)* D'you usually keep all these snakes and lizards and things in your house?

YODA: *(DISHING IT UP)* My friends they are, and harm nothing. *Usually.* Wiser you would be not to sit upon them. *(LAUGHS)*

LUKE: Mm. Thanks for the warning.

YODA: On the table is your spoon.

LUKE: Look, I'm sure that stuff's, uh, delicious. I just don't understand why we can't go see Yoda right now. I wouldn't mind traveling in the rain, if that's the problem.

YODA: Here: Your bowl take! For the Jedi it is time to eat as well. Hm? *(LAUGHS)*

LUKE: Oh, all right . . .

Sound: Luke's spoon on the bowl, etc.

YODA: Eat! *(LAUGHS)* Eat! Hot! Good food, hm? Good, hm?

LUKE: *(EATING)* Uh-huh. How far— *(SWALLOWS)* how far away is Yoda? Will it take us long to get to him?

YODA: Not far. Yoda not far. *(LAUGHS)* Patience! Soon you will be with him. Eat now. Rootleaf, it is; I cook! *(LAUGHS)*

LUKE: Um, thanks; it *is* good . . .

YODA: Yes! Thank you! Now, why you wish to become Jedi? Hm? *(LAUGHS)*

LUKE: Y'know, pal, you ask a lot of questions.

YODA: In my home are you! A guest, eating my food!

LUKE: But I never asked you to bring me to this hut! I never even—

YODA: Polite should you be! Nothing would it cost you! *(LAUGHS)* Why a Jedi, then?

LUKE: Mmm. Mostly because of my father, I guess.

YODA: Ah, your father! Powerful Jedi was he. Mm-hm; *powerful* Jedi!

LUKE: Huh? Aw, c'mon; how could you know my father? Y'don't even know who *I* am. Ah-hh—

Sound: Luke tosses his bowl and spoon onto the table.

LUKE: I don't even know what I'm doing here. I've got friends who're waiting for me, counting on me! I should be with the Rebel Alliance.

YODA: So-oo?

LUKE: Yeah, that's so! You say you knew of my father? Well, the man . . .

YODA: Speak on! Speak on!

LUKE: The man who murdered him's gotta be stopped. And I'm sitting around a mud hut on a swamp planet!

YODA: Aha! And find this murderer you would? For revenge?

LUKE: I—there's so much I should be doing. This's getting me no place. We're wasting our time here!

YODA: *(SIGHS, TAKING ON HIS OTHER PERSONA)* I cannot teach this one. The boy has no patience, Obi-Wan!

LUKE: *What?*

BEN: *(SPECTRAL, DISEMBODIED)* He will learn patience, Master.

LUKE: Huh—*Ben?* Wh— how—

YODA: *(TO HIMSELF)* Hm. *(TO BEN)* Much anger in this one, Obi-Wan. Like his father is he.

BEN: And was I any different when you taught me, Master?

YODA: Hmm, haa . . . This one is not ready, Obi-Wan!

LUKE: Yoda! . . . *you!* You're—I *am* ready, Yoda! *(TO THE ROOM AT LARGE)* Ben! I *can* be a Jedi! Ben, tell him I'm ready . . .

YODA: *Ready* are you? Loud, unthinking youngster are you! What know you of "ready"?

LUKE: But Ben told me to come to you so that I could—

YODA: For eight hundred years have *I* trained Jedi! My own counsel will I keep on who is to be trained!

LUKE: Yoda—*Master*, I didn't mean to sound like I—

YODA: No right have you to call me by that word! You have not earned it! A Jedi must have the deepest commitment. *Hm?* The most serious mind!

LUKE: How can I convince you?

YODA: *(SIGHS)* Obi-Wan, this one a long time have I watched. All his life has he looked away to the future, to the horizon. Never his mind on where he was. Hm? What was he doing? *(WITH THE EFFORT OF PRODDING LUKE WITH HIS GIMER STICK)* What were you doing, eh, boy?

LUKE: *(REACTING)* Ow! Uh, I didn't see it like that. Maybe you're right. But, Yoda, *I never had anyone to teach me any different*!

YODA: And so you dreamt of adventure, eh? Excitement, eh? A Jedi craves not these things. Reckless are you, son of Skywalker!

BEN: So was I, if you'll remember, Master.

YODA: He is too old, Obi-Wan. *(AIRILY)* Yes. Too old to begin the training, Luke Skywalker!

LUKE: But I've learned so *much*, Mast— Yoda! Ben! If I can't do it, if I'm not—not *worthy*, then why was I brought here? Won't you both at least let me understand *why I had to go through this*? *Please?*

YODA: *(BEAT) (SIGHS)* Obi-Wan, will he finish what he begins?

BEN: Luke must answer for himself, and live by his answer.

LUKE: I won't fail you, Yoda! Or you, Ben! I don't want anything the way I want this.

YODA: So? So-oo?

LUKE: Yes! Yoda, I'm not afraid!

YODA: But you will be, son of Skywalker. *You . . . will . . . be!*

SCENE 6-7 YODA'S HOUSE

Sound: Brief transition. Yoda's hut comes up again. Food bubbling, fire. Luke's asleep off, grunts as he turns over. Yoda stirring his cauldron.

YODA: Hmm, hm. *(SLURPS A SAMPLE OF HIS COOKING)* Tastes good, but—not enough moss extract, no.

ARTOO: SIGNALS AND BLEEPS FROM OFF.

YODA: Eh? Who is at my window?

ARTOO: BLEEPS AGAIN.

YODA: Artoo-Detoo! Little droid! *(POINT OF VIEW MOVES CLOSER TO ARTOO)* Inside would I invite you, but bend down you cannot!

ARTOO: SIGNALS A QUESTION.

YODA: Your master? He sleeps. Hush now! He will awaken soon.

ARTOO: WHISTLES WORRIEDLY.

YODA: Yes; he is well. You worry for him, Artoo-Detoo?

ARTOO: CONFIRMS IT.

YODA: Good, such loyalty! Artoo-Detoo: Curious little droid! Brave little droid! Dangerous and lonely is the path Luke Skywalker must follow now. But follow it he must. Upon him rest the greatest matters.

ARTOO: RESPONDS UNCERTAINLY.

YODA: Yes, yes, it must be. By the Force has that been decided. Go now; with you will we be shortly.

ARTOO: ACKNOWLEDGES, MOVING OFF.

LUKE: *(SLIGHTLY OFF, AWAKENING)* Yoda? *(YAWNS)* Master?

YODA: *(POINT OF VIEW MOVING TOWARD LUKE)* Here am I, young Skywalker. How feel you?

LUKE: Uh . . . good. In fact, I feel great.

YODA: Good! Your strength will you need. Later will we eat.

LUKE: Breakfast can wait. I want to start learning, right away. I have so many questions—

YODA: Patient must you be! *(HANDING HIM THE KNAPSACK)* Here . . .

LUKE: Huh?

Sound: As the knapsack's passed over.

YODA: On your shoulders put this.

LUKE: A knapsack? What'm I carrying?

YODA: In it will I ride, while you train your body, to train your mind.

LUKE: Oh. Awright.

Sound: Buckles, etc.

LUKE: *(AS HE SHRUGS INTO THE STRAPS, BUCKLES, ETC.)* Master, Dagobah doesn't show up on any chart, and instruments can't penetrate the cloud layer. How can that be?

YODA: My privacy, do I appreciate!

LUKE: Oh. Um, where's my weapons belt—oh—

Sound: Clanking, rattling of the belt.

LUKE: Got it.

YODA: Think you that you must have weapons?

LUKE: Well, I thought that—there're a lot of mean, hungry things running around on Dagobah. I know you only carry your gimer stick, but I'm not so used to—

YODA: Hmm. Bring them then, if you feel you must: Now bend down, that onto your back I may climb . . .

LUKE: *(BENDING)* But—would you rather I didn't take them along on this—

YODA: No more questions! Come: The growing begins! The Way of the Jedi!

SCENE 6-8   DAGOBAH EXTERIOR

Sound: Brief transition to exterior Dagobah.

LUKE: PANTING AS HE APPROACHES

YODA: *(APPROACHING, RIDING IN THE PACK)* Stop; stop here! Rest you may, for a time. Sit!

LUKE: BREATHING RAGGEDLY, LOWERING HIMSELF

YODA: Tired are you, hm? With Yoda on your back?

LUKE: Whoo! It's been . . . quite a workout! Running and . . . jumping and . . . swinging through this swamp all morning. Y'know, though . . . Dagobah's beautiful . . . in a way.

YODA: What? Not a "slimy mudhole"?

LUKE: *(LAUGHS TIREDLY)* Maybe I'm seeing it through different eyes.

YODA: So? Fine! Strong are you in strength of the body, young Skywalker. But that is as nothing to strength of the spirit!

LUKE: How do I use it?

YODA: Reach out with your feelings, you must. The Force have you used before.

LUKE: Yes; when Ben taught me to use my lightsaber. When he helped me blow up the Death Star. Ben . . .

YODA: Reach out to the universe around you, and to the universe within you.

LUKE: Ben said that the Force controls us, partly, but obeys us, too.

YODA: Tell you things your senses cannot, it will! Bear you up when your body will not, it can! Use it now. Concentrate . . .

LUKE: DEEP, REGULAR BREATHING

YODA: And feel the flow of the Force.

LUKE: I do, Master.

YODA: No fatigue is there. Your commands will your body obey. Stand up.

LUKE: *(RISING, WITH LITTLE EXERTION)* It's like you say; I'm not tired. It's like when I woke up this morning.

YODA: Then . . . run. Open yourself to the Force. Now run . . . *run!*

SCENE 6-8A   DAGOBAH EXTERIOR

Sound: Brief transition. Luke, with Yoda still on his back, approaching point of view at a run, breathing evenly.

YODA: *(APPROACHING)* Stop, stop here. Be still for a moment, young Skywalker.

LUKE: All that exercise, and I'm still not tired out. Am I doing it right, Master?

YODA: Hmm. Yes. A Jedi's strength flows from the Force. Feel it; contemplate it. But beware of the dark side of the Force.

LUKE: The dark side. That's what won *Vader* over, and made him murder Father . . .

YODA: Anger. Fear. Aggression. The dark side of the Force are they. Easily they flow, quick to join you in a fight. If once you start down the dark path, forever will it dominate your destiny. Consume you, it will, as it did Obi-Wan's apprentice.

LUKE: I see him in my dreams. I think his name so often: Darth Vader. Is the dark side of the Force stronger, Master?

YODA: No; no! Quicker. Easier. More seductive. To weakness it appeals. But yours must be the strength that does *not* flow from rage!

LUKE: But—how am I to know the good side from the bad?

YODA: You will know. When you are calm. At peace . . . passive, mm. A Jedi uses the Force for knowledge and defense; never for attack.

LUKE: Mmm. Master, tell me why I can't use it so that I can—

YODA: No! No, there is no "why." Nothing more will I teach you today. Set me down.

LUKE: But there's so much that I need to know about how I can—

YODA: Clear your mind of questions, and set me down.

LUKE: *(WITH THE EFFORT)* All right. Here . . .

ARTOO: WHISTLING, SLIGHTLY OFF.

LUKE: *(POINT OF VIEW MOVING CLOSER TO ARTOO)* Hi, Artoo. Been watchin' after my gear, hm? I'll take it, thanks . . .

ARTOO: BEEPS.

Sound: Luke's weapons belt clanks, as he takes it up.

LUKE: Master, I'm gonna take Artoo and recharge his power reserves. I'll, uh . . . I'll be back in about . . .

YODA: What is it?

LUKE: There's something . . . not right in this place, Master. I feel cold, all of a sudden. Master? Please look at me.

YODA: *(SOFTLY)* What do you sense?

LUKE: Death. That cave there—under the tree. Something . . . I can't quite see . . .

YODA: That place is strong with the dark side of the Force. A domain of evil it is.

LUKE: I can feel it, almost smell it. And you brought me here.

YODA: Into it you must go.

LUKE: But why?

YODA: Told you I have. There is no "why."

LUKE: What's in there?

YODA: Only what you take into the cave with you, Luke Sky-walker.

LUKE: All right. If you say so, I'll go.

YODA: Your weapons; you will not need them. Your blaster not, nor your lightsaber.

LUKE: Do I have to leave them behind?

YODA: You will need them not. But yours is the decision.

LUKE: *(SHIVERING)* Then, I'll keep them.

ARTOO: YODELS.

LUKE: Wait here, Artoo. I'll be back.

SCENE 6-9 TREE CAVE

Sound: Brief transition to the cave. Luke's footfalls in dank, dripping, echoing cave.

LUKE: EXERTION, AS HE LOWERS HIMSELF INTO THE CAVE, OFF

Sound: Off, Luke's entrance, with loosened clots of soil, gravel, etc. falling. Critters.

LUKE: *(BREATHING MORE RAPIDLY) (APPROACHING)* Who's here? Answer me! I know you're here; I can feel it! Show yourself!

VADER: APPROACHING—MASK-BREATHING NOISES

LUKE: Vader . . . *Vader!*

Sound: Luke's lightsaber activates. Vader's breathing comes to point of view, as his lightsaber activates.

LUKE: If you only knew how I wanted this! Dreamed of it!

Sound: Moan of Luke's weapon coming en garde.

LUKE: I'm gonna kill you, Vader.

Sound: The duel begins. Swords flare and spit back and forth under Luke's lines.

LUKE: For my father . . . for Ben . . . for the Jedi!

Sound: Indicates that Vader's caught Luke's sword in bind, rotating it, trying to disarm him.

LUKE: *(EXTREME EFFORT)* Uh! No!

Sound: Luke forces the swords back out of bind.

LUKE: *(BREATHES HEAVILY)* Not good enough, traitor!

Sound: One exchange, and the duel pauses.

LUKE: Well? Why don't you say something? You know who I am, don't you?

Sound: Brief dialogue of blades.

LUKE: I'm Ben Kenobi's friend! *I'm Skywalker's son!*

Sound: Furious phrase of fencing.

LUKE: I don't know how you got here, Vader—

Sound: An exchange.

LUKE: But *you die here*! *Now!*

Sound: The duel intensifies. Luke makes Vader retreat.

LUKE: *(WITH THE RHYTHM OF THE DUEL, BEATING VADER BACK)* Huh! Huh! C'mon! Stand . . . your . . . *ground*!

Sound: The blades clash; Luke's finds access.

LUKE: Huh-hh!

Sound: Luke's blade connects, with a burst of energy, beheading Vader. Sound reverberates. Silence.

SCENE 6-10   DAGOBAH EXTERIOR

Sound: Luke scrabbling up out of the cave, slightly off, worming free, exhausted.

LUKE: *(APPROACHING)* No . . . no; it . . . couldn't be! Couldn't be!

ARTOO: ALARMED, BEEPS.

YODA: Luke, to me listen! A battle this is, for your*self*!

LUKE: Hm? Hmm?

YODA: What happened? What saw you, in the cave?

LUKE: *(BREATHLESS)* Darth Vader. We fought—lightsabers. Ah! I swung and . . . his helmet came off. Then his mask blew away and—ah! His face!

YODA: *What?*

LUKE: His face—it was *mine*! *Vader's face was mine!*

YODA: *Think! Feel!* Calmly: Focus yourself, and all other things will come to you. What said I to you?

LUKE: You said—you said—that what was in the cave was—only what I took in with me.

YODA: Yes! Deal with this you must!

LUKE: Did any of it happen, Master? Did any of it really happen?

YODA: Shapes your thought it does. Lives in your memory. It is as real as your thought, Luke Skywalker.

LUKE: *(MOANS)* Did I fail you? I took my weapon—I fought with him when what I *should* have done was—I don't know! Have I failed you, Master?

YODA: You have grown. A lesson have you learned, and grow from it you must.

LUKE: I fought . . . I *saw* . . . But what've I learned?

YODA: You must say.

LUKE: My enemy's face . . . my enemy's face—is my own.

NARRATOR: Across the gulfs of interstellar space, Luke's friends are about to come into terrible danger. Darth Vader prepares to strike, in the name of Imperial tyranny. But no battle is more fierce than the one raging within Luke Skywalker. And from the Force will flow trials, knowledge, and the Way of the Jedi.

Music: Closing theme under credits.

NARRATOR: CLOSING CREDITS.

EPISODE SEVEN:

"NEW ALLIES, NEW ENEMIES"

CHARACTERS:

Luke	Vader	Needa
Han	Boba Fett	Sentry
Chewbacca	Lando	Cloud City Control
Leia	Yoda	Droid
Threepio	Imperial Lieutenant	Trooper
Artoo	Piett	Ben

ANNOUNCER: OPENING CREDITS.

Music: Opening theme.

NARRATOR: A long time ago in a galaxy far, far away, there came a time of revolution, as Rebels united to challenge a tyrannical Empire. Now, it is a dark time for the Rebellion. Their fortress on the planet Hoth destroyed, the survivors of the Rebel Alliance are being hunted across the galaxy. Luke Skywalker, moved by the Force, has gone to the mysterious planet Dagobah, to further his Jedi training.

Sound: Falcon *zooming.*

NARRATOR: One Rebel starship, the *Millennium Falcon*, is now being pursued through an asteroid field by an Imperial starfleet. Aboard her are the Princess Leia Organa, the droid See-Threepio, Captain Han Solo, and his Wookiee first mate, Chewbacca. Giant warships and swift TIE fighters close in for the capture, at the command of Darth Vader.

SCENE 7-1 *FALCON* COCKPIT

Sound: Falcon*'s cockpit comes up, with alarms wailing, etc.*

HAN: Can'tcha give me any more power, Chewie? They're practically on top of us!

Sound: Explosions against the Falcon*'s shields.*

LEIA: Han, they're firing!

HAN: What'd you expect 'em to do, Princess? Wave?

Sound: Another explosion.

THREEPIO: Look, the asteroid field is thinning! Can't we escape into hyperspace now?

HAN: Nah, still too much junk floating around us, Threepio.

LEIA: Well we'd better do something, Han! Deflectors are hitting the overload mark!

Sound: More alarms. Chewbacca howls.

LEIA: What'd Chewbacca say?

HAN: Imperial Star Destroyer, comin' straight at us! Don't those guys ever take a day off?

LEIA: Can we stay ahead of it long enough to make lightspeed?

HAN: We're gonna find out. If we can't, you'll be among the first to know. Gimme everything she's got, Chewie!

CHEWBACCA: ROARS.

THREEPIO: What did Chewbacca say?

HAN: He said, "Here's where the fun begins!"

Sound: Engines build. The Falcon *shakes, jolts to cannonfire.*

THREEPIO: I'm sure this vessel was not designed to endure this sort of abuse! This is well beyond its capabilities.

HAN: Watch it, Threepio; she's one o' the family! Sit tight, everybody!

Sound: Engines build, then fade.

SCENE 7-2   STAR DESTROYER BRIDGE

Sound: Vader's Dreadnaught's bridge comes up.

IMPERIAL LIEUTENANT *(APPROACHING)* Admiral Piett, the bounty hunters have come aboard for their audience with Lord Vader.

PIETT: Have them wait here on the bridge, Lieutenant. And Lieutenant . . .

LIEUTENANT: Yes, sir?

PIETT: They're hired killers. I want them watched at all times.

LIEUTENANT: Very good, sir. *(TO OFF)* Sentry!

SENTRY: *(FROM OFF)* Yes, sir?

LIEUTENANT: Give the—*civilians* permission to enter.

SENTRY: At once, sir!

Sound: Power door slides open. Bounty hunters enter, approach to middle distance, under next lines. Among them are mechanical, human, and reptilian footfalls and sounds. Muttering, hissing, beeping, etc.

SENTRY: *(FROM OFF)* In here, all of you. Wait over there.

LIEUTENANT: *(ASIDE, TO PIETT, AS BOUNTY HUNTERS STOP SLIGHTLY OFF)* The big lizard-man is Bossk, Admiral. Twelve captures, eight of them alive. That droid is IG-88, modified battle robot.

PIETT: And the human with the scars?

LIEUTENANT: Dengar, former gladiator. Twenty-three captures, six alive. The one in the helmet is called—

PIETT: Boba Fett; I know.

LIEUTENANT: They've lost count of his captures. Very few of them were alive.

PIETT: *(TO OFF)* Lord Vader will give you your instructions in a moment!

Sound: Hunters murmuring, beeping, etc.

PIETT: *(TO LIEUTENANT)* As if that scum could do this job better than the starfleet! The Rebels will not escape us.

Sound: Commo signal.

LIEUTENANT: Sir, we have a priority signal coming in from the Star Destroyer *Avenger*.

Sound: Vader's approach. Breathing, heavy bootsteps, etc.

PIETT: Lord Vader. We have assembled the bounty hunters as you requested.

Sound: Chatter dies except for occasional hiss or bleep.

VADER: You bounty hunters! Heed me well! There will be a substantial reward for the one who finds the *Millennium Falcon*. You may use any methods necessary, but *I want those Rebels alive*! Is that clear?

Sound: General murmurs and noises of assent, except Fett.

VADER: I wish to hear from you in particular, Boba Fett. I will tolerate *no disintegrations*!

FETT: *(VOICE ALTERED BY HIS HELMET)* It shall be as you command, Lord Vader.

VADER: Then go, all of you. And do not forget what I have said; your lives depend upon it.

Sound: Bounty hunters leaving, under next lines.

PIETT: My Lord Vader!

VADER: Well, Admiral Piett?

PIETT: My lord, the Rebels are within our grasp. Captain Needa, aboard the *Avenger*, has the *Millennium Falcon* under close pursuit.

VADER: I want that ship, Piett! Relay that to Captain Needa. Whatever the cost, *I want the* Millennium Falcon!

Sound: Bridge fades.

SCENE 7-3 *FALCON* COCKPIT

Sound: Falcon, *running for her life, comes up. Alarms, engines, etc.*

THREEPIO: Oh, thank goodness we're coming out of the asteroid field!

Sound: Jarring of Imperial fire.

LEIA: But the Imperials are still on us, and they're getting closer, Han!

HAN: Relax, sister. We're about to lose 'em. Ready for lightspeed, Chewie?

CHEWBACCA: CAROLS AN AFFIRMATIVE.

HAN: Hah! G'bye, starfleet! We'll keep in touch! Right, partner: One—

Sound: Hyperdrive builds.

HAN: Two—

Sound: Drive increases. Chewie howls.

HAN: and . . . three-eee—

Sound: Hyperdrive revs down, dies.

HAN: —eeee—ohhh—Uh-oh. *(BEAT)* It's not fair.

CHEWBACCA: BARKS DISCONSOLATELY.

Sound: Falcon *rocked by fire.*

THREEPIO: The moment of our doom is upon us!

LEIA: Han, where's the lightspeed?

THREEPIO: Oblivion! Total oblivion!

HAN: Transfer circuits are working. It's not my fault.

LEIA: No lightspeed?

HAN: It's not my fault!

Sound: Falcon's hit again.

CHEWBACCA: HOOTS.

THREEPIO: Sir, we just lost the main rear deflector shield. One more hit on the *Falcon*'s stern and we're done for!

HAN: Chewie, bring 'er about!

CHEWBACCA: OBJECTS.

HAN: I said *bring 'er about*! I'm gonna put all power to the forward shields!

LEIA: Hold it, hold it; *you're* going to attack *them*?

Sound: The Falcon zooms.

HAN: Inspiration is my specialty! Ready the landing claw, Chewie!

LEIA: "Landing claw"?

THREEPIO: Sir, the odds of surviving a direct assault on an Imperial Star Destroyer are on the order of—

LEIA: Threepio, shut up!

Sound: Incoming fire.

THREEPIO: The Imperials have their deflectors at full power; they've cut their speed!

HAN: *(LAUGHS NERVOUSLY)* Yeah; gettin' cautious. Got any objections, Leia?

LEIA: I've already *been* an Imperial prisoner, remember? Run or fight them or do anything you want except surrender, Han.

THREEPIO: We're on a collision course!

HAN: Not quite. Hang out the landin' claw, Chewie! Brace yourselves!

CHEWBACCA: ROARS.

Sound: Falcon *loops suddenly, firing steering thrusters.*

LEIA: Ohh!

THREEPIO: Ahh!

HAN: Engage the claw, Chewie. Kill the engines!

Sound: Engines die almost instantly. Scraping as claw locks onto the destroyer's hull.

HAN: Shut 'er down, Chewie! Lights out!

Sound: Falcon *goes to total silence, as Chewie throws switches.*

HAN: *(UNCONSCIOUSLY SOFT)* The claw's secure.

THREEPIO: Yes, but to the hull of an Imperial Star Destroyer! Our existence is nearly over!

HAN: Nope. We're on their upperworks, see? A blindspot. We came in so fast, they lost track of us.

LEIA: You picked a perfect place, I'll give you that, flyboy.

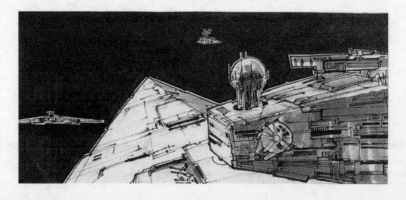

HAN: Yeah. I always wondered if this'd work.

LEIA: I thought you said it was an inspiration.

HAN: Y'got any complaints, save 'em. The Imperials'll think we got to lightspeed somehow.

LEIA: And *now* what d'we do?

HAN: We wait it out. Just trust me.

THREEPIO: I knew it! I knew he'd say that! Oh, dear, dear, dear . . .

SCENE 7-4 STAR DESTROYER BRIDGE

Sound: Brief transition to Vader's ship's bridge. Mask-breathing.

PIETT: *(FROM OFF)* Captain Needa has come aboard, Lord Vader!

VADER: Bring him before me at once!

Sound: Power door opens.

NEEDA: *(APPROACHING)* Lord Vader, the *Millennium Falcon* has eluded us; we're not sure how. She's too small a vessel to carry a cloaking device.

VADER: Is that so, Captain Needa?

NEEDA: I—yes, My Lord. I accept full responsibility and extend my deepest apology. Her crew was very resourceful. They— *(BEGINS CHOKING)*

VADER: They are minor criminals! Marginal outlaws! You are inept!

NEEDA: *(CHOKING)* N-no—Lord Vader—please . . .

VADER: And ineptitude is of no use to me or the Empire.

NEEDA: My lord—I beg you—no-oo— *(NEEDA EXPIRES)*

Sound: Needa hits the deck.

VADER: Your apology is accepted, Captain Needa. *(TO OFF)* You men! Remove his body! Admiral Piett! Your report!

PIETT: *(APPROACHING, SHAKEN)* The—the starfleet has completed its scan of the area and found nothing, Lord Vader. If the *Millennium Falcon* went to lightspeed, she could be on the other side of the galaxy by now.

VADER: Alert all commands. Calculate every possible destination along their last known course.

PIETT: Yes, My Lord! We'll find that ship.

VADER: Do not fail me again, Admiral Piett.

PIETT: *(TO OFF)* Alert all commands! Deploy the fleet! Make preparations for lightspeed at once!

Sound: Wild lines, etc., then bridge fades.

SCENE 7-5 DAGOBAH EXTERIOR

Sound: Dagobah exterior comes up.

YODA: Use the Force, young Skywalker.

LUKE: I'm ready, Master.

YODA: Feel what you are about to do—then do it. Now: Hands on the ground, feet in the air!

LUKE: A handstand—*(WITH THE EFFORT)* Uh! Like this?

YODA: Lift yourself not with your body alone. Remember the balance within, and the balance without! Yes; feet in the sky!

Sound: Luke in minute shifts of balance, exertion, etc.

YODA: Good!

LUKE: What now, Master?

YODA: Burdens must you learn to bear! The first will be your teacher. Hold still!

LUKE: Hey! Whoops!

YODA: *(WITH THE EFFORT OF CLIMBING LUKE'S LEG)* Perch on your big foot, I will! Steady; do it, you can!

LUKE: Oops—uhh . . .

YODA: Steady down there, that the view up here I might enjoy!

LUKE: Whoa—

YODA: Rely not on your muscles alone! To what you are doing must you attune yourself!

LUKE: Mmm— *(STEADY)* Ummm . . .

YODA: Good! Now: All your weight and mine, on your left hand alone. One hand, one hand!

LUKE: EFFORT

YODA: Yes! Focus; focus yourself! Bear you up, the Force will!

LUKE: I—yes; like this . . .

YODA: Precisely! Now: That stone. Into the air will you raise it, with your mind alone.

LUKE: But—but—

YODA: Use the Force, as you have; as you can. Yes. Now; the stone.

LUKE: *(EXERTION)* It's—rising!

YODA: To the Force are all other things subordinate. Even gravity. Feel the Force.

ARTOO: *(APPROACHING)* WHISTLING WORRIEDLY.

YODA: Feel the stone float in the air.

ARTOO: *(CLOSER)* BEEPS.

YODA: And concentrate . . .

LUKE: Artoo-Detoo! What's wrong?

ARTOO: BEEPS ALARM.

YODA: Con . . . cen . . .

LUKE: What's the mat—whoa—oo

YODA: —tra—aeee—woooo!

Sound: Impact as Yoda and Luke hit the ground, roll, etc.

YODA AND LUKE: OOF AND UMPH!, ETC.

ARTOO: WHISTLES HIS CONCERN.

LUKE: Ohh. No, I'm okay, Artoo. Master, are you all right?

YODA: Warn me you should, before you decide to collapse.

LUKE: But I didn't—Master, Artoo's trying to tell us something.

YODA: Into the marsh is your fighter sinking. Have you no ears?

LUKE: My ship! *(SCRAMBLING UP)* Artoo, c'mon . . . *(MOVING OFF AT A RUN)* We've gotta save 'er. Hurry!

SCENE 7-5A   DAGOBAH EXTERIOR

Sound: Brief transition. Sound of bubbling bog comes up, sucking down the X-wing.

LUKE: *(APPROACHING AT A RUN, PANTING)* No! Aww—no! Lookit that!

ARTOO: WHISTLES A RESPONSE.

Sound: The ship disappears into the bog.

LUKE: There it goes. We'll never get the ship out of there now, Artoo.

YODA: *(APPROACHING)* "Never"? So impossible is it? So certain are you?

ARTOO: BEEPS MOURNFULLY.

YODA: Young Skywalker: Always with you it cannot be done. Hear you nothing that I say? If you wish to lift it out, do so!

LUKE: Master, raising stones into the air is one thing. Raising my fighter out of the swamp . . . that's totally different.

YODA: No! No different! Only different in your mind! Unlearn! You must unlearn what you have learned before.

LUKE: But this is so much—

YODA: Do it. Raise it; bring it here, to the shore.

LUKE: I—all right; I'll give it a try.

YODA: No! *Do!* Or do not. There is no "try." Now: focus . . .

LUKE: *(FALLING INTO CONCENTRATION)* Yes. I'll raise it . . .

198

YODA: *Know*. Feel the ship.

LUKE: The ship . . .

YODA: Concentrate.

Sound: Waters begin to stir and roil.

YODA: Mmm! Open yourself to the Force.

LUKE: *(WITH THE EFFORT)* So heavy. Can't— *(EXHALING, EX-PLOSIVELY)* I can't hold it up—

Sound: Swamp gurgles to stillness.

ARTOO: *(SLIGHTLY OFF)* BEEPS DISAPPOINTMENT.

LUKE: Master, the fighter's too big.

YODA: Size matters not! Look at me. Judge *me* by my size do you?

LUKE: Of course not; I never meant that you—

YODA: And well you should not! For my ally is the Force. And a powerful ally it is!

LUKE: I know that—I'm *trying* to know that . . .

YODA: Life creates it! Makes it grow. Ah! Its energy surrounds us and blinds us. *Luminous* beings are we! See: this arm of yours?

LUKE: *(AS YODA PRODS HIM)* Uh?

YODA: We are not this crude matter; not flesh and bone! You must feel the Force around you. Here. Between you . . . me . . . this tree . . . that rock. Everywhere!

LUKE: Everywhere.

YODA: Yes! Mmm. Even between the land . . . and your ship.

LUKE: Master, I truly wish I could raise it but . . . you want the impossible.

YODA: Told you, did I not? All things are subordinate to the Force. *(DRAWING A DEEP BREATH)* Now: *see!*

Sound: The waters bubble again.

YODA: *(SERENE)* Bigger than the stone are you; smaller than the ship am I. And yet . . .

Sound: Waters boil, part.

LUKE: *(AMAZED)* What . . . ?

YODA: —what is that, to the Force?

Sound: The ship lifts clear of the water.

LUKE: The ship!

ARTOO: WHISTLES INCREDULOUSLY.

Sound: Ship dripping. Humming slightly.

LUKE: You're doing it!

YODA: Said I not? The land . . . and the ship. Ashore, it comes . . . because it *will*. And so: It is here.

Sound: X-wing coming to rest, landing gear sighing, wings dripping, etc.

LUKE: But, *this*! I don't . . . I just don't believe it!

YODA: Yes. Luke; that is why you fail. Come.

SCENE 7-6 *FALCON* COCKPIT

Sound: Silent Falcon *comes up.*

THREEPIO: Captain Solo, would you be so kind as to stop ignoring me? This time you have gone too far!

LEIA: Calm down, Threepio. You're only running down your power reserves.

THREEPIO: I'm afraid I must insist, Princess Leia. Captain Solo has endangered your life.

LEIA: He saved it, Threepio.

THREEPIO: Master Luke was quite specific in commanding me to look after your well-being, Your Highness. Captain Solo's actions are beyond any rational justification.

CHEWBACCA: GROWLS.

THREEPIO: No, First Mate Chewbacca, I will *not* be silent! *(TSKS)* Why, oh why, doesn't anyone ever listen to me?

HAN: *(IGNORING THREEPIO)* Look! Here we go; the starfleet's breaking up.

LEIA: What does it mean, Han?

HAN: Means they're gettin' ready to move into hyperspace. Just what we been waitin' for.

THREEPIO: And what ill-considered move are you contemplating now, may I make so bold as to inquire?

HAN: Chewie, go aft and stand by the manual release for the landing claw.

Sound: Chewie, rising, moves off, hooting.

THREEPIO: I really don't see how all this is going to help.

LEIA: Threepio, control yourself.

THREEPIO: Your Highness, I must point out that surrender is a perfectly acceptable alternative in extreme circumstances.

HAN: *(INDICATING THREEPIO) Leia . . .*

THREEPIO: The Empire may be gracious enough to reconsider—

Sound: Leia throwing Threepio's cutoff switch.

THREEPIO: *(VOICE SLOWING TO A HALT)* —it's at—ti—tude—urrrr.

LEIA: Sorry, Threepio.

HAN: Ah, the nap'll do 'im good. He's been through a lot. Anyway, thanks for the peace and quiet, Princess.

LEIA: Anyway, what'd you have in mind for your next move, genius?

HAN: Well, if the fleet follows standard Imperial procedure, they'll dump their garbage before they go to lightspeed. And then we just let loose and float away.

LEIA: With the rest of the garbage. Han, their sensors will pick up a metal object as big as the *Falcon*.

HAN: Uh-uh. They suffered a lot of damage chasing us through that asteroid field. There'll be burnt-out deflector generators, contaminated shielding, cracked hull plate . . .

LEIA: Well, well; you're actually thinking instead of reacting! What d'we do then?

HAN: Then we've gotta find ourselves a safe port somewheres. Got any ideas?

LEIA: You're really asking for an opinion? Are you feeling all right?

HAN: C'mon, Leia.

LEIA: Anyway, no. Where are we?

HAN: The Anoat system. Let's see what the data banks say.

Sound: He switches on the data screen. Soft beep of computer printing under next lines.

LEIA: Anoat system. There's not very much around here.

HAN: No. Well, wait . . .

LEIA: I'm getting pretty good at that.

HAN: No, this is interesting. Lando!

LEIA: "Lando system"?

HAN: Lando's not a system; he's a man. Lando Calrissian. He's, oh, a card player, gambler, *scoundrel—*

LEIA: Don't push your luck, Solo.

HAN: You'd like him.

LEIA: Oh, thanks!

HAN: He's on the planet Bespin. That's pretty far from here, but I think we can make it on sublight engines.

LEIA: *(READING THE SCREEN)* What does it say? "Cloud City"? It's a mining colony?

HAN: Yeah, a Tibanna gas mine. Floating refinery, suspended in the atmosphere.

LEIA: How'd one of *your* friends get into an honest line of work?

HAN: Lando conned somebody out of Cloud City. We go back a long way, Lando 'n' me.

LEIA: Can you trust this Lando?

HAN: 'Course not.

LEIA: No, " 'course not!"

HAN: But he's got no love for the Empire.

LEIA: My kind of criminal . . . Look; they're jettisoning their junk!

HAN: *(TO OFF)* Hey, Chewie, here we go! Stand by the claw!

CHEWBACCA: *(FROM OFF)* ACKNOWLEDGES.

LEIA: Well, will you look at that! Just like you said!

HAN: Looks like a zero-gravity scrapyard, doesn't it? Wish the taxpayers could see this. *(TO OFF)* Detach the claw, partner!

CHEWBACCA: GROWLS.

Sound: Claw releases. Slight scraping of hulls.

LEIA: It's working. What d'you know?

HAN: See 'em forming up? Like good little clones. *So* predictable!

LEIA: You *do* have your moments, Han. Not many of them—but you *do* have them.

HAN: Clean livin' and a pure heart triumph again!

LEIA: The fleet's accelerating . . .

Sound: Distant thunder of the fleet booming into hyperspace under next lines.

HAN: Into hyperspace. And good riddance to 'em.

LEIA: Now, if our luck will just hold out, we can—

HAN: Will you quit that kinda talk?

Sound: Switches, etc., as the Falcon's *engines rise, systems come on.*

HAN: It's a piece a cake from here on in. We hit Bespin, Lando fixes the *Falcon*, and we head for the rendezvous. *(TO OFF)* Stand by, Chewie!

CHEWBACCA: ANSWERS.

LEIA: At least I get to find out if it's true.

Sound: Engines build.

HAN: If what's true?

LEIA: All that stuff about honor among thieves.

HAN: Why don't you buckle in and give it a rest?

Sound: Engines boom as the ship accelerates.

HAN: It's in the bag!

Sound: Falcon *fades.*

SCENE 7-7   DAGOBAH EXTERIOR

Sound: Brief transition.

LUKE: Like this, Master?

YODA: Yes; prepare yourself, young Skywalker.

ARTOO: *(OFF)* BEEPS.

YODA: Quiet, little droid! He practices; he grows. Interrupt him not!

LUKE: I'm ready.

YODA: Now will your control of the Force lift you from the ground.

LUKE: DEEP, REGULAR BREATHING

YODA: Let it raise you up.

LUKE: Mmm. Yes . . .

YODA: Good . . . doing it, you are!

LUKE: Up! *(LAUGHS SOFTLY)* Yeah . . .

ARTOO: WHISTLES IN ASTONISHMENT.

YODA: Because you believe! To your concentration, hold! Turn! Head down! Feet in the air! Your control, remember!

LUKE: Umm—turn . . .

YODA: Well done! No limits are there, to one who reaches out to the Force. Your equipment, there: Raise that box.

LUKE: Mmmm . . .

Sound: Rumble of box jostling from pile.

YODA: And another! Your ally now, is the Force.

Sound: Another case lifting off.

LUKE: Ohh . . . there . . . up!

YODA: Yes; effort must there be; but within you is the power.

ARTOO: WARBLES.

LUKE: Stand still, Artoo-Detoo; up you go!

ARTOO: BEEPING IN SHOCK AS HE'S LEVITATED.

LUKE: Don't worry; I won't let you fall.

YODA: Be serene; there is your strength.

LUKE: BREATHING BECOMES EVEN

YODA: Through the Force, things will you see. Other places. The future . . . the past. Old friends long gone.

LUKE: How do I—*Han!* And Leia! *Leia, no!* Uhhh—

Sound: Artoo whoops in surprise as he falls. Impact as boxes, Artoo, and Luke fall the short distance. Boxes tumble, Artoo resounds.

LUKE: GRUNTS IN PAIN AS HE LANDS

YODA: Control. You must learn control.

ARTOO: SIGNALS.

YODA: You do not concentrate.

LUKE: I saw . . . I saw a city in the clouds, a floating city.

YODA: Mm. Friends have you there?

LUKE: Han and Leia and the others. They were in pain.

YODA: It is the future you see.

LUKE: Future? Will they die? Please, Master, I have to know!

YODA: Difficult to tell. Always in motion is the future.

LUKE: I've got to go to them.

YODA: You act in haste. All calm have you lost, all wisdom.

LUKE: I can't just let them be killed!

YODA: Decide you must how to serve them best. If you leave now, help them you could. But you would destroy all for which they have fought and suffered.

LUKE: *(BEAT)* All right, Master. I believe you. But—I feel as if I'm being torn in half. They have to live. They *have* to!

Sound: Dagobah fades.

SCENE 7-8 *FALCON* **COCKPIT**

Sound: Falcon's cockpit comes up, as the ship zooms.

HAN: *(TO COMLINK)* Now look, Cloud City Control, I'm only gonna say this one more time: I don't *have* a landing permit! I'm trying to reach Lando Calrissian. This is the *Millennium Falcon.* You can check with Lando.

LEIA: Han, look! Interceptors!

Sound: Twin-pod cloud cars swoop by, firing a warning shot.

LEIA: They're shooting at us! Some friends you've got!

THREEPIO: I might have known!

CHEWBACCA: MOANS.

Sound: Another shot.

HAN: Oh, whoa-a, wai-wait a minute! Cloud City Control, call 'em off me! Lemme explain!

CLOUD CONTROL: *Millennium Falcon*, this is Cloud City Control. You will not deviate from your present course. Our interceptors will escort you for landing. There will be no further *warning* shots!

THREEPIO: Well, really! Rather touchy, aren't they?

LEIA: Han, I thought you were friends with this Lando person.

Sound: Falcon zooms.

CHEWBACCA: BARKS.

HAN: Aww, be quiet, Chewie. After all, that was a long time ago. I'm sure Lando's forgotten about all that by now.

LEIA: "About all" *what*? What're you getting us into? *Han?*

HAN: Nothin', nothin'.

THREEPIO: There: Just as I said! We're in dreadful peril once again!

HAN: You really gotta do somethin' about your morale problem, Threepio.

LEIA: Solo, if you don't level with me right this second, I am going to—

HAN: Little misunderstanding me 'n' Lando had, awhile back.

CLOUD CONTROL: *Millennium Falcon*, this is Cloud City Control. You're cleared for landing on platform 3–2–7.

HAN: See, Leia? Nothin' to worry about.

CLOUD CONTROL: Be advised: You are being tracked by our weapons systems.

LEIA: Who's worried, Han?

THREEPIO: I, for one, I must confess! This escort is a dubious honor at best!

HAN: There's Cloud City.

LEIA: I'll give you this much: It's beautiful.

THREEPIO: What holds it up in the air? *Are you certain it's safe?*

CHEWBACCA: GROWLS.

HAN: Chewie says not to forget you've still got that cutoff switch on your back, Threepio. Okay; there's the landing platform—

Sound: Falcon*'s engines blare, easing her in for a landing.*

SCENE 7-9 CLOUD CITY EXTERIOR

Sound: Brief transition to exterior Cloud City. Bespins winds, etc.

HAN: Right, Chewie; lock up the ship.

CHEWBACCA: BARKS.

Sound: The ramp lifts and locks, seals with a clang.

THREEPIO: Shouldn't we have waited inside the *Falcon*, Princess Leia? There's no one here to meet us. It seems rather ominous.

LEIA: I don't like it either, Han.

HAN: Well, what *would* you like, Your Highness?

THREEPIO: Perhaps it will be all right. After all, they did permit us to land.

LEIA: Lots of predators hunt that way, Threepio.

HAN: Don't worry. Everything's gonna be fine. Trust me.

THREEPIO: Every time you employ that phrase, my circuitry becomes erratic!

Sound: Power door opening, distance.

THREEPIO: Look over there!

HAN: Yeah; it's Lando.

LEIA: And who are all those surly gentlemen with the guns?

CHEWBACCA: GRUNTS.

THREEPIO: Oh dear! This *is* going to be a congenial reunion, isn't it?

HAN: Right. Hugs 'n' kisses.

LANDO: *(FROM OFF)* So; Han Solo. It is you!

HAN: *(ASIDE)* See? My friend. Um, Chewie, keep your eyes open, huh?

CHEWBACCA: SOFT GUTTURAL MOAN.

LANDO: *(APPROACHING)* You slimy, double-crossing no-good swindler! Guards, cover them!

HAN: Uh-oh.

THREEPIO: Oh; we're done for!

HAN: Been a long time, Lando—

LANDO: Solo, you've got a lot of guts, coming to Cloud City after what you pulled on me!

HAN: Who, *me*?

LANDO: You might as well put your fists up. I'm gonna knock you down, either way.

HAN: Well—no—wait—*hey!*

LANDO: *(LAUGHS)* I just wanted to see if you can still duck as fast as you used to. How y'doin', you old pirate? So good to see you!

HAN: Y'just took a couple years off my life!

LANDO: I never thought I'd catch up to you again. Where you been?

THREEPIO: *(ASIDE)* He seems very friendly, doesn't he?

HAN: Here and there. Business as usual.

LANDO: Nothing honest?

LEIA: *(ASIDE)* Yes, Threepio; *very* friendly.

HAN: 'Course not. The profit margin's too low.

LANDO: But what're you two doing here?

HAN: Ah, repairs, Lando. To the *Falcon*. I thought you could help me out, Lando.

LANDO: What've you two lunatics done to my ship?

HAN: *Your* ship? Hey, you lost 'er to me fair and square!

LANDO: Lucky day for you! Only thing you ever did right. *(TO CHEWIE)* And how you been doin', Chewbacca?

CHEWBACCA: HOOTS A GREETING

LANDO: You still hangin' around with this loser?

CHEWBACCA: BARKS.

LANDO: *(WHISTLES IN ADMIRATION)* Hel-lo! Who have we here? What a charming young lady!

HAN: Oh. Uh, Lando, this, ah—

LANDO: Welcome my dear. I'm Lando Calrissian, administrator of Cloud City. And who might you be?

LEIA: I'm Leia. How do you do?

LANDO: Then, welcome, *Leia*. You have definitely improved my day!

HAN: Awright, awright, y'old smoothie!

LANDO: *(LAUGHS)* Come in, all of you!

HAN: Thanks. C'mon, Leia. *(MOVING OFF)* I knew we could count on you, Lando!

THREEPIO: Hello, Administrator Calrissian. I am See-Threepio, human-cyborg relations. My facilities are at your—

LANDO: Yes, yes. *(MOVING OFF)* Come along, Chewbacca! *(CALLING AHEAD)* Leia, you'll have to tell me what these two did to the prettiest starship that ever graced the skies . . .

THREEPIO: *(SIGHS)* I suppose I should resign myself to human discourtesy!

Sound: Exterior fades.

SCENE 7-10   CLOUD CITY INTERIOR

Sound: Cloud City main concourse comes up. Aliens, humans, machines. Males and females laughing, chattering. Eighth Avenue and 42nd Street, downtown Oz.

THREEPIO: What a remarkable place! So many life-forms and automata!

LANDO: What's wrong with the *Falcon*, Han?

HAN: Hyperdrive. It let us down twice, now.

LANDO: That's all? No problem. I'll get my people right to work on it.

HAN: Listen, Lando: This's really one I owe you.

LANDO: My pleasure. You know, Leia, that ship saved my life any number of times.

LEIA: She has a habit of doing that sort of thing.

LANDO: She's the fastest hunk o' junk in the galaxy.

HAN: How's the gas mine? Still payin' off for you?

LANDO: Oh, not as well as I'd like. We're a small outpost here by Imperial standards, and not very self-sufficient.

THREEPIO: And yet you appear to be prospering, sir.

LANDO: I've had supply problems of every kind, I've had labor difficulties, I've been forced to go to—

HAN: LAUGHING.

LANDO: What's so funny, Han?

HAN: You! Listen to you; you sound like a businessman, a responsible leader. Who'd've thought that, huh?

LANDO: Now, Leia, don't you laugh at me, too!

LEIA: I won't, Administrator Calrissian.

LANDO: We're going to have to get you to use my first name. Come; I'll show you to your quarters. *(MOVING OFF)* It's true: I am responsible, these days.

LEIA: *(MOVING OFF)* How unfortunate for you.

LANDO: It's the price you pay for being successful.

Sound: Chewie, moving off with them.

THREEPIO: *(CALLING AFTER)* Sirs! Your H— *ma'm!* What shall I—do . . . *(SIGHS)* I should've expected this sort of thing!

Sound: Power door opens nearby. Another droid moves past.

THREEPIO: Another relations droid! How nice to see a familiar face! Hello, there!

OTHER DROID: *(MOVING PAST)* E chu ta! Nee do raa! Pha oo coh! On bee ruh!

THREEPIO: Well, how rude! Obviously an inferior design! What's this?

Sound: Tech facility heard as Threepio approaches the open door.

THREEPIO: A technical facility! How marvelous!

Sound: R2 sounds, distance.

THREEPIO: Why, that sounds like an R2 unit in there. I wonder . . .

Sound: Threepio's point of view moves into the facility. Power door shuts behind.

THREEPIO: Hello? Is anyone—oh! How interesting!

TROOPER: *(FROM OFF)* *(IN HELMET)* Hey! Who're you?

THREEPIO: Oh my! Oh, er, I'm—I'm terribly sorry, sir. I didn't mean to intrude. I'll just be on my way—

TROOPER: Come back here, you!

THREEPIO: No, please don't get up!

TROOPER: Hold still!

THREEPIO: Wait! This is all a terrible misunderstanding, I assure—Ahhh!

Sound: Blaster bolt, and the explosion of Threepio's body. Tech facility fades.

SCENE 7-11   DAGOBAH EXTERIOR

Sound: Dagobah exterior comes up.

LUKE: *(TO OFF)* All right, Artoo; let's see how the engines sound!

ARTOO: *(OFF)* ACKNOWLEDGES FROM X-WING SOCKET.

Sound: Engines come up to low idle.

LUKE: Not bad, considering she was underwater. Okay; shut 'em down!

Sound: Engines die away.

ARTOO: BEEPS IMPATIENTLY.

LUKE: Calm down, Artoo! Lemme load the survival gear, and we'll lift off.

Sound: Boxes and stuff being loaded into the cargo well.

LUKE: *(WITH EFFORT)* There we go.

Sound: Hatch creaks closed, locks.

YODA: *(APPROACHING)* Luke. Luke, will you not your mind change? You must stay on Dagobah; complete your training.

LUKE: I'm sorry; I can't keep that vision out of my head. Leia and the others—They're my friends; I've got to help them.

YODA: You are being impulsive, unthinking. No help is that!

LUKE: Master—I wasn't there when my aunt and uncle needed me, and the stormtroopers murdered them. I can't *go* through that again; *not again*! Han saved my life! and Leia—Leia . . .

YODA: You must not go!

LUKE: But they'll die if I don't!

BEN: *(SPECTRAL)* You don't know that for certain, Luke.

LUKE: Ben!

BEN: Even Yoda cannot see their fate, there in Cloud City.

LUKE: But I can help them. I feel the Force.

BEN: But you cannot control it. This is a dangerous time for you, Luke, when you will be tempted by the dark side of the Force.

YODA: Yes, yes. To Obi-Wan you listen, Luke. The cave! Remember your failure at the cave!

LUKE: But I've learned so much since then! Master—Yoda, I promise to return and finish what I've begun. You have my word!

BEN: It is you and your abilities the Emperor wants. That is why your friends are made to suffer.

LUKE: That's why I have to go.

BEN: Luke, I don't want to lose you to the Emperor the way I lost Vader.

LUKE: You won't, Ben.

YODA: Stopped they must be. On this all depends.

LUKE: Yes; and I want to—

YODA: And only a fully trained Jedi Knight, with the Force as his ally, will conquer Vader and his Emperor.

LUKE: I'm still going to try.

YODA: If you choose the quick and easy path as Vader did, you will become an agent of evil.

BEN: Patience, Luke!

LUKE: And sacrifice Han and Leia?

YODA: If you honor what they fight for—yes!

BEN: Luke, if you choose to face Vader, you will do it alone. I cannot interfere.

LUKE: I understand, Ben. *(BEAT. TO OFF)* Artoo-Detoo?

ARTOO: ANSWERS, FROM OFF.

LUKE: Fire up the converters.

Sound: Engines come up, idling.

BEN: Luke! Don't give in to hate! That leads to the dark side of the Force. No matter what, you must remember that!

YODA: Strong is Vader. Mind what you have learned, youngster! Save you, it can!

LUKE: I will, Master.

Sound: Luke's flight boots on the ladder rungs, as he climbs to cockpit.

LUKE: *(MOVING OFF)* And I'll return. I promise! You'll see!

YODA: *(SIGHS)* Obi-Wan! Told you I did. Reckless is he. And now . . . matters are even worse than before.

Sound: Engines up. X-wing lifts off slowly. X-wing moving off under next lines.

BEN: Yoda, that boy is our last hope.

YODA: No, Obi-Wan. There is another!

NARRATOR: The workings of the Force draw its principals towards a future that no Jedi Master, Dark Lord or Emperor can predict or control. And in Cloud City are the man to whom Luke Skywalker owes his life, the woman whose image has led him into tragedy and triumph, and the enemy whose destiny was tied to his own before his birth.

Music: Closing theme under credits.

NARRATOR: CLOSING CREDITS.

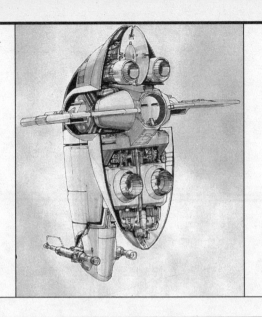

EPISODE EIGHT:

"DARK LORD'S FURY"

CHARACTERS:

Luke	Vader	Commander
Leia	Threepio	First Trooper
Han	Artoo	Second Trooper
Chewbacca	Lobot	First Guard
Lando	Boba Fett	Second Guard

ANNOUNCER: OPENING CREDITS.

Music: Opening theme.

NARRATOR: A long time ago in a galaxy far, far away, there came a time of revolution, when Rebels united to challenge a tyrannical Empire. Now, it is a dark time for the Rebellion, as the Empire hunts scattered and demoralized Rebel units across space. While Luke Skywalker has gone off on his own to further his training as a Jedi Knight, Han Solo, Leia Organa, Chewbacca, and See-Threepio have been forced to seek refuge on Cloud City, a huge gas-mining complex floating in the atmosphere of the planet Bespin.

Sound: X-wing zooms.

NARRATOR: But Luke is now speeding towards Bespin in his X-wing fighter, convinced by glimpses of the Force that his friends are in horrible danger.

SCENE 8-1   CLOUD CITY QUARTERS

Sound: The Rebels' luxurious quarters in Cloud City. Fountains. Wind chimes. A power door opens.

HAN: *(APPROACHING)* Well, I just talked to the tech supervisor, Leia. Everything's goin' great!

LEIA: Oh? Everything always seems to be going "just great" in Cloud City.

HAN: *(SIGHS)* Things go bad, you worry. Things go good, you're suspicious. Why don't you try bein' happy for a change, Princess?

LEIA: I will be—when we're out of here. And I hope nobody finds out about the "princess" part.

HAN: Hey, what more d'ya want from Lando? He took us in, he's gettin' the *Falcon*'s hyperdrive repaired, and he's puttin' us up in luxury quarters.

LEIA: Oh yes, Lando's been generous to a fault, I'll grant you that.

HAN: I mean, look at this place; three times as much room as we need, all this art, view of the whole city, the works! Pretty classy, even for a princess, isn't it?

LEIA: And *dazzling* to a smuggler, I imagine.

HAN: I take the good life when it comes my way, yeah! And I see you don't mind wearing those fancy robes he had sent over.

LEIA: There's something about the way Lando Calrissian smiles . . .

HAN: Listen, Lando's just a crook like me who went straight. I thought that's what you're always sayin' *I* should do.

LEIA: Being in business doesn't make him honest. And what about that creepy assistant of his, "Lobot," or whatever his name is?

HAN: What about him?

LEIA: What kind of man allows himself to be implanted with computer ancillaries?

HAN: If Lobot wants to let 'em wire up his head so he can keep a steady job, that's up to him, isn't it?

LEIA: It makes me nervous just looking at him.

HAN: Look, the *Falcon*'s almost repaired. Two or three more details to take care of and we'll be in great shape.

LEIA: The sooner the better. Something's wrong here, Han. I can feel it. Have you seen See-Threepio?

HAN: No, I haven't seen him since we landed.

LEIA: Well, nobody seems to have heard of him or have any idea where he is.

HAN: Well, he probably wandered off sightseeing and got lost. Lando'll turn him up for us.

LEIA: He's been gone too long to have simply gotten lost. Chewbacca's out looking for him now.

HAN: Stop worrying. Leia . . . Leia, come here . . .

LEIA: Romance is not going to solve our problems, Solo!

HAN: Can't hurt.

LEIA: *Han* . . .

HAN: Ah, relax. I'll go talk to Lando right now, see what I can find out.

LEIA: I don't trust Lando.

HAN: Well, I don't trust him either! But he *is* my friend. And like I say, we'll be gone soon.

LEIA: Then you're as good as gone, too, aren't you, Han? You drop me at the Rebel rendezvous point and you're off on your own again.

HAN: We've been over all this already.

LEIA: I know: Jabba the Hutt; the money you owe him; the bounty hunters. Good way to justify leaving . . . *the Rebellion* . . . with a clear conscience.

HAN: Leia—

LEIA: I don't know why I ever thought you'd change, Han!

HAN: The things that happened between us—if you think they don't matter to me, you're wrong. But like I said: I'm no good to you or the Rebellion until I take care of this . . .

LEIA: Don't you *dare* pull that "outlaw" routine on me! You can't fool me any better than you can fool yourself!

Sound: Power door opens. Chewie enters, snarling, approaching point of view.

HAN: Chewie! What's the matter? What d'ya got there?

CHEWBACCA: YOWLS.

LEIA: Threepio!

HAN: What's left of him. Boy, Threepio, somebody blasted you good.

CHEWBACCA: SNARLS.

HAN: Chewie says he found the pieces in a scrap reclamation center. He had to fight off a buncha those little "Ugnaughts" for 'em.

LEIA: I told you something was wrong. Are all Threepio's pieces here?

Sound: Sorting through the junk.

HAN: Looks like. Not too much damage.

LEIA: Oh, what a mess! Can Chewbacca repair him?

HAN: Uh, looks like his emergency releases blew when the blaster shot hit 'im; sluffed off most of the impact.

LEIA: So he can be fixed?

HAN: Yeah; Lando's got people who can do it.

LEIA: No thanks! Wake up, Han! Lando's people probably *did* this!

HAN: Look, there's no reason to think Lando was in on this; those Ugnaughts are nasty little creatures . . .

Sound: Power door opens.

LANDO: *(APPROACHING)* Good afternoon, folks. I came to see if you, uh . . . Am I interrupting something?

CHEWBACCA: WOOFS.

LEIA: Not really, Administrator Calrissian.

LANDO: Leia, you look absolutely magnificent in those robes! You truly *belong* with us here among the clouds.

LEIA: *(COOLLY)* I can't agree, but thank you.

LANDO: Would you care to join me in the banquet hall for a little refreshment? Everyone's invited, of course.

CHEWBACCA: AGREES.

HAN: Sounds good, Lando; I'm always one for a free feed.

LANDO: Splendid! By the way, Han: Are you having trouble with your droid there?

HAN: No. No problem. He comes apart once in a while. Why?

LANDO: Oh, nothing. Ready, Princess? Gentlemen? *(MOVING OFF)* Right this way!

Sound: Quarters fade.

SCENE 8-2   CLOUD CITY THOROUGHFARE

Sound: Cloud City thoroughfare comes up. Passing throngs, automata, aliens, etc.

LANDO: *(APPROACHING POINT OF VIEW)*—so you see, Han; Leia: Since we're a small operation, we don't fall into the, er, jurisdiction of the Empire.

LEIA: So you're part of a mining guild, then?

LANDO: No, as a matter of fact. Our operation is small enough not to be noticed.

HAN: Yeah; the Empire's sorta busy right now.

LANDO: Yes, which is advantageous since my, um, customers are anxious to avoid attracting attention to themselves.

HAN: Lando, aren't you afraid the Empire's gonna find out about this little racket of yours? Shut you down?

LANDO: It's always been a danger. It looms like a shadow over everything we've done here.

LEIA: "We"?

LANDO: Most of the personnel here just want to work their jobs and lose their past.

CHEWBACCA: HOOTS.

LEIA: That's not always so easy.

LANDO: No, but something has developed that will ensure our security.

HAN: Oh yeah?

LANDO: I've just made a deal that will keep the Empire out of Cloud City forever.

LEIA: Congratulations! Perhaps you'll reveal your secret to us. I'd enjoy hearing just how it's done.

LANDO: Ah; here's the banquet hall . . .

Sound: Lando throws a switch. Door slides up.

LANDO: Enter, please.

HAN: Y'don't haveta ask twice, when it comes to a meal for—

Sound: Vader's breathing.

LEIA: Han!

VADER: *(SLIGHTLY OFF)* Greetings, Princess Leia; Captain Solo! It has been a long chase. Would you care to sit at my table?

CHEWBACCA: GROWLS.

HAN: Well, hiya, Vader . . .

LEIA: Han, we can't let him take us—

HAN: He won't. So long, black-mask!

Sound: Han fires a shot. Sputtering, as Vader deflects it with his palm.

HAN: That's impossible. Nobody stops a blaster bolt with his hand . . .

VADER: Would you care to try again, fool?

HAN: Don't mind if I do . . .

Sound: Bolt, turned aside, and another, same.

HAN: It can't be . . .

LEIA: Han, it's no good.

VADER: As you well know, Princess Leia; Solo, I weary of this game. You won't be needing your precious weapon ever again! *Here! To me it flies!*

Sound: Blaster zips from Han's hand, through the air.

HAN: Hey! Ahh!

Sound: Blaster slaps into Vader's gauntleted palm.

VADER: You see? Firearms are of no consequence to *me*!

LANDO: Lord Vader has won, Han. It's over for you.

HAN: Oh yeah? You agree, Chewie?

CHEWBACCA: ROARS ANGRILY.

HAN: I'm with you, partner. *Let's take 'im* . . .

LANDO: Han, *no*!

LEIA: It's suicide!

LANDO: That's *Vader*, Han! Nobody can stand up to—

HAN: I thought you knew, Lando: Me 'n' the Wookiee don't *go* to jail!

CHEWBACCA: HOWLS.

LANDO: Don't be stupid!

HAN: *(TO OFF)* Hey, you in the funeral outfit! Let's find out what you got besides parlor tricks! *(STALKING FORWARD SLOWLY)* Chewie! You get 'im on the left! I'll handle the right . . .

CHEWBACCA: CONCURS.

VADER: Yes; come, both of you!

HAN: We're on our way, big boy . . .

LEIA: He can tear you apart with his hands! *He'll kill you both, you idiots!*

LANDO: Listen to her, Han!

HAN: *(PAUSING)* "Listen to her; listen to you; listen to *him*!" *We* only get in trouble when we listen to people! Ready, partner?

CHEWBACCA: WOOKIEE'S WAR CRY.

VADER: I await you, Solo. If you dare!

HAN: *(MOVING)* Don't flatter yourself! *You* ain't the biggest thing me 'n' the *Wookiee* ever tackled, pal!

VADER: The Wookiee's life is forfeit, Solo. I need you, but I shall strangle him before your eyes!

LEIA: He'll do it! *Han, believe me!* It's Chewie's life!

VADER: You capitulate, Princess Leia?

LANDO: Lord Vader, give him a chance to surrender; he can see there's no . . .

VADER: His chance is this moment!

LANDO: But he's no good to you dead; you said so. In a fight, you might kill him.

VADER: Yes. I shall make this simple for you, pilot. *(TO OFF)* Commander! Bring in your men!

LEIA: Stormtroopers!

Sound: Stormtroopers, off, running to take up positions. Wild lines.

LANDO: Yes. Cloud City's filled with them.

COMMANDER: *(OFF. IN HELMET)* You men, cover the doorway! Keep your weapons trained on the Rebels!

VADER: Here's someone else you'll recognize, Solo. *(TO OFF)* Come in, bounty hunter!

229

THE EMPIRE STRIKES BACK: THE NPR DRAMATIZATION

BOBA FETT: *(IN HELMET. APPROACHING)* Hello, Solo. Jabba the Hutt sends his warmest regards. He's looking forward to seeing you.

HAN: Boba Fett. What'd somebody do, kick over a rotten log?

FETT: Joke while you can, Solo!

VADER: I await your decision, Solo. Does the Wookiee die?

LEIA: Han, it was a good run, but—he has us. Don't throw Chewie's life away.

CHEWBACCA: ROARS.

HAN: No, Chewie; she's right. I guess you win, Vader.

VADER: Of course, Captain. Although—I am disappointed. I would have enjoyed our little contest.

HAN: Another time, then. Lando, I hope the word gets out about you.

LEIA: No wonder you called *Han* a double-crosser, Lando; the word must've been very much on your mind.

LANDO: I had no choice. Vader and Fett and the others arrived right before the *Falcon*. I'm sorry, Han.

HAN: I'm sorry, too.

VADER: Not nearly as sorry as you're going to be, Captain Solo. For every insult, you will scream a dozen times!

Sound: Banquet hall fades.

SCENE 8-3 CLOUD CITY—OUTSIDE TORTURE CHAMBER

Sound: Corridor, outside torture chamber, comes up. Sounds of Han's torture in the next room. Sparks, crackling, humming, snapping electricity, etc.

HAN: IN THE NEXT ROOM. SCREAMS INTERMITTENTLY AS HE'S TORTURED

LANDO: *(APPROACHING)* What're they doing in there? Where's Han, Fett?

FETT: *(HELMET)* Lord Vader is . . . chastising him, Calrissian.

LANDO: Torture was never part of the bargain!

FETT: Then, why don't you complain to Vader? I would enjoy seeing the Dark Lord lose his patience with you.

LANDO: Is it true that gun of yours only works when somebody's got his back turned?

FETT: Don't push me!

LANDO: Someday, bounty hunter, you and I are going to meet when you haven't got a division of stormtroopers to back you up!

FETT: And what will happen then, Calrissian?

LANDO: See this face? Memorize it; it's going to be the last thing you ever see!

Sound: Power door opens. Vader enters, mask-breathing.

HAN: OFF. SCREAMS.

LANDO: Lord Vader! I've done what you wanted! You've *got* to stop torturing Han . . .

VADER: Presently, Calrissian. Boba Fett, you may take Solo to Jabba the Hutt after I have Luke Skywalker in my grasp.

FETT: Lord Vader—with all respect, *I* was the one who found the *Falcon* for you. You made certain promises. Jabba wants to make an example of Solo; he's no good to me dead.

VADER: Solo will not be permanently damaged.

LANDO: But what about Leia and Chewbacca?

231

VADER: They must never again leave Cloud City.

LANDO: But that was never a condition of our agreement! Nor was giving Han to this bounty hunter!

VADER: Perhaps you think you are being treated unfairly, Calrissian? Perhaps you would prefer to dissolve our little . . . understanding?

LANDO: I never said that . . . No; no, Lord Vader.

VADER: Good! It would be unfortunate if I had to leave a garrison of stormtroopers here in Cloud City.

LANDO: Yes. "Unfortunate."

VADER: You; bounty hunter! *(MOVING OFF)* Come with me. We have final arrangements to make.

FETT: *(MOVING OFF)* As you wish, Lord Vader.

LANDO: *(TO HIMSELF)* This deal is getting worse all the time! *(TO OFF)* Lobot! Come here!

LOBOT: *(APPROACHING)* What is your command, Lando?

LANDO: Tell my guard force to be ready. I don't like the way things are going. And you stay on constant alert.

LOBOT: It will be as you command, Lando.

LANDO: I've got a bad feeling about all of this!

Sound: Corridor fades.

SCENE 8-4   CLOUD CITY CELL

Sound: Holding chamber comes up, with sound of Chewie working on Threepio's parts. Growling, pieces grating and clanking, etc. Sound of a switch being thrown.

THREEPIO: BURSTS OF INCOMPREHENSIBLE GARBLE, STATIC, ETC.

CHEWBACCA: GROWLS, THROWS ANOTHER SWITCH.

THREEPIO: *(SPEECH SPEEDING UP TO NORMAL)* Th—rr aarre stormtroopers! Stormtroopers! We're in danger! I must warn the others—oh no! I've been shot!

CHEWBACCA: BARKS.

THREEPIO: Oh, First Mate Chewbacca! What's happened? I'm all in pieces!

CHEWBACCA: WOOFS.

THREEPIO: Oh dear! Please, reassemble me!

CHEWBACCA: WORKING, GRUNTING.

THREEPIO: Yes, yes; my head goes on my body like that! Truly, you haven't any idea how grateful I am! Now; throw the connecting switch!

CHEWBACCA: HOOTS.

Sound: Switch being thrown.

THREEPIO: Oh yes; that's very good. I like that! But—something's not right, because now I can't see!

CHEWBACCA: GRUMBLING, ADJUSTING THREEPIO.

THREEPIO: Oh, oh, oh! That's much better. Wait, wait! Oh my! What have you done? *You've put my head on backwards!*

CHEWBACCA: IRRITATED WOOF.

THREEPIO: You stupid furball! Only an overgrown mophead like you could make such a ridiculous mistake! How could you do such a thing—

Sound: Power door opens. Han is shoved into the cell, sprawling. Grunts of effort from stormtroopers as they throw him in.

HAN: MOANS AS HE HITS THE DECK

FIRST STORMTROOPER: *(IN HELMET)* Rest up while you can, Solo!

SECOND STORMTROOPER: *(IN HELMET)* We'll be back. With some company! *(LAUGHS)*

Sound: Power door closes.

CHEWBACCA: MOANS.

HAN: *(SLIGHTLY OFF)* Hoo! I feel *terrible*! Chewie, gimme a hand here, will ya?

CHEWBACCA: GRUNTS.

Sound: Laying aside of Threepio's bits, which clank and rattle.

THREEPIO: Chewbacca, please be careful where you're putting me!

CHEWBACCA: BARKS *(MOVING SLIGHTLY OFF TO HAN)*.

HAN: Right! *(WITH EFFORT OF BEING HAULED UP)* What'd you say?

CHEWBACCA: REPEATS.

HAN: *(STILL GROANING)* As a matter of fact, yeah; the sleeping platform looks pretty good, right about now. *(AS HE'S LOWERED ONTO IT)* Oof! You're not lookin' so hot either, professor . . .

THREEPIO: I was accosted and blasted by stormtroopers!

HAN: Figured it was somethin' like that . . .

THREEPIO: Chewbacca is attempting to reassemble me, with mixed results.

HAN: *(GROANS)* Well, with your head on that way, you'll always know where you've been.

THREEPIO: That's not particularly amusing, Captain; I was just trying to correct the situation! But what of you?

HAN: Torture chambers. Take a tip from me, Threepio, don't ever get on Vader's bad side.

THREEPIO: That advice is rather tardy, Captain Solo!

HAN: *(GROANS)* No argument there!

Sound: Power door. Troopers' effort as they shove Leia into the cell.

LEIA: SLIGHTLY OFF. REACTING TO SHOVE

THREEPIO: Princess Leia!

Sound: Door closes.

CHEWBACCA: HOOTS SADLY.

LEIA: Threepio! *(MOVING ON)* Han! Han, what've they done to you?

HAN: Pretty much what they wanted. Made me holler a lot.

LEIA: Han, why are they doing this to you? There's nothing you can tell them.

HAN: I dunno. They never even asked me any questions. Somehow, I think I got Vader sore . . . *(GROANS)*

LEIA: You're never going to learn, are you?

Sound: Power door opens. Lando and guards enter.

FIRST GUARD: *(APPROACHING)* Stay where you are, all of you!

LANDO: *(APPROACHING)* Never mind that; the two of you just post yourselves by the door.

SECOND GUARD: Yes, Lando!

LEIA: Well, look what slithered in!

LANDO: Listen to me, all of you. We're short on time.

LEIA: Calrissian, I was wrong about you. You're an even more despicable creature than I'd thought.

HAN: Get outta here, Lando.

CHEWBACCA: GROWLS.

LANDO: Shut up and listen! Vader's agreed to turn Leia and Chewie over to me.

HAN: Leia . . . I bet you *loved* that part of the deal!

LANDO: You're wrong, Han. That's *never* been my style and you know it! Leia and Chewie'll have to remain in Cloud City, but at least they'll be safe.

HAN: *(WEAK LAUGH)* Safe!

LANDO: Yes! Leia, you have my word on that.

LEIA: Your word is worthless! Contemptible! I don't want your protection.

LANDO: That's the best I can do; I pressed Vader as hard as I could.

LEIA: What about Han?

LANDO: Vader's giving him to the bounty hunter.

HAN: What'd I do to become so popular?

LEIA: Lando, Vader wants us all dead.

THREEPIO: Oh no, it mustn't happen! Not after all this, Your Highness!

LANDO: You're wrong, Leia. Vader doesn't want you at all. He's after somebody named Skywalker.

LEIA: Luke. Of course. It had to be . . .

LANDO: Vader's set a trap for him.

LEIA: And we're the bait.

LANDO: Yes. And this Skywalker's apparently on his way here.

HAN: Perfect. Works out great for you, doesn't it, Lando?

LANDO: No. But you should've looked around more, Han. You'd have recognized a lot of faces. My operation isn't just illegal. Almost everyone here is on the run or making a last try for some kind of a life.

LEIA: And that makes you a philanthropist, is that it?

LANDO: It means I can't lose this place! *Cloud City is all we have!*

HAN: *(GROANS AS HE SITS UP)* Well, you fixed us real good, didn't you, Lando? Gimme a hand up, here, will ya?

LANDO: *(WITH THE EFFORT)* Sure. Look, Han . . .

HAN: *(WITH EFFORT, RISING)* Thanks . . . *(SWINGING)* My *friend*!

Sound: Long roundhouse suckerpunch.

LANDO: REACTS.

Sound: Lando goes down.

FIRST GUARD: *(SLIGHTLY OFF)* Hold it, or you're dead, Solo! *(TO HIS PARTNER AS HE APPROACHES POINT OF VIEW)* Cover the others!

SECOND GUARD: *(SLIGHTLY OFF)* I got 'em. No one moves!

CHEWBACCA: GROWLS.

FIRST GUARD: This'll be a real pleasure, Solo . . .

Sound: Guard rifle-butt-strokes Han.

HAN: REACTS.

Sound: Han goes down.

CHEWBACCA: SNARLS.

LEIA: Han!

THREEPIO: No! No! There's no reason to resort to violence!

LANDO: *(PAINFULLY)* Stop, guards! Leave them alone . . .

LEIA: Han, are you all right?

HAN: I've felt better . . .

LEIA: You've looked better, too!

LANDO: Han, I've done all I can for you. I'm sorry I couldn't do more, but I've got my own problems.

HAN: Yeah, Lando. You're a real hero. You think I don't understand you? I used to *be* you!

LANDO: Save your breath, Han. You're gonna need it.

LEIA: What's Vader going to do with him?

LANDO: I don't know. I have to go meet Vader now. He's promised me that you won't be hurt, though.

LEIA: You can't trust Vader! Haven't you discovered that yet?

LANDO: *(MOVING OFF)* I have no choice! None of us has, now!

LEIA: There's always a choice, Lando. *There is always a choice!*

Sound: Power door closes.

LEIA: You certainly have a way with people, Han!

HAN: *(GROANS)* You gotta understand somethin' about Lando: He came down here to give me a chance to take that poke at 'im.

LEIA: Didn't work out too well for you, did it?

HAN: No. *(LAUGHS WEAKLY)* Sorry; me 'n' Chewie can usually pull off this kinda stuff . . .

LEIA: Stop it. You did all that anyone could do.

HAN: Wasn't enough. Maybe in the old days, I wouldn't've fallen for this trap.

LEIA: That's what comes from hanging around with idealists, hmm?

HAN: There're a lot of things I never got to say t'you, Princess.

LEIA: Shh! We have to hang on until Luke gets here.

THREEPIO: But, it's a trap for Master Luke as well!

LEIA: No! I think they're underestimating him. Even Vader! Luke's been trained in the Way of the Jedi.

HAN: Maybe you're right. If anybody can get you outta this, it's Luke. But I think Vader's got other plans for me.

CHEWBACCA: BARKS.

THREEPIO: Don't be downcast, Captain Solo! Master Luke won't fail us!

Sound: Cell fades.

SCENE 8-5   CLOUD CITY FREEZING CHAMBER

Sound: Freezing chamber comes up. Gas projections, echoing machinery, sputtering connections, etc.

LANDO: *(APPROACHING)* Lord Vader, Lobot tells me that you have my techs preparing the carbon-freezing chamber. What's going on?

VADER: This carbon-freezing facility is crude, but it should be adequate for my purposes. Skywalker must be made comfortable for his journey to the Emperor.

LANDO: You're gonna *freeze* Skywalker?

VADER: I do not wish him to harm himself or inflict unnecessary losses. This is a useful means of avoiding that.

FIRST TROOPER: *(APPROACHING. IN HELMET)* Lord Vader! Sensors report a spacecraft approaching Bespin! X-wing class; a Rebel snubfighter.

VADER: Excellent; that will be Skywalker. Monitor his progress and allow him to land unchallenged and unopposed. I shall deal with him when he arrives!

FIRST TROOPER: *(MOVING OFF)* Yes, Lord Vader. I'll see to it at once!

LANDO: What if he has other Rebels with him, or more ships appear? I don't want any battle damage to Cloud City. I have my people to think about.

VADER: Skywalker will be alone. He has been learning the Way of the Jedi. The confrontation will involve only us two.

LANDO: But—we only use this facility for carbon-freezing, not life-suspension! You put Skywalker into a block of carbonite in that pit, and it might kill him.

VADER: Unlikely. And yet, I don't want the Emperor's prize captive damaged. We will test the process, on Captain Solo.

LANDO: Now, wait; you never told me you were going to . . .

VADER: I can quite easily destroy this entire city, or have you executed, Calrissian. Is that your desire?

LANDO: No; it's not.

VADER: Splendid! Have Solo brought here, and the other prisoners as well. I wish them to witness the fate of an enemy of the Empire.

LANDO: The droid's still not reassembled, but he's activated.

VADER: Then the Wookiee can carry the pieces. Bring them all up here at once, and prepare the pit for a carbon-freezing.

LANDO: Just as you say. *Lord* Vader.

VADER: *(TO OFF)* Guard!

FIRST TROOPER: *(FROM OFF. IN HELMET)* Yes, Lord Vader?

VADER: You will keep me informed constantly of Skywalker's progress.

FIRST TROOPER: Yes, My Lord!

Sound: Chamber fades.

SCENE 8-6   LUKE'S X-WING COCKPIT

Sound: Luke's X-wing cockpit, with engine sounds, background, comes up.

LUKE: How're the converters holdin' out back there, Artoo-Detoo?

ARTOO: *(AFT)* ANSWERS THAT THEY'RE OKAY.

LUKE: Good! I've got Bespin on the scopes. We'll be there soon. I just hope we get there in time.

ARTOO: ASKS A QUESTION.

LUKE: Yes, I'm *sure* See-Threepio's with the others. I didn't leave *you* behind, did I?

ARTOO: BEEPS.

LUKE: No, I can't get a sense of whether they're all right. But they have to be! Just hang on, Artoo; we may have to fight our way in. Charge up the guns and get ready to bring up the deflector shields.

ARTOO: ANSWERS.

Sound: The fighter zooms, fades.

SCENE 8-7   CLOUD CITY FREEZING CHAMBER

Sound: Freezing chamber comes up. Ugnaughts, techs, steam valves, servos, etc.

FIRST TROOPER: The Rebels are being brought in now, My Lord. Skywalker's ship is entering the atmosphere.

VADER: Good. Have the others stand here, so that they may have a perfect view of the proceedings.

FIRST TROOPER: *(TO OFF)* Bring in the prisoners!

VADER: *(TO OFF)* Calrissian! Come here; you will stay by me as well.

LANDO: With your permission: I don't want any part of this. I'm going to—

VADER: Stand over here! You and everyone else will learn what defiance of the Empire brings down upon traitors!

SECOND TROOPER: *(APPROACHING)* Move along there, all of you!

CHEWBACCA: *(APPROACHING)* SNARLS.

LEIA: *(APPROACHING)* Easy, Chewie, easy.

THREEPIO: *(BEING BORNE CLOSER ON CHEWBACCA'S BACK)* Yes, Chewbacca! Do be reasonable! If you'd only attached my legs, you wouldn't need to carry me strapped to your back. Now remember: You have a responsibility to think of my well-being, so don't do anything foolish!

HAN: *(APPROACHING)* Well, Lando; what's goin' on, *buddy*? Don't tell me they're throwin' this bash just for *me*?

LANDO: You're being put into carbon-freeze, Han.

CHEWBACCA: REACTS.

LEIA: I hope you're proud of yourself, Lando.

HAN: Well, Vader, this time you outdid yourself.

VADER: I lack the time to punish you properly, Solo. But Boba Fett will deliver you into the hands of Jabba the Hutt—*if* you survive the freezing. I'm told that Jabba can be . . . most inventive, when it comes to vengeance. Is that not so, Fett?

BOBA FETT: *(APPROACHING)* Lord Vader, what if Solo doesn't survive the freezing process? He's worth a lot of money to me!

VADER: The Empire will compensate you if he dies. Now stand aside, bounty hunter!

HAN: Y'know what, Vader? I'm only sorry I won't be there when the Rebel Alliance finally gives you and the Empire what you got comin'.

VADER: Empty words, Solo!

LEIA: No, they're not, Han! They're not at all . . .

VADER: Put him onto the lift and lower him into the pit!

FIRST TROOPER: All right, you men: Take him away!

CHEWBACCA: SCREAMS.

THREEPIO: No! Chewbacca don't! No fighting!

CHEWBACCA: ROARS.

Sound: Chewie strikes trooper.

SECOND TROOPER: REACTS IN PAIN, IN HELMET

TROOPERS: WILD LINES: "LOOK OUT!" "GRAB 'IM!" ETC.

HAN: Stop, Chewie! Stop!

THREEPIO: You're getting *me* involved in this as well, Chewbacca!

Sound: Thud, etc., as Chewie smacks troopers around. Wild lines, etc.

LEIA: Chewbacca, you mustn't do this! Please!

VADER: Calm the Wookiee or I'll kill him, Solo!

HAN: Stop! Chewie, hear me? *Stop!*

THREEPIO: Yes, Chewbacca: *stop!* I beg you!

HAN: Chewie, this won't help me! *Hey!*

LANDO: *They're right, Chewbacca!*

CHEWBACCA: STOPS ROARING.

HAN: Save your strength, partner.

THREEPIO: By all means, *do!*

HAN: There'll be another time, Chewie. The princess—you haveta take care of the princess for me. D'you hear me? *Hah?*

CHEWBACCA: RESIGNED WOOF.

HAN: Stay with her, Chewie! You know what she means to me . . .

CHEWBACCA: WAILS.

VADER: Stormtroopers! Proceed! Remove his bonds! Take him away!

LEIA: Wait! Oh, wait—Han! Han . . . *(THEY KISS)*

HAN: *(AS THEY KISS)* Leia . . . good-bye, Princess . . .

VADER: *Take him!*

SECOND TROOPER: *(MOVING OFF TO MIDDLE DISTANCE WITH HAN)* The prisoner is in position! Ready to commence!

LEIA: Han! Han, I love you . . .

HAN: *(FROM SLIGHTLY OFF)* I know that, Leia. And I love you!

VADER: Lower him into the pit! Prepare for the carbon-freezing cycle!

Sound: Lift platform as it lowers Han into the pit.

LEIA: Han . . .

CHEWBACCA: KEENS.

Sound: Lowering sounds grow louder.

VADER: Commence the freezing cycle!

Sound: Ugnaughts grunt. Gushing of gas projectors, thumping of generators as freezing begins.

HAN: OFF. YELLS IN AGONY

CHEWBACCA: HOWLS.

Sound: Freezing sounds rise.

LEIA: *Han!*

Sound: Scene fades.

NARRATOR: Han Solo will live or die, as the carbonite block hardens around him, encasing him. For Luke Skywalker, whose X-wing fighter approaches Cloud City, the same fate is planned. And Lando Calrissian is about to learn what it means to strike a bargain with the Empire as Leia, Threepio, and Chewbacca await the cruelty of Darth Vader. Inexorably, designs of the Force are shaping the long-awaited duel of Luke Skywalker and the Dark Lord of the Sith.

Music: Closing theme under credits.

NARRATOR: CLOSING CREDITS.

EPISODE NINE:

"GAMBLER'S CHOICE"

C H A R A C T E R S :

Luke	Chewbacca	Second Trooper
Leia	Lobot	Third Trooper
Lando	Boba Fett	Supervisor
Threepio	Lieutenant	Bespin Guard #1
Artoo	Commander	Bespin Guard #2
Vader	First Trooper	Bespin Guard #3

ANNOUNCER: OPENING CREDITS.

Music: Opening theme.

NARRATOR: A long time ago in a galaxy far, far away, there came a time of revolution, as Rebels united to challenge a tyrannical Empire. Now, it is a dark time for the Rebellion. Using Han, Leia, Chewbacca, and See-Threepio as bait, Darth Vader has lured Luke Skywalker to Cloud City, a mining colony of the planet Bespin.

Sound: Luke's X-wing landing on exterior city platform.

NARRATOR: As Luke makes his landing approach, the Dark Lord has gathered his prisoners in the carbonite-freezing chamber, where he means to place Luke in suspended animation for transportation to the Emperor. But first, he has chosen to test the process on Han Solo.

Sound: Freezing sounds, turbines, hissing gas, etc., come up.

NARRATOR: As his companions watch helplessly, Han undergoes the agony of carbonite encasement, perhaps to survive, perhaps to die in the freezing pit.

SCENE 9-1   CLOUD CITY FREEZING CHAMBER

Sound: Freezing sounds all the way up, Ugnaught techs grunting, off, other techs' wild lines, off. Vader's breathing, point of view.

VADER: *(TO OFF)* You there; Supervisor! Report!

SUPERVISOR: *(FROM OFF)* Freezing process nearly complete, Lord Vader!

LEIA: Is he alive? Vader, is Han alive?

VADER: We shall know that presently, Your Highness.

THREEPIO: What—what's happening? Chewbacca, strapped to your back like this, I can't see a thing! Turn 'round! Turn 'round! I want to see!

CHEWBACCA: WAILS.

THREEPIO: Oh, if only you'd reattached my legs! Administrator Calrissian, I beg of you, tell me what is taking place!

LANDO: It's nearly over, Threepio.

LEIA: Yes. Nearly over.

SUPERVISOR: *(FROM OFF)* Carbonite freezing completed! Secure from freezing mode!

VADER: *(TO OFF)* Hoist the carbonite block out of the pit and place it here.

Sound: Hoist descends, grabs the block, lifts it out, and deposits it near them with a boom under next lines.

SUPERVISOR: *(FROM OFF)* Stand clear of the hoist!

LEIA: Look! The block is still smoking!

THREEPIO: Oh dear! Poor Captain Solo! Well, he should be quite well protected if he survives the freezing process, that is.

LEIA: How you must be enjoying this, Vader! Cruelty and pain and grief: All the things you live by!

LANDO: Leia . . .

VADER: If you try my patience any further, Your Highness, I shall have you silenced. *(TO LANDO)* Calrissian!

LANDO: Yes, Lord Vader?

VADER: You will examine the sensors on the block, and determine Solo's condition.

LANDO: I—as you say, My Lord . . .

SUPERVISOR: *(FROM OFF)* All right, set it down!

LANDO: *(TO OFF)* Carefully there!

Sound: The block is set down on the metal floor.

VADER: Release the hoist! Let the block fall flat!

Sound: Hoist releases. Block falls onto its back with a huge clang and thud.

THREEPIO: Oh, goodness! His face is quite visible through the carbonite. Is he alive, Your Highness?

VADER: Let us find out. Calrissian, read the sensors.

LANDO: *(MOVING SLIGHTLY OFF)* At once, My Lord.

LEIA: Do you see his face, Vader? Does it give you pleasure to see the pain you have inflicted?

VADER: He was an ememy of the Empire. He deserves his fate. Well, Calrissian?

LANDO: He's alive! The sensors indicate that he's in perfect hibernation.

CHEWBACCA: ROARS.

THREEPIO: Oh, thank the Maker! No, calm down, Chewbacca! Don't forget, if you initiate more violence, you'll involve me as well as yourself!

LEIA: Threepio's right, Chewie. It's too late for that now.

THREEPIO: But Captain Solo will be—will be—all right, won't he?

LEIA: He's trapped inside that thing forever unless someone releases him. I think I would almost prefer that he'd died.

VADER: *(TO OFF)* Boba Fett! Bounty hunter! Come here!

FETT: *(APPROACHING. IN HELMET)* Yes, Lord Vader!

VADER: You heard Calrissian's report. Solo has served my purposes, and now he is all yours. You may take him, with my compliments, to Jabba the Hutt.

FETT: My thanks, My Lord. My starship is docked out on the east landing platform.

VADER: *(TO OFF)* Lieutenant!

LIEUTENANT: *(FROM OFF. IN STORMTROOPER HELMET)* Yes, My Lord?

VADER: Fit the carbonite block with a null-gravity field. Escort Boba Fett to his ship with a detail of your stormtroopers. See that he gets off safely.

LIEUTENANT: As you command, Lord Vader.

VADER: Calrissian, your crew will now reset the freezing pit for Skywalker.

LANDO: Very well, My Lord. If you no longer need me here I beg your permission to resume my normal responsibilities.

VADER: It is granted.

COMMANDER: *(APPROACHING. NO HELMET)* Lord Vader, we've just received word! Skywalker's X-wing fighter has landed!

VADER: Excellent, Commander. Has this part of the city been evacuated?

COMMANDER: Yes, My Lord. All doors and corridor exits have been sealed, except for those that will lead Skywalker here.

VADER: See to it that he finds his way into the freezing chamber. After that I shall deal with him alone.

COMMANDER: *(MOVING OFF)* It shall be as you command!

LANDO: Come, Leia. There's no point in your staying here—

LEIA: *(SHAKING HIM OFF)* Get your hand off my arm! You sicken me! You let Han think you were his friend—and you let them do this to him!

LANDO: But it would've happened anyway! If I'd tried to stop it I'd have got my own people killed into the bargain!

LEIA: Go back to your cloud towers, Lando. Go back to your business and enjoy your luxuries—until Vader snaps his fingers again.

LANDO: I'm taking you and Chewie to your quarters . . .

CHEWBACCA: HOWLS.

THREEPIO: Please, *listen* to him, Chewbacca! There's nothing more we can do here!

VADER: Calrissian, you will take Princess Leia and the Wookiee to my ship. The droid as well; they will be leaving with me.

THREEPIO: Oh, no!

LANDO: Lord Vader, you agreed to leave them in Cloud City, in my custody. That was our deal.

VADER: I am altering it. And you may pray, Calrissian, that I do not see fit to alter it any further. *(TO OFF)* Commander!

LEIA: I don't know why you look surprised, Lando. Did you expect him to keep his word?

COMMANDER: *(FROM OFF)* What are your orders, Lord Vader?

VADER: Have a squad of stormtroopers escort the prisoners to my ship. Make certain that the Wookiee's wrists are securely bound!

COMMANDER: It shall be done, My Lord! *(TO OFF)* You men! Fall in over here . . .

VADER: *(MOVING OFF)* Technical crew! See that all things are in readiness for freezing Skywalker, then evacuate the area!

FIRST TROOPER: *(OFF. IN HELMET)* Stand clear of the block.

LEIA: Take one last look at Han's face, Lando.

SECOND TROOPER: *(OFF. IN HELMET)* Okay, raise it—easy now!

LEIA: Han was your friend. And you sold him out.

FIRST TROOPER: All right; let's float it out to the east platform! Fall in!

LANDO: Leia, I know you loved him, but what could I do?

COMMANDER: *(OFF)* Prisoner detail, stand by. You, Calrissian! Get those prisoners over here!

LEIA: What could you know about love, Lando? *(MOVING OFF)* Come on, Chewbacca. We wouldn't want to keep the *real* owners of Cloud City waiting!

CHEWBACCA: *(MOVING OFF)* SNARLING.

THREEPIO: *(MOVING OFF)* Now be careful you don't bump into something with me, Chewbacca!

LANDO: *(TO SLIGHTLY OFF)* Lobot, come here . . .

LOBOT: *(APPROACHING)* What are your orders, Lando?

LANDO: Alert my personal guardsmen. Stand by for orders and move fast when you get them.

LOBOT: We shall be waiting, Lando. We shall be ready.

Sound: Transition.

SCENE 9-2   CLOUD CITY CORRIDOR

Sound: Cloud City corridors, empty but for Luke and Artoo. Artoo approaches with rolling, servo sound, treads, etc.

LUKE: *(APPROACHING)* Over this way, Artoo! This corridor's open!

ARTOO: *(APPROACHING)* BEEPS A QUESTION.

LUKE: No; there's nobody around. No opposition when we landed, no guards, no citizens. I wonder who set *this* trap!

ARTOO: WHISTLES.

LUKE: No, don't worry. We're not leaving until we find Han and Leia and the others. Maybe if we could locate a computer terminal, you could get some information—Somebody's coming! Get back!

ARTOO: BEEPS.

Sound: Artoo rolls briefly. Procession with Han's block goes by. Marching, hum of gravity field under next lines.

LUKE: *(QUIETLY)* Stormtroopers! I knew it—Artoo, stay back outta sight!

ARTOO: BLEEPS SOFTLY.

LUKE: They've got something on a lifter field—metal crate, statue—something big.

FETT: *(OFF. IN HELMET)* Be careful! He must not be damaged!

LUKE: There's a civilian with 'em—with a rifle . . .

FETT: Inform control that I will be lifting off at once!

LUKE: Stay back . . .

ARTOO: WHISTLES.

LUKE: Search me; I dunno what it was about. *(EDGING OUT OF HIDING)* I wonder if they were—*get back, Artoo!*

Sound: Boba Fett's shot streaks toward Luke, from off. Impacts the wall, sputters, and smolders.

LUKE: Take cover!

ARTOO: SQUEALS WITH FRIGHT.

Sound: Another shot from Fett.

LUKE: Watch out!

Sound: A third incoming round.

LUKE: That one was 'way off. *(INDICATING HE'S SNEAKING A PEEK AROUND THE CORNER)* They're gone. Phew! Whoever saw stormtroopers retreating? And it was the civilian who fired, a guy in a helmet? What's it mean?

ARTOO: WHISTLES IMPATIENTLY.

Sound: Artoo rolls back and forth, bumping Luke, to urge him on.

LUKE: Artoo, will ya quit bumping me? We'll find 'em, don't worry! But if we just go charging around this place, we're askin' to get ourselves blasted, don't you understand?

ARTOO: BEEPS MOURNFULLY.

LUKE: Well, I'm worried, too. C'mon—but be careful . . .

ARTOO: *(FOLLOWING)* WHISTLES SOFTLY.

SCENE 9-2A   CLOUD CITY COORDINATOR

Sound: Brief transition to another corridor.

LUKE: *(APPROACHING)* Yes, I'm sure this is the way, Artoo.

ARTOO: ASKS ANOTHER.

LUKE: Don't ask me why; it'd only strain your logic circuits. Shh! More stormtroopers!

Sound: Troopers, Leia, Lando, Chewie, and Threepio moving by, off.

LUKE: *(SOFTLY)* They've got prisoners or—somebody with 'em . . . It's them! *Leia.* And Chewie and Threepio!

ARTOO: BEEPING EXCITEDLY.

LUKE: *Shhh!* They'll hear you! *(REACTING TO TROOPER AIMING AT HIM)* Duck!

Sound: Blaster bolt comes at them from off.

ARTOO: WARBLES IN FEAR.

LUKE: They saw us! Get back!

THREEPIO: *(FROM OFF)* Artoo-Detoo! Is that you?

Sound: Another bolt from the trooper.

ARTOO: BEEPS.

LUKE: I *can't* shoot, Artoo! I might hit Leia or Chewie—

Sound: Another round, incoming.

LUKE: They're using Leia as a shield!

LEIA: *(OFF)* Luke! Luke, go back! It's a trap!

LUKE: *(TO OFF)* Leia!

LEIA: *(FROM OFF)* Luke, no! Get away while you still can! It's a trap! *(REACTS TO BEING PULLED THROUGH THE DOOR)*

Sound: Another shot at Luke. Power door closes, off.

LUKE: *Leia!* Leia . . .

ARTOO: HOOTS SADLY.

LUKE: Forget it, Artoo. That door'll be sealed just like all the others. Everyone's coming from that direction. That's where I have to go.

ARTOO: BEEPS.

LUKE: No, Artoo. You try to follow Leia and the others; you can't go with me. *(MOVING OFF)* This is what I came here for, and I have to go alone. So long, little friend.

Sound: Power door slams down. Artoo signals furiously, then hoots in despair.

SCENE 9-3 CLOUD CITY FREEZING CHAMBER

Sound: Sound of freezing chamber comes up. Luke's echoing steps approach.

LUKE: *(APPROACHING)* Vader! You might as well speak up. I know you're here somewhere!

Sound: Point of view Vader's breathing.

VADER: Come; up here to me, young Skywalker. The Force is with you.

Sound: Luke approaching, up metal staircase.

LUKE: *(COMING ON)* The Force brought me here.

VADER: Indeed it did. And you have chosen to holster your blaster? Quite correct; firearms have no place here. As your friend Solo found out.

LUKE: Lightsabers, of course.

VADER: Of course.

LUKE: What've you done with Han? And where are Leia and the others going?

VADER: It is pointless to concern yourself with your friends now. The Force has ordained this moment. But remember, you are not a Jedi Knight yet!

LUKE: And you ceased to be one a long time ago.

VADER: Come, Skywalker—

Sound: Vader's saber activates.

VADER: Time to prove to you just how little distance you've come in your learning.

LUKE: D'you think you're the only one who knew it would come to this?

Sound: Luke's blade activates.

LUKE: You're wrong. We both did.

VADER: You miss the point: We both *wanted* it! *(INDICATES EFFORT OF A SLASH)*

Sound: Lightsabers clash, spatter, spit, crackle, etc.

LUKE: INDICATES EFFORT OF THE EXCHANGE

Sound: Dueling pauses.

VADER: You have been learning. You're young and quick; you offer me better sport than the old man, Obi-Wan.

LUKE: You are fighting us both, Vader. But let's see how you do with me . . . *(EFFORT INDICATES ATTACK-IN-ADVANCE)*

Sound: Lightsabers crash.

VADER: Too much confidence, young Skywalker! *(INDICATES EFFORT OF ATTACK)*

Sound: Lightsabers whirl, Luke's carried around in bind.

LUKE: REACTS, AS HIS BLADE'S CARRIED AROUND AND HE'S FORCED BACKWARD OFF BALANCE

Sound: Lightsabers part as Luke lands with a thud.

VADER: You see? Stand up! Perhaps now is the time for you to concede the match!

LUKE: *(INDICATING EFFORT OF RISING)* Now who's too confident? It's only just begun, Vader . . .

Sound: Their weapons engage.

LUKE: It's only just begun.

Sound: Dueling.

LUKE AND VADER: EFFORT FROM BOTH, AS LUKE DRIVES VADER BACK

LUKE: Let's see *you* . . . give up some ground!

VADER: INDICATES EFFORT OF A WIDE SLASH

LUKE: EFFORT, DODGING THE SWING

Sound: Vader's blade parts an upright, melting it, etc.

LUKE: Well, you're not bad at hacking girders in two. It's a little harder to hit me, hmm?

VADER: Not very. I shall demonstrate—

LUKE AND VADER: EFFORT OF DUEL

Sound: Intense fighting.

Sound: Pause in the duel.

VADER: You have learned much, young one!

LUKE: You'll find I'm full of surprises!

Sound: Brief exchange, Vader pressing hard.

LUKE AND VADER: INDICATING.

Sound: Break in the duel.

VADER: Your surprises are few, and insufficient. You will no longer need your lightsaber! *(INDICATES, AS HE WHIRLS LUKE'S BLADE)*

Sound: Spitting and screaming of blades.

LUKE: REACTS TO BIND AND LOSS OF HIS WEAPON

Sound: Luke's lightsaber flies off. Vader's moans, threatening, under next lines.

VADER: No weapon, young Skywalker? No hope! Is it any wonder that you feel such fear?

LUKE: You haven't won yet . . .

VADER: You charged up those stairs so boldly—*(INDICATING: THREATENING LUKE WITH HIS SABER)*

LUKE: REACTING

VADER: —only to go down them even more abruptly!

LUKE: No-oo! *(REACTS TO FALL, AS HE TUMBLES OFF)*

Sound: Luke's fall down the metal staircase.

LUKE: OFF, MOANS.

VADER: But stairs are unnecessary—to one who controls the Force! *(INDICATES COMPOSURE, CONCENTRATION OF LEVITATING DOWN STAIRS)* Behold!

Sound: Vader swoops. Hum of sword, snap of cloak. Impact of his landing on lower deck. Point of view approaches Luke.

LUKE: *(AS VADER SWOOPS DOWN)* No-oo! *(PANTS, SCRAMBLING BACK AS VADER'S POV APPROACHES)* How could you do that?

VADER: This is nothing, to one who is in complete control of the Force.

LUKE: No one controls it completely!

VADER: That is the foolish and obsolete belief of senile minds! Now; get to your feet!

Sound: Vader's lightsaber threatens.

LUKE: EFFORT, AS HE SCRAMBLES TO HIS FEET

VADER: Your destiny lies with me, young Skywalker! Obi-Wan knew this to be true.

LUKE: No! Not with you! *Never!*

VADER: Back you go, young Skywalker—

Sound: Vader's saber swings, forcing Luke back.

LUKE: REACTS.

VADER: —into the pit! *Back!*

Sound: Wide, close swing of the saber.

LUKE: REACTS, AS HE'S DRIVEN OFF THE EDGE, FALLING, VOICE MOVING OFF ABRUPTLY.

Sound: Luke's impact, in pit.

LUKE: OFF. MOANS.

VADER: *(TO HIMSELF)* All too easy, son of Skywalker! Perhaps you are not as strong as the Emperor thought you to be. And now: The carbonite. You, too, will be—

LUKE: OFF. EXERTION OF HIS LEAP OUT OF THE PIT, INTO THE APPARATUS OVER IT.

Sound: Luke among the hoisting tackle, chains, running gear, etc.

VADER: —nothing more than a block of . . .

LUKE: *(FROM OFF)* You'll have to do better than that, Vader!

VADER: Impressive! Far higher and faster than a mere human could leap. Most impressive! And I *shall* do better! Come down from the mechanism—

Sound: Vader's sword swings, cutting chains, cable, carbonite hose, etc. Hose steam-whistles, gas gushes, etc.

VADER: Come down, or I'll cut you down!

Sound: Another sword-swipe through the apparatus.

Sound: From Luke: Another sword-swipe.

LUKE: OFF: EXERTION AS HE SOMERSAULTS CLEAR.

Sound: Luke lands on his feet, off.

VADER: Again: most adroit! But a duel cannot be won by all this leaping and evading.

LUKE: *(OFF, PANTING)* I know that . . .

VADER: Come! Here is your lightsaber, at my feet. Take it up, if you dare. If you're not afraid!

LUKE: *(APPROACHING TO SLIGHTLY OFF, VOICE STEADYING)* The Jedi and his lightsaber; the two are one . . .

Sound: Luke's saber begins ringing like a tuning fork, drawn toward him.

LUKE: The Force calls my lightsaber to me . . .

VADER: No, it does not! Not to a frightened boy! It sends you only to your doom!

Sound: Vader's sword swings.

LUKE: *(REACTING, DUCKING)* Here! Try some carbonite!

Sound: Carbonite gushes from the pressure hose at Vader.

VADER: REACTS IN PAIN.

LUKE: The Force calls my lightsaber—

Sound: Tuning fork to the top. Saber zaps through the air, smacks Luke's palm, under next.

LUKE: —to me!

Sound: Luke's saber activates.

LUKE: EXERTION, AS HE ATTACKS.

Sound: Quick, intensive interchange.

VADER: And so it has! Very quick! The carbonite hose was very inventive! Obi-Wan taught you well; you have controlled your fear.

LUKE: Too bad you missed your chance. You won't get another . . .

Sound: Brief clash. Swords feint, moaning.

VADER: Now: Release your anger! Only your hatred of me can give you the power to destroy me!

LUKE: *(LAUGHING, PANTING)* You're telling me how to beat you, is that it? *(LAUGHS AGAIN)* You underestimated Ben—and you underestimate me!

Sound: Another short phrase of fencing.

VADER: Skywalker! Vengeance is like sunfire within you! Yield to it! The Force will help you!

LUKE: Yes! The dark side would! Knowledge and defense: That's what a *Jedi* uses the Force for. Are there ever times when you remember that?

VADER: You have no concept of the power you are ignoring.

LUKE: You can keep the hatred—hatred and fear. *(INDICATES AN ATTACK)*

Sound: Passage-at-arms.

LUKE AND VADER: EFFORT OF THE DUEL.

VADER: AS HE'S DRIVEN OFF THE EDGE OF THE PLATFORM, FALLING—INDICATES, FALLING OFF.

Sound: Luke's lightsaber deactivates, leaving relative silence in the freezing chamber.

LUKE: *(PANTING) (TO OFF)* Vader! *Vader, answer me! (MASTERING HIS BREATHING, ETC.) (TO HIMSELF)* All right—*Lord* Vader . . . *(TO OFF)* You wait down there, in the shadows! *(WITH THE EFFORT OF JUMPING A SHORT DISTANCE DOWN, TO THE BRINK)* I'll come down. Are you just angry—or are you *afraid*, too? I'm gonna find you . . . and we'll see . . .

Sound: Chamber fades.

SCENE 9-4 CLOUD CITY CORRIDOR

Sound: Cloud City corridor comes up. Stormtroopers' marching.

CHEWBACCA: *(APPROACHING)* HOOTING.

THIRD TROOPER: Keep moving! Prisoners! Move quickly!

THREEPIO: *(APPROACHING)* That was Master Luke, wasn't it, Your Highness? And Artoo-Detoo?

LEIA: *(APPROACHING)* Yes, it was.

THREEPIO: Unless Chewbacca turns around, I have to guess what's going on. I . . .

LANDO: *(A MUTTER, AS HE APPROACHES)* Keep quiet and stay ready: We'll have to move fast.

LEIA: *(A MURMUR)* What d'you mean? What are you talking about, Lando?

LANDO: Just stay ready.

BESPIN GUARD #1: *(APPROACHING VERY QUICKLY)* Hold it right there, stormtroopers, or we fire! *Hold it!*

BESPIN GUARD #2: *(APPROACHING QUICKLY, OVERLAPPING)* Don't move, or you're dead. Don't move, I said!

BESPIN GUARD #3: Hand your weapons over, *now*! *Hand 'em over!*

TROOPERS: REACT. HELMETS WILD LINES: "DON'T SHOOT!" ETC.

LEIA AND THREEPIO: REACT.

Sound: Chewbacca does, too.

LOBOT: *(APPROACHING)* Guards, give me the stormtroopers' weapons. Don't forget to deactivate their helmet comlinks.

Sound: General hubbub. Weapons handed over. Comlink switches.

LEIA: Lando, what *is* all this?

CHEWBACCA: HOOTS.

LANDO: Well done, Lobot! Here; give me a couple of those blasters . . .

Sound: Passing guns.

LOBOT: I received your signal. It was fortunate that the Imperials didn't take your wrist comlink from you.

THREEPIO: What a wonderful turn of events!

LEIA: Lando, are you going to tell me why Cloud City guards are ambushing stormtroopers?

LANDO: I sent an emergency signal to Lobot while the troopers were firing on your friend.

THREEPIO: Oh, how marvelous! A miracle!

CHEWBACCA: GRUNTS, UNIMPRESSED.

LOBOT: What are your orders, Lando?

LANDO: Take the stormtroopers and hold them in the security tower. And keep it quiet! Move!

LOBOT: *(TO OFF)* You: guards! Let's move.

Sound: Shuffling, etc.

EXTRAS: WILD LINES, SHOVING, ETC., AS GUARDS HERD TROOPERS OFF.

LOBOT: *(MOVING OFF)* I will await your further instructions, Lando!

LANDO: Here, Leia: Hold the guns.

Sound: Guns passed. Leia reacts.

LANDO: I've gotta get these wrist binders off Chewbacca . . .

Sound: Lando working on the bracelets.

LEIA: Lando? What d'you think you're *doing*?

LANDO: What's it look like? If Vader can renege on a deal, so can *I*! We're all getting out of here.

THREEPIO: I knew it all along! It had to be a mistake! Administrator Calrissian, I always knew you were trustworthy!

LEIA: Well, I am yet to be convinced.

CHEWBACCA: SNARLS AS LANDO WORKS.

LANDO: *Will ya hold still, Chewie?*

LEIA: Why should we believe you, Lando?

LANDO: *(INDICATING EFFORT OF OPENING CUFFS)* Open your eyes, Leia! There's no going back for me now! You think I enjoyed what they were doing?

Sound: Chewbacca's wrist binders snap open.

LANDO: *(INDICATING)* There y'go, Chewie! *(TO LEIA)* That's only one of the ways you had me wrong, Leia.

LEIA: It is? What's another?

LANDO: Keeping prisoners isn't my style. Never was.

THREEPIO: I liked him from the first! From the very first!

LANDO: How you feelin' there, Chewie? You getting your circulation back—

Sound: Chewbacca, enraged, as he seizes Lando by the throat, snarling. Ditto, under next lines.

LANDO: *(REACTING, CHOKING)* Chewie! No! No!

THREEPIO: Release him, you furry oaf! *You'll strangle him!*

CHEWBACCA: SAYS "YEP!"

LEIA: Lando, do you think that after what you did to Han, we're gonna trust you?

LANDO: *(CHOKING)* I had no choice, Leia . . . y'don't understand . . .

THREEPIO: What are you doing, Chewbacca? Trust him! Trust him!

LEIA: Oh, *we understand!* Don't we, Chewie? "He had no choice!"

CHEWBACCA: HOOTS AMID THE STRANGULATION.

LANDO: I'm trying to help . . .

LEIA: We don't need your help, traitor!

THREEPIO: Oh, *yes!* Yes we do, Princess Leia!

LANDO: . . . Han . . . *Han!*

THREEPIO: I think he's trying to tell us something about Captain Solo. Let him speak, Chewbacca!

Sound: Chewie relents a bit.

LANDO: *(CATCHING A LITTLE BREATH—WOOKIEE'S PAWS STILL ON HIM)* We can *still save Han* . . .

LEIA: Let him talk, Chewie!

CHEWBACCA: WOOFS.

LANDO: *(AS CHEWIE EASES OFF)* There's still a chance to save Han. They're loading the carbonite block into Boba Fett's starship, out on the east platform . . .

THREEPIO: You see? *You see?* He *was* acting honorably!

LEIA: Let 'im go, Chewie! And here: Take a gun!

CHEWBACCA: ROARS AS HE RELEASES LANDO.

LANDO: *(REACTS, HEAVING FOR BREATH)* We . . . we have to move fast!

THREEPIO: Administrator Calrissian, I apologize for Chewbacca's uncouth behavior! If I could I would dissociate myself entirely . . .

LEIA: *(MOVING OFF)* This way, Chewie, come on! Hurry! Hurry!

CHEWBACCA: MOVING OFF. ROARING.

THREEPIO: *(BEING BORNE OFF)* After all, Administrator Calrissian, *he's only a Wookiee!*

SCENE 9-5   ANOTHER CLOUD CITY CORRIDOR

Sound: Brief transition to another corridor. The allies' running, as they approach.

LANDO: *(APPROACHING)* Quickly! Come on! The east platform's over that way— *(WHISPERS)* Wait! Wait! Get back!

LEIA: *(APPROACHING)* What is it?

LANDO: A stormtrooper patrol.

CHEWBACCA: HOWLS SOFTLY.

LEIA: No, Chewie; he's right! We can't afford a firefight now! They'll be gone in a moment . . .

ARTOO: *(APPROACHING)* SIGNALING FURIOUSLY.

THREEPIO: Eh? What? *I'd know that signal anywhere! Artoo-Detoo!* Oh, praise the Maker!

ARTOO: WHISTLES, OVERJOYED.

LEIA: Be quiet, you two!

THREEPIO: Artoo, where have you been? Wait— *(TO CHEWIE)* Chewbacca, turn 'round so that I can see my counterpart, would you please?

CHEWBACCA: GRUNTS SOFTLY.

LEIA: Shhh! Welcome back, Artoo . . .

LANDO: Strange friends you've got, Leia. Now come on! There isn't much time. The stormtroopers're about to move out.

LEIA: Maybe I was wrong about you, Lando.

THREEPIO: Artoo, follow us! We're trying to save Captain Solo from a bounty hunter! Chewbacca, you great behemoth, be careful with me!

LEIA: There go the Imperials!

ARTOO: WHISTLES.

THREEPIO: What do you mean *you're* not in the best of condition, Artoo? At least *your* components aren't strapped to the back of an irresponsible Wookiee!

LANDO: Here we go: C'mon, everybody. . . . *(MOVING OFF)* Leia! Chewie! This way; follow me!

LEIA: *(MOVING OFF)* Quickly, Chewbacca! There's no time left!

CHEWBACCA: *(MOVING OFF)* GROWLS.

THREEPIO: *(BEING BORNE OFF)* Come along! Make haste, Artoo!

ARTOO: SIGNALING, GOING AFTER.

SCENE 9-6   CLOUD CITY LANDING PLATFORM

Sound: Brief transition to a doorway, at the east landing platform. Winds.

LANDO: *(APPROACHING)* This way! The east platform's out here—

Sound: Off, Fett's ship lifts off on thrusters, preparing to accelerate.

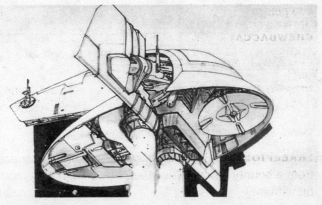

LANDO: That's it! That's Boba Fett's ship! Han must be aboard!

LEIA: We can't let it blast off! Chewie, open fire on it!

Sound: Leia fires. Chewie, roaring. More blaster bolts.

LANDO: It's useless, Leia . . .

LEIA: Disable it, Chewie! Aim for the lifters!

Sound: More shots.

THREEPIO: Your Highness . . . the ship has its deflectors up.

CHEWBACCA: HOOTS.

Sound: Another bolt.

LANDO: *It's no use, Leia!* But if we move fast, we might be able to catch them. My people repaired the *Millennium Falcon.* Let's go.

LEIA: When you change sides, you don't fool around, Lando.

THREEPIO: Look! More stormtroopers!

Sound: Blaster shots ranging close.

CHEWBACCA: HOWLS.

THREEPIO: No, no! Chewbacca, they're behind you, *behind you*!

LEIA: Over there! There! Chewie, *fire*!

Sound: More blaster bolts, incoming, outgoing.

LANDO: There's a way around them! We can still reach the *Falcon*!

LEIA: What about Luke?

LANDO: Every stormtrooper in Cloud City's between him and us, Leia!

Sound: More blaster shots.

CHEWBACCA: HOWLS.

LANDO: We can't stay here! Believe me! Believe me, or—

Sound: Blaster bolts.

LANDO: There's a way around the stormtroopers!

THREEPIO: If we perish here, all is lost, Princess Leia!

LEIA: All right, *all right*! Lead the way, Lando . . .

LANDO: Side door, over there . . .

Sound: More shooting.

CHEWBACCA: HOOTS UNHAPPILY.

LANDO: Keep your heads down!

THREEPIO: Keep your entire *body* down, Chewbacca! I do not wish to be annihilated!

CHEWBACCA: HOOTS.

THREEPIO: And Artoo! Use your maximum speed!

ARTOO: AGREES.

LEIA: Ready, Lando . . .

LANDO: You're not bad at this! Figures. *(MOVING OFF)* Keep close, everybody . . . and move it, *move it*!

Sound: Firefight fades.

SCENE 9-7 ANOTHER CLOUD CITY CORRIDOR

Sound: Another corridor comes up.

LANDO: *(APPROACHING)* There it is over there! Landing platform number 3–2–7!

LEIA: *(APPROACHING)* The blast door is closed!

LANDO: Yeah; but one set of auxiliary controls works from over here. Take cover; the stormtroopers're right behind us!

CHEWBACCA: *(APPROACHING)* WOOFS.

THREEPIO: *(BEING BORNE ON)* Artoo! Artoo-Detoo! *Increase your speed!*

ARTOO: *(APPROACHING)* WHISTLES.

LEIA: Lando, *open the blast door!*

LANDO: Take it easy; let me work, here . . .

Sound: Touchpad beep tones.

THREEPIO: Why isn't the blast door opening? *What's wrong?*

LANDO: Somebody's changed the security code on it.

LEIA: I bet you can guess who . . .

CHEWBACCA: HOWLS.

THREEPIO: Artoo-Detoo! You can tell the Cloud City computers to override the security system! Here's a computer terminal!

ARTOO: WHISTLES.

Sound: Servos whine as he extends his connector arm.

LANDO: There's a linkup to the public address system, too . . .

Sound: Beeping as Lando engages the P.A. system.

THREEPIO: Artoo, hurry!

274

LEIA: What're you doing, Lando?

LANDO: I owe you and Han a lot, Princess. But I owe something to my people, too . . .

Sound: P.A. engages.

LANDO: *(AMPLIFIED THROUGH CORRIDORS)* Attention, all personnel. This is Lando Calrissian. The Empire has taken control of Cloud City. I am advising you all to leave, before more troops arrive! All Cloud City spacecraft are hereby released for evacuation service.

THREEPIO: That's it, Artoo! Engage the computer system!

Sound: Artoo plugging in.

LANDO: *(AMPLIFIED)* Please, please: Try to help each other! May—may luck go with all of us . . . Lando Calrissian, out.

Sound: P.A. system goes down.

CHEWBACCA: WOOFS.

LEIA: Lando—I'm sorry about your people.

LANDO: Well, it's not your fault.

ARTOO: IN PAIN, BEEPING, SPUTTERING, AND SO FORTH . . .

THREEPIO: Artoo, break contact! That's a power socket, not a computer terminal! You'll burn out! *Break contact!*

LEIA: Chewie! Pull Artoo away from it!

CHEWBACCA: YOWLS.

Sound: Contact broken. Sparks.

ARTOO: *(DAZED)* BEEPS ACCUSINGLY AT THREEPIO.

THREEPIO: Well, don't blame me, Artoo! *I'm* just an *interpreter*! *I'm* not supposed to know a power socket from a computer terminal!

LANDO: C'mon! I *know* there's a terminal down there by the blast door!

LEIA: We won't have much cover down there, and there's no way out . . .

LANDO: I can't help that . . . You comin', Chewie?

CHEWBACCA: AFFIRMS.

THREEPIO: *(BORNE OFF)* Artoo, move quickly! Quickly!

ARTOO: BEEPS.

SCENE 9-8   ANOTHER CLOUD CITY CORRIDOR

Sound: Brief transition. Chaos in corridor, off, comes up, as crowds push, shove, stampede and, well . . . crowd.

THREEPIO: *(APPROACHING)* But Your Highness, shouldn't we try to take some of those evacuees with us?

LEIA: *(APPROACHING)* We'd be taking them *into* a lot more danger than we'd be taking them *out* of, Threepio!

LANDO: Look out, everybody!

Sound: Blaster bolt.

THREEPIO: Stormtroopers! As though our plight were not sad enough! Is there no end to them?

CHEWBACCA: HOWLS.

LEIA: Artoo-Detoo! Open the blast door!

ARTOO: WHISTLES RESPONSE.

Sound: More blasters.

LANDO: Leia! Chewie! Cover the corridor from that side!

Sound: Lando fires.

LANDO: Hold 'em back!

Sound: Blasterfire, outgoing.

LEIA: One over there by the column, Chewie!

CHEWBACCA: HOWLS.

Sound: Chewbacca fires. Impact, off.

TROOPERS: OFF: REACT. HELMETS.

LANDO: Not bad . . . Watch 'em on the right!

THREEPIO: Artoo, will you *please open that door*?

ARTOO: SIGNALS.

LEIA: Threepio, what's wrong?

THREEPIO: Artoo is having difficulty with the Cloud City computer again!

Sound: More incoming rounds.

CHEWBACCA: BARKS.

LEIA: Artoo, you must!

ARTOO: ALL AT SEA.

LANDO: Artoo-Detoo, it's now or never!

Sound: More firing.

ARTOO: WHISTLES HIS PERPLEXITY.

THREEPIO: *Yes*, Artoo! As Lando says: *Now or never!*

Sound: Firefight rises, fades.

NARRATOR: Deeper into the shadows, Luke Skywalker follows Darth Vader towards the very core of Cloud City. Han Solo, encased in carbonite, is being taken away to new and even worse torment by Boba Fett. At blast door 3–2–7, a Wookiee's strength and ferocity, a gambler's cunning and courage, and the beauty and wisdom of a princess are not enough in this moment. Not for the first time, galactic events hinge on the deeds of a simple astro-droid. And the Force has drawn its principals together, for battle, and for revelation.

Music: Up and under.

ANNOUNCER: CLOSING CREDITS.

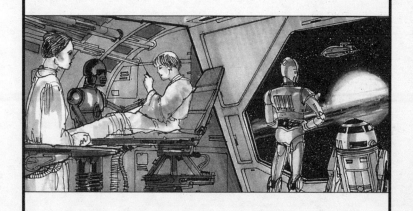

EPISODE TEN:
"THE CLASH OF LIGHTSABERS"

CHARACTERS:

Luke   Lando
Leia   Vader
Threepio   Too-Onebee
Artoo   P.A. System
Chewbacca

ANNOUNCER: OPENING CREDITS.

Music: Opening theme.

NARRATOR: A long time ago in a galaxy far, far away, there came a time of revolution, when Rebels united to challenge a tyrannical Empire. Now, it is a dark time for the Rebellion. Deep inside Cloud City, Luke Skywalker fights a desperate lightsaber duel against Darth Vader. Han Solo, encased in a block of carbonite, is in the charge of the bounty hunter, Boba Fett. And, attempting to escape to the *Millennium Falcon*, Leia, Lando, Chewbacca, See-Threepio, and Artoo-Detoo, are trapped by a locked blast door, as Imperial stormtroopers open fire on them.

SCENE 10-1   CLOUD CITY CORRIDOR

Sound: The firefight comes up.

NARRATOR: Their only hope lies with the astro-droid Artoo-Detoo, who is trying to use Cloud City's computer system to open the door.

THREEPIO: Artoo, the stormtroopers are closing in on us! If you don't get that door open, we're finished!

ARTOO: BEEPS.

Sound: A blaster bolt comes at them.

THREEPIO: Well, *try harder*!

LEIA: Lando! Stormtrooper by that doorway!

LANDO: I see him, Leia—

Sound: Lando fires.

LEIA: You got 'im!

Sound: Another incoming shot.

LEIA: That only leaves a dozen or so . . .

LANDO: Chewie! Watch that other corridor! They may try to come at us from two directions at oncc!

CHEWBACCA: HOOTS.

Sound: More shots.

LEIA: Threepio, how's Artoo doing?

THREEPIO: He is attempting to countermand the security program now, Your Highness.

ARTOO: WHISTLES.

THREEPIO: No, Artoo; we are *not* interested in information on the *Millennium Falcon*'s hyperspace drive! It's been fixed.

Sound: More shooting.

LANDO: Watch it! They're getting ready to rush us!

THREEPIO: Artoo! Just open the blast door, you stupid little lump!

ARTOO: BEEPS.

Sound: The door whooshes up.

LANDO: He did it! Leia, the door's open!

THREEPIO: I never doubted you for a second, Artoo! Wonderful!

LANDO: Quick, everybody! Run for the *Falcon*!

LEIA: We'll be out in the open, the whole way!

LANDO: It can't be helped!

THREEPIO: But what about Master Luke? Your Highness, surely . . .

LEIA: No, Lando's right; we have to try for the *Falcon*. We can't do anything for Luke here!

ARTOO: WHISTLES.

Sound: More shooting.

THREEPIO: What do you mean, Artoo, you'll "cover our retreat"? You're not a combat machine!

ARTOO: BEEPS.

Sound: Artoo's extinguisher starts belching.

THREEPIO: What are you . . .

LANDO: That droid's a sawed-off genius! He's laying down a smoke screen!

THREEPIO: Your firefighting aerosol! How *do* you think of these things, Artoo?

LEIA: It won't last long. Chewie, get moving! Run for the ship!

THREEPIO: And Chewbacca, please do keep in mind the fact that I am strapped to your back! You've exhibited little regard for my safety, thus far!

CHEWBACCA: *(MOVING OFF)* WAILING.

THREEPIO: *(BEING BORNE OFF)* Hurry, Artoo! Don't be left behind! Oh, if only Master Luke were here! Hurry, Artoo!

Sound: Artoo, going after, signaling distress, as shots range around him. Fades.

SCENE 10-2   CLOUD CITY CONTROL ROOM

Sound: Interior, Cloud City control room, comes up. Luke's footsteps, approaching.

LUKE: *(APPROACHING)* All right, Vader . . . show yourself! How long do I have to hunt for you down here? I know you weren't hurt in that fall . . .

Sound: Vader's breathing, off.

VADER: *(OFF)* As you thought: I was not. You were prudent, in not rushing down headlong after me.

Sound: Vader's saber activates.

VADER: *(APPROACHING)* But caution will be of no help to you now.

LUKE: I've learned other things besides caution.

Sound: Luke's blade activates.

VADER: You have learned wishful thinking, and a few partial insights! As for your lightsaber . . . there are many weapons available to one who *truly* commands the Force.

LUKE: No one commands it! Not even you!

VADER: You think not? Then, observe that control bar . . .

Sound: The bar trembles and creaks as Vader's Force-commands tear it loose.

VADER: The Force can tear it loose. The Force allows me to use it for any purpose I choose—even as a missile!

Sound: Relay breaks loose, zips through the air, smashing into a bulkhead.

LUKE: REACTS, DUCKING IT.

VADER: I can do the same with any object in this control room. Do you think you can evade them all?

Sound: Stanchion ripping loose.

VADER: That stanchion, for example?

Sound: Stanchion flies. Luke's lightsaber hits it, sputtering, deflecting it. Stanchion clatters off the bulkhead.

LUKE: *(INDICATING THE DEFLECTION)* I don't have to dodge 'em all. I still have my lightsaber.

VADER: And can you parry missiles—and fight at the same time?

Sound: They cross swords.

LUKE AND VADER: INDICATING IT.

VADER: Can you defend yourself—and evade that connecting tube?

Sound: Power tube rips loose, flies, hits Luke a glancing shot, bounces.

LUKE: GROANS.

VADER: Or that? *Or that?*

Sound: Machinery being torn loose and hurled at Luke by Vader's will. Steam from broken main. Luke's saber, as he deflects them.

LUKE: PARRYING THE MACHINERY, GROGGY.

VADER: You see, Skywalker? You are helpless.

LUKE: *(PANTING)* I thought you said . . . lightsabers. What's the matter? Lost your confidence? Changing the rules?

VADER: "The rules" are what I ordain them to be! The contest may take any form! Defend yourself if you can!

Sound: Another piece of machinery is hurled. It glances off Luke and crashes through the viewport, shattering it. The air howls as it rushes out the opening into the shaft.

LUKE: *(REACTS TO IMPACT)* The viewport . . .

VADER: You see? The contest may take any form. Can you stand your ground *now*?

LUKE: *(INDICATING EFFORT OF HOLDING HIS PLACE)* Yes . . . I can . . .

VADER: No! These winds will pull you through the viewport—into the reactor shaft. But they are nothing to me! *Nothing!* And *your strength will fail you*!

LUKE: *No!*

VADER: Your willpower fails you! You can do nothing!

LUKE: I can . . . *can— (AS HE'S BLOWN OUT THE SHATTERED VIEWPORT, AND FALLS DOWN THE SHAFT)* Ah-hh!

Sound: Control room fades.

SCENE 10-3 *FALCON* COCKPIT

Sound: Falcon*'s interior comes up. Sounds of engines being warmed up.*

THREEPIO: Oh, Artoo-Detoo, I thought that being strapped to the back of that great hairy beast, Chewbacca, would be the end of me!

ARTOO: TWEEDLES.

THREEPIO: He forgot to duck when he came up the ramp, and bumped me into the hatchway! Are you *certain* he didn't dent my cranial housing?

ARTOO: REPLIES.

THREEPIO: Well, of *course* I've "looked better"!

Sound: Small-arms fire splashing off the ship, off.

THREEPIO: Listen! The stormtroopers are firing on the *Falcon*! If only our deflectors will hold until we can blast off!

Sound: Engines rise as the Falcon *lifts.*

THREEPIO: Oh! We're lifting off! I simply *knew* that Administrator Calrissian would get us into the air! Now, if he can just elude Imperial pursuit, we may still survive.

ARTOO: BURBLES.

THREEPIO: Have you seen my other components lying about anywhere, Artoo? I expect you to get me reassembled without delay!

Sound: Falcon *shudders as she's hit.*

THREEPIO: Oh my! We're being fired upon again. Oh, we must escape; we simply must! Master Luke will be lost without us.

Sound: Another volley.

THREEPIO: We can only hope that Administrator Calrissian is as good a pilot as Captain Solo!

ARTOO: BEEPS.

Sound: The ship is hit again. Falcon *fades.*

SCENE 10-4   CLOUD CITY REACTOR SHAFT

Sound: Cloud City reactor shaft comes up: Moaning of air through the shaft, rumbling machinery, turbines, distance. Vader's breathing, approaching.

VADER: So, Skywalker: Once again you have managed to save yourself. Fortunate for you that this gantry broke your fall.

LUKE: There was more to it than luck.

VADER: Oh, yes; your agility, your Force training. But they can help you no more. You have no room left for retreat. Or do you think to battle your way past *me*!

Sound: Vader's sword ignites.

VADER: Look, there, down the reactor shaft! A long, long fall to Bespin. *If* you're not sucked into an exhaust port, or killed by an energy discharge!

LUKE: I don't plan to take that fall, Vader.

Sound: Luke's sword flares. They fight briefly.

LUKE AND VADER: INDICATE THE FIGHT.

VADER: You can only lose! It is inevitable! *(WITH EFFORT OF SHOVING LUKE)*

Sound: Luke sprawls.

LUKE: REACTS.

VADER: Get to your feet. You are beaten, Skywalker!

LUKE: You killed Ben, and . . . you still didn't beat him!

VADER: It is useless to resist! Don't let yourself be destroyed, as Obi-Wan did!

LUKE: Don't worry— *(INDICATING EFFORT OF RISING)* I won't. *(EFFORT OF SWINGING LIGHTSABER)*

Sound: They duel. Burning, searing sounds as Luke's blade scores on Vader's arm.

VADER: Ah-hhrrr!

LUKE: Ha! How do *you* like it? The fire of a lightsaber blade?

VADER: INDICATING EFFORT OF A VICIOUS ATTACK.

Sound: Quick, furious exchange. Vader's blade explodes instrument pod. Pause.

VADER: I did not wish to damage you, but—you leave me no alternative . . .

Sound: Another passage-at-arms.

LUKE AND VADER: INDICATING IT.

VADER: INDICATES A SLASH, TAKING OFF LUKE'S SWORDHAND AT THE WRIST.

Sound: The slash, sputtering, explosive discharge of sword, etc.

LUKE: *(SCREAMS AS HE'S STRUCK, GROANING)* My hand! *My hand . . .*

VADER: No sword! *No swordhand!* No hope left for you, Sky-walker! *Surrender!*

LUKE: *(SOBBING)* No . . . *no . . .*

VADER: There is no escape!

LUKE: *(MOANS)* Yes—yes, there is . . .

VADER: Luke, don't make me destroy you. You do not yet realize your importance. You have only begun to discover your powers!

LUKE: You might as well get it over with . . .

VADER: Join me, and I will complete your training! With our combined strength, we can end this destructive conflict, and bring order to the galaxy!

LUKE: *Your* kind of "order"? I'll never join you! I'll die first!

VADER: If only you knew the power of the dark side!

LUKE: I've seen it! Hatred and fear and cruelty!

VADER: Obi-Wan never told you what happened to your father . . .

LUKE: He told me enough! He told me *you* killed my father!

VADER: No, Luke. *I* am your father!

LUKE: No. No, that's not true! *That's impossible!*

VADER: Search your feelings. The Force gives you knowledge. You know what I say to be true.

LUKE: No, oh, no-oo!

VADER: Luke, you can destroy the Emperor. He has foreseen this. It is your destiny!

LUKE: I reject it! *I renounce it!*

VADER: Join me, and together we can rule the galaxy as father and son!

LUKE: Stay back . . . *stay back!*

VADER: Come with me, Luke. It is the only way this can end.

LUKE: There's one other . . . I can jump . . .

VADER: Is *that* the wisdom of a Jedi?

LUKE: I won't be the first to die—to keep you from winning!

VADER: Luke, no!

LUKE: I will never let you win, Vader. *(FALLING OFF)* Never . . .

VADER: *(UNDER)* Luke!

Sound: Transition to underside Cloud City.

SCENE 10-5   CLOUD CITY EXTERIOR

Sound: Exterior howling winds, distant tornadoes, etc. Quiet beeping of aircraft warning light on vane. Luke's sliding approach, along exhaust chute.

LUKE: MOANING, REACTING, AS HE APPROACHES, SLIDING.

Sound: Exhaust chute opens as Luke plummets out, landing on the small vane, point of view, rattling it.

LUKE: MOANS, INDICATING EFFORT OF CATCHING, DESPERATE EFFORT OF GRABBING VANE. MOANS.

Sound: Vane rattles and clatters as Luke tries to pull himself back up, clawing at the exhaust port.

LUKE: *(MOANS, PANTS AS HE TRIES TO HAUL HIMSELF BACK IN- SIDE CLOUD CITY, SCRABBLING AT CLOSED EXHAUST PORT, AND NEARLY FALLS) (BEGINS TO FOCUS BREATHING, CONTROL)* Ben . . . Ben, please let me hear you. Tell me what to do, Ben! I know you couldn't help me against Vader, but—Ben . . . Ben . . . *(MOANS)* Leia. You're my only hope. You have to hear me! Leia! Leia! Leia!

Sound: Cross fade to Leia's voice. Falcon cockpit background.

SCENE 10-6 *FALCON* COCKPIT

Sound: Falcon's cockpit comes up.

LEIA: Luke! *Luke!*

LANDO: Don't worry, Chewie. Before those TIE fighters can close with us, we'll be in hyperspace.

LEIA: *(REACTING TO LUKE'S CONTACT)* Lando!

LANDO: Huh? What's wrong?

LEIA: It's *Luke*! We've got to go back to Cloud City!

CHEWBACCA: GROANS.

LANDO: Hey! I thought we'd settled all that!

LEIA: *(URGENT)* I know where he is, Lando. He's on the underside of Cloud City. He was falling, but he caught hold of— something; I couldn't see what.

LANDO: Leia, calm down . . .

LEIA: He can't get back inside, and he can't hold on much longer. He needs us!

LANDO: Well, what about all those TIE fighters on our tail?

LEIA: Never mind the fighters! Chewie, we've got to do it, or Luke will die! Just do it!

CHEWBACCA: YOWLS.

LANDO: Leia, Chewie: wait! Well, what about Vader? He's still there, you know . . .

CHEWBACCA: HOWLS, ROARS.

LANDO: All right, all right, all *right*, Chewie! Comin' about!

Sound: Falcon's steering thrusters blast.

LANDO: I hope you know what you're doing, Leia. But I doubt it . . .

LEIA: Lando, make your approach *underneath* Cloud City!

LANDO: Chewie! Gimme more power to the engines; cut back on the shields. We're gonna have to outrun those fighters if we're gonna make a pickup!

Sound: Engines blast. Brief transition.

SCENE 10-6A *FALCON* COCKPIT

Sound: Cockpit comes up again.

LANDO: Okay, Leia, show me where you thought.

LEIA: Look up there! Someone's hanging from the vane!

LANDO: You were right!

LEIA: It's Luke! Chewie, slow down and ease the *Falcon* up under him!

CHEWBACCA: SNARLS.

Sound: Thrusters blare.

LEIA: Lando, open the top hatch!

LANDO: Listen, I'll go topside through the airlock and grab him! *(INDICATES GETTING OUT OF SEAT) (TO CHEWIE)* Chewie, gimme that comlink! When I've got Luke *(MOVING OFF)* get us out of here right away. Those TIEs'll be on us any second!

Sound: Falcon *maneuvering slowly, easing up.*

LEIA: Easy, Chewie . . . good . . . *(TO HERSELF)* Just hang on a few seconds more, Luke. *(TO COMLINK) Lando, hurry!*

LANDO: *(OVER COMLINK)* I have to cycle the airlock!

LEIA: Override the lock controls.

LANDO: Okay. Going up now.

LEIA: Easy, Chewie.

LANDO: Almost got 'im . . . Ease her up, Chewie. Hold it . . . that's good . . . we're there! Got 'im!

CHEWBACCA: HOOTS HAPPILY.

Sound: Alarm on control board starts bleeping.

LEIA: Chewie, look! Sensor alarm! The TIE fighters are almost on us!

Sound: Intercom activates, as she contacts Lando.

LEIA: Lando, get 'im back inside. TIE fighters approaching!

LANDO: *(OVER INTERCOM)* Okay, I've got 'im in the airlock! Let's go! *Get us outta here!*

LEIA: *Hit it, Chewie!*

CHEWBACCA: SNARLS.

Sound: Falcon*'s engines howl.*

LEIA: Those fighters are practically on us. Chewie, divert more power to the shields!

LUKE: OFF. GROANS IN PAIN.

LEIA: Luke!

LANDO: *(OFF)* Leia, you'd better take him aft. *(MOVING ON)* I've gotta give Chewie a hand, here.

LEIA: Oh, Luke . . .

LUKE: *(DELIRIOUS)* Leia . . . you heard me! Vader . . .

LANDO: *(WITH THE EFFORT OF SHIFTING LUKE'S WEIGHT)* Get 'im back to a bunk in the crew quarters. And hang on!

LEIA: *(WITH THE EFFORT OF SHOULDERING LUKE'S WEIGHT)* I'll be right back, Lando . . . *(MOVING OFF)* Easy, Luke.

Sound: Power door shuts.

LANDO: *(APPROACHING POINT OF VIEW)* All right, Chewie: Set up the jump to lightspeed.

Sound: A cannon round rocks the ship. TIE howls past.

LANDO: Here come the Imperials! Watch it! Get that jump ready!

Sound: Brief transition.

SCENE 10-7 *FALCON* HOLD

Sound: Ship shudders to TIEs' fire.

LEIA: Oh, Luke, what have they done to you?

LUKE: . . . Vader . . . *Vader!*

LEIA: Shh; hold still, Luke. I've got to get an autotourniquet onto your . . . your arm . . .

LUKE: Ben told me Vader had *killed*, had *killed* my father . . .

Sound: Falcon's hit again.

LEIA: *(REACTS)* Luke, I've got to get back to the cockpit! *(MOVING OFF)* Try not to move. I'll be back as soon as I can!

Sound: Brief transition.

SCENE 10-8 *FALCON* COCKPIT

Sound: Door opens as Leia enters.

LEIA: *(APPROACHING)* Lando, you've got to get us into hyperspace, or—

Sound: Another volley rocks the ship.

CHEWBACCA: REACTS.

LEIA: —or they'll blow us apart!

LANDO: Almost ready; it took me a little fancy maneuvering to get around those TIE fighters, but we're coming out of Bespin's gravity field.

Sound: Alarm flashing, beeping.

LEIA: What's the alarm for?

LANDO: Take a look, right out there . . .

LEIA: Imperial Star Destroyer. Only . . . it's . . .

LANDO: Yeah. Biggest ship I ever saw; must be three times the size of Cloud City.

Sound: TIEs swoop by, firing.

LANDO: And the TIE fighters're still with us! Awright, Chewie: Get set to go to lightspeed!

Sound: Switches being thrown, etc.

LEIA: Assuming your people fixed the hyperdrive, Lando!

LANDO: Don't worry; I gave *that* order myself!

LEIA: Well, all the coordinates are set. It's now or never.

LANDO: Now sounds preferable! Okay, Chewie! *Punch it!*

Sound: Hyperdrive revs and coughs out once again.

LANDO: Oh no . . .

LEIA: Not again. I should've known . . .

CHEWBACCA: WOOFS.

LANDO: They said they fixed it! They were *supposed to* fix it! Hey, c'mon, Chewie! Leia! It's not my fault!

LEIA: Where've I heard *that* before? Chewie, what're you doing? Where're you going?

CHEWBACCA: CARPING, MOVING OFF.

LANDO: He's gonna try to repair the hyperdrive; I've gotta keep those TIE fighters off our tail.

LEIA: That Star Destroyer's closing on us . . .

LANDO: And you know who's gotta be in it, don't you?

LEIA: We can't let him catch us, Lando! I'm not sure what Luke is talking about, but he keeps mentioning Vader's name, over and over.

Sound: Ship jolts to blaster cannon.

LANDO: I can't evade 'em forever . . .

Sound: Falcon *maneuvers.*

LEIA: They'll have a tractor beam locked onto us any minute now.

LANDO: And if we're *really* unlucky, they'll take us alive.

LEIA: We can't let them take the *Falcon*! Especially for Luke's sake. *We can't let Vader take us!*

Sound: Brief transition to aft.

297

SCENE 10-9 *FALCON* HOLD

LUKE: ON BUNK, BREATHING IRREGULARLY, MOANING.

VADER: *(DISEMBODIED)* Luke . . . *Luke!*

LUKE: Hmm—wha—*Father!*

VADER: Son, come with me! *Return to me!*

LUKE: Ben—why didn't you tell me? Why didn't you warn me? *Ben . . .*

Sound: Brief transition.

SCENE 10-10 *FALCON* MIDSHIPS

Sound: Chewbacca, off, trying to repair the ship. Steam escaping, alarms, circuitry sputtering. Point of view is Artoo working on Threepio: tool noises, Artoo beeping.

THREEPIO: Carefully, Artoo; carefully! Now, connect the relay switch to my leg.

ARTOO: BEEPS.

Sound: Throws switch.

THREEPIO: There; that's much better! That's *one* of my legs back in a useful configuration!

Sound: Chewbacca, off, working and tooling, howling in despair.

THREEPIO: Do you hear that noisy brute, Artoo-Detoo?

ARTOO: ANSWERS.

THREEPIO: What *can* Chewbacca be doing? Why don't we just go to lightspeed?

ARTOO: CHIRPS.

THREEPIO: What do you mean, we *"can't"*? How would you know the hyperdrive's been "sabotaged"?

ARTOO: BEEPS EXPLANATION.

THREEPIO: The Cloud City central computer told you? Artoo-Detoo, how many times must I tell you not to trust a strange computer?

ARTOO: OBJECTS.

THREEPIO: Oh, never mind! Just attach my other leg, this instant!

ARTOO: AGREES.

Sound: Sounds of Artoo's endeavor.

THREEPIO: Ouch! And watch what you're doing! Oh, there's surely no hope for us this time! No hope whatsoever!

Sound: Brief transition.

SCENE 10-11 *FALCON* COCKPIT

LANDO: Leia, get Chewie on the comlink. They're gonna nail us any second.

LEIA: He's on.

LANDO: *(TO INTERCOM)* Chewie, how's it goin' back there?

Sound: Door whooshes open.

LEIA: Luke!

LUKE: *(APPROACHING)* I'm all right, Leia.

LEIA: I told you to stay in the bunk . . .

LUKE: Where's his ship? Yeah; I see. He's there.

LANDO: The Star Destroyer?

LUKE: Vader. It's Vader.

VADER: *(DISEMBODIED. ONLY LUKE HEARS)* Luke! It is your destiny!

LUKE: No, it's not! *(SOFTER)* Why didn't you *tell* me, Ben? Why?

LANDO: "Ben?" *(TO LEIA)* What's he talking about?

LEIA: Luke! You . . . you should be resting.

LANDO: No point worrying about that now. Everybody: Grab hold! The Imperials're boxing us in!

Sound: Falcon's engine blast.

LANDO: *(TO INTERCOM)* Come on, Chewie! Get the hyperdrive working or we've had it!

Sound: Brief transition.

SCENE 10-12 *FALCON* MIDSHIPS

Sound: Chewie still working, and swearing in Wookiee, off. Artoo's torch.

THREEPIO: Artoo, will you please pay attention to what you're doing? Ow, my leg!

ARTOO: SIGNALS.

Sound: Torch shuts off. Artoo drops same, with a clank.

ARTOO: *(MOVES OFF)* BEEPING.

THREEPIO: Artoo, come back here! Pick up that tool! *You still have to reattach my other leg!*

ARTOO: *(OFF)* HALLOES.

Sound: Artoo goes to work on circuitry of the Falcon.

THREEPIO: Get away from that control wiring! You'll only burn yourself out again! *You* don't know how to repair the *Falcon*'s hyperdrive!

ARTOO: THINKS HE DOES.

Sound: Artoo working, connecting, under next.

THREEPIO: Oh, no you *don't*! Chewbacca, perhaps, but not you! And in the meantime, I'm standing here, tottering, in pieces, and you're having delusions of grandeur! *(PAUSE)* What . . .

ARTOO: TRIUMPHANT YOODLE.

THREEPIO: Artoo, what are you—

Sound: Positive contact, off, as Artoo's arm finds the sabotaged leads.

THREEPIO: What are you meddling at now—

ARTOO: CHEERS.

Sound: Hyperdrive starts to kick in.

THREEPIO: Oh, my goodness! You did it! The *hyperdrive*! Artoo-Detoo—OOO!

Sound: Hyperdrive building, Threepio and Artoo upended. Artoo falls, yelping, sliding.

THREEPIO: Artoo, *you fixed it*! You did it!

ARTOO: WHISTLES.

Sound: Hyperdrive builds.

VADER: *(OVER, DISEMBODIED)* Luke. . . . It is your destiny!

Sound: Hyperdrive booms as Falcon *rates lightspeed. Fades.*

SCENE 10-13   REBEL CRUISER MED-CENTER

Sound: Sick bay, inboard Rebel cruiser, comes up. Med-center sounds.

TOO-ONEBEE: If you please, hold your arm *very* still, Commander Skywalker; I have to locate all the nerve endings in your wrist precisely, in order to fit your powered prosthetic hand.

LUKE: All right; you're the doctor, Too-Onebee.

Sound: Medi-sensors reading Luke's stump, for linkup.

P.A. SYSTEM: Attention, all personnel and automata! *Millennium Falcon* ready for departure!

TOO-ONEBEE: Perhaps, Commander, when all Rebel Alliance units have gathered here in rendezvous orbit, it will be possible to organize a complete medical center; in that event other procedures will become available for the treatment of your injury. But for the foreseeable future, this prosthetic hand must suffice.

LUKE: Believe me, I'm not complaining, Too-Onebee . . .

Sound: Power door opens.

CHEWBACCA: *(OFF)* SNARLS.

LANDO: *(OFF)* Hiya, stranger!

LUKE: Lando! Chewie! How's it goin'?

CHEWBACCA: HOOTS, APPROACHING.

LANDO: *(APPROACHING)* We've got the *Millennium Falcon* all repaired—the *right* way, this time—so we're ready to shove off.

LUKE: Are you sure about this, Lando? Maybe if you waited a little longer, there'd be enough of us at the rendezvous for the general to spare you two some help.

LANDO: Chewie and I prefer it this way, Luke. For one thing, we can't waste any more time; we don't know where Boba Fett's taken Han. But more than that: Chewie and I are used to the kind of places where we'll be going—the sort of opposition we'll be up against. Right, Chewie?

CHEWBACCA: CONCURS.

LANDO: Anybody else'd just slow us down, Luke . . .

LUKE: Well, good hunting.

LANDO: Thanks. We could use you; you've been through it all before. But the Alliance can't spare anybody right now—especially you.

LUKE: Where d'you start?

LANDO: Well, Chewie and I are gonna check around with a few folks who *owe* us.

Sound: Power door slides open.

THREEPIO: *(APPROACHING)* Artoo, look! Master Luke, Artoo and I are delighted to see that you are your old self once again!

LUKE: Well, not quite . . . but close enough. You're looking better too, Threepio.

THREEPIO: Yes; the Rebel technicians have completely repaired me, but—

LUKE: "But" what, Threepio?

THREEPIO: Well, it's Artoo-Detoo, sir. He appears to have developed the most illogical imagination!

ARTOO: BRISTLES.

LUKE: "Illogical"?

THREEPIO: Yes, Master Luke. His account of his and your own experiences on some nonexistent planet called "Dagobah."

LUKE: Oh. Yeah, that . . .

THREEPIO: As I demonstrated to Artoo, sir, no such planet is mentioned in any navigational data bank!

LUKE: We can straighten it out later, Threepio. At least you're repaired.

THREEPIO: But are you certain that you're all right, sir?

LUKE: Uh-huh. But there're other things we should be thinking about.

THREEPIO: Oh, yes, I'd heard. Administrator Calrissian, may I—

LANDO: "Lando."

THREEPIO: Thank you, sir. "Lando," my best wishes, and Artoo's as well, go with you and Chewbacca.

CHEWBACCA: WOOFS.

LANDO: You and your friend can ship with me anytime, Threepio. Artoo, you have yourself a distinct talent for pulling things off at the last second.

ARTOO: WHISTLES.

THREEPIO: Artoo thanks you, sir, although I personally am of the opinion that he has an overdeveloped sense of the dramatic!

ARTOO: BRIDLES.

LANDO: Look, Chewie and I will meet you at the rendezvous point on Tatooine.

LUKE: I'll be there, Lando. If you need help, you know how to reach me.

THREEPIO: Yes, Master Luke; the details of rendezvous arrangements are safely stored in Artoo's memory banks.

LUKE: Isn't that how all this started?

ARTOO: AGREES.

LUKE: Take care of yourself, Chewie . . .

CHEWBACCA: HONKS, AS HE HUGS LUKE.

LUKE: Oof! *(LAUGHS)*

Sound: Power door opens.

LEIA: *(APPROACHING)* Lando, they're ready for your launch.

LANDO: So're we. You folks'll be able to see it from here.

LUKE: That all right, Onebee?

TOO-ONEBEE: All that remains is the final attachment of the prosthetic. You will then be able to return to duty status, Commander.

THREEPIO: May I ask what is the latest word on the rallying of our forces?

LEIA: It's better than we'd thought at first, Threepio. Just about everyone who got off Hoth made it here. So, we've got some supplies, a bit of fighter cover. Our losses in ships and lives weren't as bad as they might've been. Most of the starfleet was busy chasing the *Falcon*.

LANDO: So you're not just gonna sit out here on the rim of the galaxy much longer, hmm?

LEIA: Figure it out for yourself, high-roller.

LANDO: Did anyone mention the Cloud City evacuation ships? Did any get clear?

LEIA: We've had scattered reports. We're afraid a great many of them were killed or captured by Imperials. The Alliance is doing its best to locate the others.

LANDO: All we ever wanted was to be left alone.

LUKE: I'm truly sorry, Lando.

THREEPIO: We all are, Lando!

LEIA: But the Emperor and Vader have to be stopped. They have to be—

LANDO: The Empire isn't going to leave anybody alone. Maybe I knew it all along. Personal treaties, a place to lie low: Those things don't work anymore.

P.A. SYSTEM: Attention, *Millennium Falcon* crew. Please report for launch.

LANDO: Ready, Chewie?

CHEWBACCA: BARKS.

LUKE: Take care of 'im, Chewie. Make sure he doesn't lose the *Falcon* again.

LANDO: You hang onto your pay, Commander. Next time I see you, I'll teach you a little something about the odds of numbers.

LUKE: It's a deal.

THREEPIO: Good luck, *Captain* Calrissian!

LANDO: Thanks very much—*See*-Threepio.

ARTOO: WHISTLES.

LEIA: Good luck, Lando.

LANDO: We'll find Han, Leia.

LEIA: I know—and I thank you.

LANDO: *(MOVING OFF)* C'mon, Chewbacca. Take care, all of you!

CHEWBACCA: SNARLING, MOVES OFF.

Sound: Power door closes.

TOO-ONEBEE: Commander Skywalker, I am ready now to fit your prosthetic hand.

LUKE: The sooner the better, Onebee.

TOO-ONEBEE: Hold still please, Commander . . .

Sound: Onebee fitting bio-synergic hand onto Luke. Test beeps, compometer sounds of the gizmos, under next lines.

TOO-ONEBEE: You will feel slight pain as I test the nerve responses, sir.

LUKE: I've had sore fingers in that hand ever since I lost it, Onebee. Go right ahead.

TOO-ONEBEE: Yes, sir . . .

Sound: Test beeps, etc.

THREEPIO: Sometimes I wish that I, too, had been programmed as a medical droid, Onebee. You are most proficient!

TOO-ONEBEE: Thank you, See-Threepio . . .

LUKE: *(AS ONEBEE TESTS)* Ouch!

TOO-ONEBEE: I'm sorry, Commander, but—

LUKE: You may not believe this, but it almost feels good.

LEIA: Luke, I'm worried about Lando and Chewbacca. I suppose I want you to tell me that they'll be all right.

LUKE: A professional gambler and con artist, and a Wookiee smuggler, flying "the fastest hunk of junk in the galaxy"? They'll be all right.

P.A. SYSTEM: *Millennium Falcon*, prepare for departure.

Sound: Onebee's test beep.

LUKE: Oo! Good, Onebee! Uh, where's that comlink?

THREEPIO: Here you are, Master Luke! Oh, and, er, Artoo still maintains that you have been engaged in rather—well, illogical activities.

LUKE: Understatement!

LEIA: LAUGHS.

Sound: Comlink activating.

LUKE: Skywalker, to *Millennium Falcon*. *(ASIDE, AS ONEBEE WORKS)* Ouch!

TOO-ONEBEE: Nearly finished, Commander.

THREEPIO: At any rate, Master Luke, Artoo has decided that, despite his own logical circuitry, he is gaining confidence in your—your predictions, sir.

LUKE: Thanks, Artoo. *(TO COMLINK)* Repeat, Skywalker to *Falcon*.

LANDO: *(OVER COMLINK)* Lando here. We'll see you on Tatooine, Luke. *With* Han!

CHEWBACCA: *(OVER COMLINK)* ROARS.

LANDO: *(OVER COMLINK)* We'll bring him back to you, Leia. I swear it.

THREEPIO: Quick, Artoo! To the viewport! We'll be able to watch the blastoff.

LEIA: Take care, Lando. Chewbacca.

LUKE: May the Force be with you both.

LEIA: May it be with us all.

TOO-ONEBEE: The procedure is complete, Commander Sky-walker.

LUKE: *(RISING)* C'mon, Leia! Threepio, Artoo . . . here they go . . .

ARTOO: BEEPS.

THREEPIO: Yes, Artoo, there is room for you right here by me.

LEIA: They'll succeed. We can't lose after all we've been through.

LUKE: The Empire threw everything it had at us, and we're still here.

ARTOO: WHISTLES.

LUKE: What'd Artoo say, Threepio?

THREEPIO: Artoo says that the existence and continued popularity of the Rebellion are in conflict with logic and statistics and—and that—

LEIA: What, Threepio?

THREEPIO: Well, an astro-droid shouldn't be capable of this, but—Artoo *claims* to be reevaluating both logic *and* statistics.

Sound: The Falcon *blasts, distance.*

LEIA: There they go. Back into the Empire.

LUKE: The Empire can't stop us. Now it's our turn.

Music: Closing music.

ANNOUNCER: CLOSING CREDITS.

ABOUT THE AUTHOR

BRIAN DALEY is the author of numerous works of science fiction and fantasy, including the Coramonde and Alacrity Fitzhugh books. He also scripted the National Public Radio serial adaptations of *Star Wars* and *The Empire Strikes Back*, dramatic recordings for Disneyland/ Buena Vista, and a number of animated TV episodes.

In collaboration with his friend and fellow Ballantine novelist James Luceno—using the pen name Jack McKinney—Brian co-wrote the *Robotech*, *Sentinels*, and *Black Hole Travel Agency* series.

Brian has in recent years been laboring over an SF saga that's grown in the telling. He and his longtime companion, historical novelist Lucia St. Clair Robson, live in a quiet riverside community near Annapolis, Maryland.

THE ORIGINAL RADIO DRAMA

By Brian Daley

You've seen the movie. But you've only heard half the story!

- How did Princess Leia and the Rebels get the plans for the Death Star?
  - Just what was so dangerous about Beggar's Canyon?
  - What kept Han Solo from double-crossing Luke and Ben?
  - What compelled Princess Leia to join the Rebellion?

Learn the answers to these questions and many others in this original script of the acclaimed US radio dramatisation. A behind-the-scenes introduction by the script's author Brian Daley takes you into the recording studio with Mark Hamill, Anthony Daniels and others. This original script, with dialogue never heard on air, is the missing chapter in the history of a tale that began a long time ago in a galaxy far, far away...

THE ART OF *STAR WARS* A NEW HOPE

Edited by Carol Titelman

A New Hope was part of the original title of the movie that became *Star Wars,* the ultimate film entertainment experience of the 1970s that is now one of the most-loved movies of all time. *The Art of Star Wars: A New Hope* contains the first film's complete script by George Lucas and is beautifully illustrated with the movie's fantastic works of art. In this unique compilation of all the imagination and beauty that went into the first of the film trilogy, the magic of *Star Wars* lives on.

This volume includes:

- Photographs
- Costume sketches
- Finished production paintings
- A selection of cartoons and spin-off art
- Many of the spectacular *Star Wars* posters
- The first rough concepts and preliminary drawings
- Storyboards of action sequences detailing the evolution of the story and characters
- Some of the creative art by the young fans who have always sustained the *Star Wars* legend

THE ART OF STAR WARS GALAXY VOLUME 2

Written & edited by Gary Gerani

All-new art! All-new visions! All-new excitement!

Journey back to a galaxy far, far away in this second all-star collection of new artwork based on the *Star Wars* trilogy – the most enduring and popular film saga of our time.

Over seventy of today's greatest comic and fantasy illustrators provide new visions of the *Star Wars* galaxy, offering their personal interpretation of the movies' imagery, and recollections of the impact the trilogy had on them and their work. In addition to volume one, this volume also features expanded coverage of the production, promotional and merchandising art that has been produced for the film and its countless spin-off products.

Featuring the work of fan-favourite artists Jack 'King' Kirby, Dave Gibbons, Kelley Jones, John Bolton and Jim Starlin (along with many others), this book is a must for all film buffs, art aficionados, comic fans and *Star Wars* enthusiasts alike.